A Textbook of Logic

A Textbook of Logic

Krishna Jain
Associate Professor
Janki Devi Memorial College
(University of Delhi)

PRINTWORLD
Publishers of Indian Traditions

Cataloging in Publication Data — DK
[Courtesy: D.K. Agencies (P) Ltd. <docinfo@dkagencies.com>]

Jain, Krishna, 1947–2019
A textbook of logic / Krishna Jain. — 5th rev. and enl. ed.
p. cm.
Includes bibliographical references (p.)
ISBN 13: 9788124606483

1. Logic — Textbooks. 2. Logic, Symbolic and mathematical — Textbooks, I. Title.

DDC 160 22

ISBN 13: 978-81-246-0648-3
First published in India in 1998
Fourth edition, 2007
Fifth revised and enlarged edition 2012
Reissued in 2014, 2015, 2016, 2018, 2020, 2021, 2023

Printed and published by:
D.K. Printworld (P) Ltd.
Regd. office : *Vedaśrī*, F-395, Sudarshan Park
(Metro Station: ESI Hospital) New Delhi - 110015
Phones : (011) 4172 2626, 98713 94815
e-mail : indology@dkprintworld.com
Web : www.dkprintworld.com

Preface to the Fifth Edition

THIS is the fifth revised and enlarged edition of *A Textbook of Logic — An Introduction*. Whereas many chapters have been further elaborated, some new ones, such as Arguments and Explanations, and Dilemma have been added, keeping in view the requirements of university syllabi. Each chapter is followed by fresh and exclusive exercises.

I am thankful to my various colleagues, particularly Dr Raj Verma Sinha (Asst. Professor, Miranda House, University of Delhi), for their help in many ways. I am equally thankful to Shri Susheel Kumar Mittal of D.K. Printworld, New Delhi for his personal care and interest in publishing the present edition of the book.

2 August 2012 **Dr. Krishna Jain**

Preface to the First Edition

THE present book is the outcome of an interaction with students over a long period of time and proposes to explain the principles and procedures of Elementary Logic in the simplest possible way. It is an attempt to introduce students to both traditional as well as Symbolic Logic. It also covers Inductive Logic and includes Informal Fallacies committed in everyday arguments.

Almost all the topics are explained with the help of lucid examples. They also carry plenty of exercises for a better grasp of the subject. Special attempts have been made to clarify basic concepts such as Validity, Reasoning, Types of Reasoning, Proposition, Term, etc. In modern logic, Existential Import, Boolean Alzebra, Venn Diagrams, Truth Table, Shorter Truth Table Method are explained in a simple and easy language. A special chapter is provided for "translating" ordinary language sentences into symbolism of modern logic.

I shall like to express my gratitude to Prof. V.K. Bhardwaj, Deptt. of Philosophy, Delhi University, who went through the first draft of the text and offered many valuable suggestions. I am also thankful to Shri Balwant of Ajanta Books International for his keen interest in publishing the book. Last but not the least my thanks are due to my husband Dr V.K. Jain for encouraging me to write the present text.

Krishna Jain

Contents

Part II

Part III

Part IV

Part I

Chapter 1

Introduction

Subject Matter of Logic

Logic is a science of reasoning. The aim of logic is to provide methods, techniques and devices which help in differentiating right reasoning from wrong, and good reasoning from bad. But it does not mean that only those who study logic can reason correctly. However, it is true that those who study logic certainly make less errors while arguing. Just as a trained athlete is a better player than an untrained one, similarly a person acquainted with logical principles is likely to put forth good arguments. Knowledge of logic helps one to face a problem in a more orderly and systematic way, and in many cases makes the solution less difficult but more certain.

Science means a branch of coherently organized body of knowledge. Since logic is the study of consistent reasoning, it is certainly a science. Through logic we can judge, for example, whether a piece of reasoning such as we find in newspapers, magazines, or in everyday life is correct or not, and also whether the conclusion follows correctly from the given evidences (premisses). Correct reasoning means to discover the right order between the evidences and conclusion. There is order and sequence in our reasoning. The moment one is concerned with the idea that one thought follows from another, he is being logical. Correct and consistent reasoning means conclusion follows from the evidences or the premisses. In other words, **correct reasoning means the premisses are strong enough to support the conclusion, and when the premisses are insufficient or inadequate to support the conclusion, then the reasoning becomes incorrect.**

Correct reasoning is the basis of all sciences, natural as well as social. In this sense it is very true to say that logic is presupposed by all sciences, and hence, it becomes a basic and primary science; a science of sciences.

But the logicians are not interested merely in the study of methods or techniques of differentiating right reasoning from wrong; it is equally important for them to acquire skill to apply these methods in determining the correctness of everyday reasoning. How efficiently or how skilfully one makes use of these methods in practical life is nothing but demonstrating the artistic aptitude. All arts are concerned with 'doing' and 'making'. Anyone who knows logic 'does' good reasoning and 'makes' sound arguments. He makes good definitions and good debates. Logic prepares a man to make right reasoning and right decisions. "Practice makes a man prefect" is true for all arts, and it is equally true for logic as well.

Traditionally logic is defined as the study of laws of thought. There are three laws which have been considered indispensable for correct reasoning by the ancient logicians. They are :

1. Law of Identity
2. Law of Non-Contradiction
3. Law of Excluded-Middle

There is no doubt that these laws are absolutely indispensable for correct reasoning; but there are other laws also which are equally important for valid reasoning, for instance, various laws of inference and deduction.*

Moreover, in defining logic as the science of laws of thought, the word 'thought' needs clarification. It refers to thinking, to mental processes, and to mental activity. Whereas it is absolutely clear that reasoning is a reflective, a mental activity, and not a physical activity like walking, talking, etc.; yet every mental activity is not reasoning. There are many mental activities, and

* These laws are discussed in detail in chapter 8.

reasoning is one of them. In other words, reasoning is merely one of the mental processes. Every piece of reasoning is a mental process (thinking) but every mental process is not reasoning. Remembering, imagining, daydreaming are various types of mental processes (mental activities) but none of them is reasoning. The following diagram makes it clear:

Mental Processes

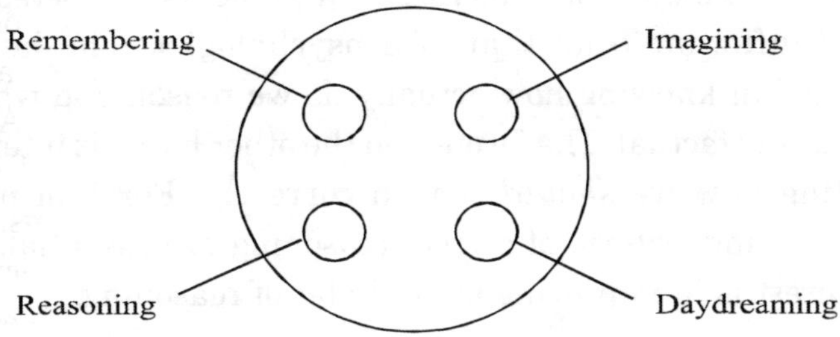

The logicians are interested in 'reasoned thinking' which takes place when we work at problems, tell stories, plan strategies and so on. It involves elements that are both deductive (when we solve problems by using a given set of rules as arithmetical task) and inductive (when one solves problems on the basis of data placed before us, as in working at a travel route).

Reasoning is a special type of thinking, a special type of mental activity and a special type of mental process. When one thought is more or less consciously *connected* with another in order to elicit the conclusion towards which our thought is directed, then it is reasoning. For reasoning to take place there should be some basis, some ground, some evidences, some premisses which imply conclusion. In non-rational thinking no evidence is provided and no conclusion follows. Thus to define logic as the science of laws of thought is too wide a definition. Though it hints what logic is dealing with, yet it does not very specifically define it.

It is more appropriate to define **logic as the science of valid reasoning.** A logician, however, is not concerned with every aspect of reasoning. For instance, he is not dealing with reasoning as a 'actual mental process'. He is concerned only with its correctness or incorrectness. A logician looks to reasoning from a special angle, that is, from the viewpoint of its validity. A psychologist, on the other hand, studies reasoning from different angle. He studies all the mental processes, and in this sense, studies reasoning also as one of the mental processes. But his interest is in the 'actual mental process' while correctness of reasoning does not bother him at all. The logician's aim, on the other hand, is merely in correctness of arguments. His perspective is thus different from that of a psychologist. The latter is interested in knowing how actually do we reason and why; his study is only factual. The former, on the other hand, is interested in telling how we *should* reason correctly. For him norms, standards and criteria of correct reasoning are essential, since his interest is in improving man's habit of reasoning.

Argument and Explanation

What does reasoning consist of ? What is an argument? Reasoning means providing evidences for the conclusion in the clearest of term and supporting the conclusion with maximum evidences. The evidences provided to substantiate the conclusion are said to be premisses. That which is drawn on the basis of the premisses is a conclusion. An argument or a piece of reasoning is thus a relational arrangement of premisses and conclusion. An argument may have just one premiss or more but both premisses and conclusion should be there to form an argument. If the premisses are given and no conclusion is drawn from them, then it is not an argument. Similarly, if conclusion is given and no premisses are cited then also it is not an argument. Let us see some examples of arguments:

All men are mortal.
Socrates is a man.
___
Therefore, Socrates is mortal.

If there is rain, then we shall not go for picnic.

There is rain.

Therefore, we shall not go for picnic.

If A then B.

If B then C.

Therefore, if A then C.

All observed crows are black.

Therefore, all crows are black.

It is very important that the student recognizes argumental form, and should be able to differentiate non-argumental sequence from an argumental presentation.

Five kinds of passages that are sometimes confused with argument are:-

- Reports
- Unsupported statements of belief or opinion
- Illustrations
- Conditional statements
- Explanations

Arguments consist entirely of statements as either true or false. Questions, commands and explanations cannot be part of arguments because they do not have truth value nor are they true or false.

Arguments sometimes resemble with explanations. People often are not themselves clear whether they are arguing or explaining something. The same type of words and phrases are used in presenting explanations and arguments. It is thus important to know what is an explanation and how it is different from an argument. An explanation is a set of statements constructed to describe some facts, events or phenomena. An explanation aims to describe how and why things occur as they do. The reason one gives for why something happened and how it happened is called an explanation. It is often underpinned by an understanding and uncovers new knowlege among the facts.

Following are the examples of explanation:

1. I am late for the meeting (x) because my train was late (y).
2. Apples fall on the ground (x) from tree because there is gravitational force in the earth (y).
3. Sita took aspirin (x) because she had headache (y).
4. She did not come to work today (x) because she was sick (y).
5. Many newcomers have won mid-term election this year even defeating strong incumbents (x) because voters are not happy with the way the ruling party is running the government (y).

In all the above examples the word 'because' is used to indicate that an explanation is being offered.

An explanation is comprised of two parts; the explanandum (x) and explanans (y). The explanandum (x) is the statement that describes the phenomenon which is to be explained. The explanans (y) is the statement or set of statements that aim to do the explaining.

The general form of an explanation is

x because of y
or
y therefore x

x is explanandum and y is explanans. Explanandum (x) is a fact or an event which has occurred. In that sense it is an accepted fact or event. The aim of explanation is to provide explanans (y) for that fact or event that had occurred.There can be various alternative explanans (y) for one explanandum (x). For instance there can be various reasons for why one is late for the meeting, or how Miss X has managed to get selected for the post.

An argument differs from an explanation. The argument can have the same form as that of explanation.

x because of y
y therefore x

Here conclusion x is not an accepted fact. Premiss y provides the grounds which prove (or establish) the conclusion x. Let us see the following illustrations:

1. Satish has just got admission in MBA course in one of the best institutes of USA, **so he will quit his job**. This is an argument. Satish has just got admission in MBA course in one of the best institutes of USA is premiss. This premiss establishes and claims to prove the conclusion that he will quit his job.

   Premiss $\Rightarrow$ claims to prove or establish $\Rightarrow$ conclusion

   y claims to prove or establish x.

2. Satish has quit his job because he has just got admission in MBA course in one of the best institutes of USA. This is an explanation.

Satish has quit his job (x) is accepted fact. This is explained and elaborated (but not proved or established) by the statement that he has just got admission in MBA course in one of the best institutes of USA.

One simple method to distinguish explanation from argument is: If the statement that precedes (comes before) 'because' describes an accepted fact or event and the other remaining statements which come after 'because' aim just to elaborate that fact or event, then it is explanation. If the statement that precedes 'because' is not accepted fact but it has to be proved and established by the other statements that come after 'because' then it is an argument.

An argument is consisted of premisses and conclusion. Both premiss and conclusion of an argument are propositions. A proposition is a sentence, but every sentence is not a proposition. Only informative or indicative sentences may be said to be propositions. Interrogative or exclamatory sentences are not propositions. A proposition is believed or disbelieved, asserted or denied whereas interrogative or exclamatory sentences are neither asserted nor denied. Questions are asked, commands are given and exclamations are uttered. But none of them can be affirmed, denied or judged to be either true or false. For instance, "Bring a glass of water" is not a proposition whereas "Water is essential for human beings" is a proposition. Hence, though every proposition is definitely a sentence, every sentence is not necessarily a proposition. Since logic deals with the propositions only, so indicative sentences find place in the preview of logic. This can be expressed as follows:

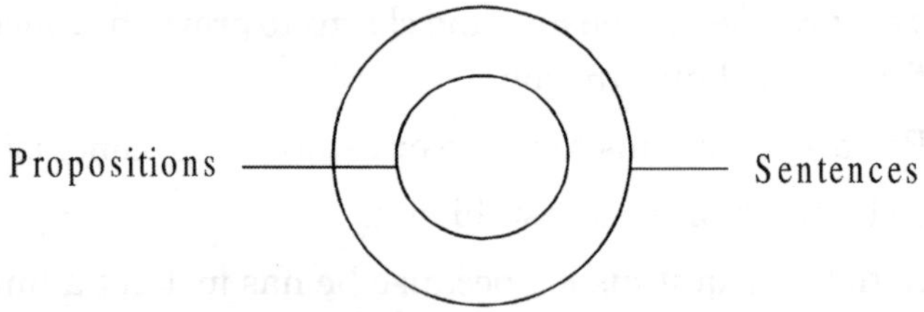

Besides, a proposition is language neutral entity. For instance, the sentence "This is a book" can be translated and expressed in various languages such as English, Hindi, German, Japanese, etc., but there is only one proposition underlying in all these differently expressed sentences. Logical propositions (statements) go beyond the language in which they are framed and expressed. The unit of reasoning is a proposition which is totally and wholly language neutral. Both premisses and conclusion of an argument are propositions; but propositions by themselves do not carry any tag suggesting that certain propositions are exclusively premisses while some other propositions are exclusively conclusions. A proposition becomes either a premiss or a conclusion only in the context of an argument. Just as by entering into wedlock a woman becomes wife, similarly by entering into an argument some propositions become premisses and some other conclusions.

It is extremely important that we recognize which propositions are premisses and which ones are conclusion in an argument. Without this any attempt to establish correctness of an argument is futile. There are words which help in identifying premisses and conclusions. The use of words like 'hence', 'therefore', 'it follows', 'thus', 'so', etc. are conclusion indicators, and words like 'because', 'for', 'since', 'implies', etc. are premiss indicators.

Validity, correctness, rightness or soundness of an argument means premisses are sufficient and efficient enough to support the conclusion. A logician is confronted with such a question, "Are the premisses good evidences for accepting the conclusion?"If premisses adequately support the conclusion, then the argument is correct otherwise not. So evidences play a very vital role in determining the correctness of an argument. In scientific inquiries also the evidences play an extremely important role. In fact, all scientific explanations are essentially evidence-based. Even in ordinary life often the evidences are produced to explain a certain situation, event or phenomenon. For instance, if a student comes late in the class, then on asking why he is late, he gives some explanation, some reason for his being late. Similarly, judges, detectives, historians and sociologists are looking and assessing the evidences for the events.

Form and Matter

Logic like pure mathematics is 'science of forms' and norms. An argument consists both form and matter. The content of an argument is matter, and the order in which the content is arranged is form. Form, thus, is the manner in which all the constituents of the reasoning (premisses as well as conclusion) are arranged. The "form is not another constituent, but is the way the constituents are put together".[1]

Not only an argument but every object on the earth is made of some type of matter and it has some kind of shape. Non-existent objects can also be conceived or thought in the **matrix of form and matter.** There is no matterless form and there is no formless matter. Both form and matter, however, are changeable. The same form can be given to different matter, for example same type of chair can be made from wood, iron, cane or plastic. Similarly different forms can be given to the same matter. For instance, to wood one may give the shape of chair, table, almirah,

1. B. Russell, "Logic as the Essence of Philosophy", *Essay in Logic* (ed.) Ronald Jager, p. 126.

etc. Take the example of admission form of a college. All the admission forms are same, but the content in each of the form is different. The same is the case in currency. For instance, all ten rupee notes are similar in form but the number on each note is different.

Subject matter of an argument is the content. We may argue about political situations, educational policies, economic systems, etc. Form of an argument is order, pattern, arrangement in which all the elements (terms and propositions) stand in relation to one another. Form is like a model, a mold, a die in which different kinds of stuff can be put. Logical methods and principles which evaluate rightness of the arguments are constituted according to the forms of arguments. Innumerable arguments can be constituted having the same form. For instance, from the following argument form, we can have many arguments:

All M is P.
All S is M.
___
Therefore, all S is P

One can make innumerable arguments by giving different values to S, P, M. All these arguments will differ from one another only in the content. They all have same form; they all have the same arrangement of the terms and propositions. The 'general pattern' of these arguments is the same. The form is 'framework' of terms like S, P, M occurring in the same position in every argument.[2] Correctness or incorrectness of the argument is not decided by the values of terms like S, P, M but by the manner in which they occupy the places in the premisses and conclusion.

The interest of all the deductive logicians lies in the form of an argument only because the correctness of an argument is decided solely by the form of the argument. The form of the argument must satisfy the logical principles in order to be correct (valid). Since the validity of an argument in deductive logic is totally decided by the form of the argument (content is absolutely irrelevant from the viewpoint of validity), it is called a formal science.

2. Cf. P.F. Strawson, *Introduction to Logical Theory,* p. 45.

The arguments in deductive or pure logic are classified into different categories according to the general form they possess. Arguments having same 'pattern' and of the same 'type' are treated similarly even if the content in each argument is different. The logicians are looking for 'formal similarity' among the arguments. The logical principles or rules which determine correctness (validity)/ incorrectness (invalidity) of an argument is devised on the basis of 'common logical features' of the argument. Thus, the logical form of an argument is the most precious thing in logic. The formal logicians frame rules and formulae for testing the validity of arguments on the basis of logical form they possess. They (the logicians) are thus hunting for 'formal analogy' among the arguments. The arguments having same 'framework' of occurring words and terms are tested by the same logical methods.[3] Logicians' task consists in 'compiling list of highly general rules' of reasoning and arguments. They (the logicians) provide 'representative formulae' for testing the validity/invalidity of the arguments. The arguments having the same kind, same type will be examined and tested by the same general formulae. This makes the logicians' job a little simpler, because if there is a separate rule for each concrete individual argument, then 'the principles of logic will be longer than a dictionary'. In order to avoid that, all arguments of the same type are bracketed together and are thus handled together. The 'representative formulae' or the 'general rules' of arguments are, however, not inconsistent to each other. They are connected and provide ideal and organic system of logic.

Truth and Validity

Two sets of evaluative notions are generally used in elementary logic: true/false and valid/invalid. A proposition is either true or false. A proposition is true when it gives correct information, 'when it mirrors the world'. If, on the other hand, a proposition states the facts incorrectly, then it is false. For example, "All men are

---

3. Cf. P.F. Strawson, *Introduction to Logical Theory*, pp. 45-46.

mortal", "All cats are mammals", "All cows are four-legged animals" are true propositions, for they describe the facts correctly whereas propositions like "All fruits are sweet", "All Indian women are literate" are false propositions for they describe the facts wrongly. A proposition, however, is never evaluated as valid or invalid.

A deductive argument instead is evaluated as valid or invalid and never as true or false. An argument is valid if its premisses necessarily imply the conclusion. In other words, when the conclusion necessarily follows from the premisses, then the argument is considered valid otherwise not. Validity and invalidity are formal notions and hence are applied to formal reasoning and formal logic only.

Though we can isolate these evaluative notions (truth and falsity, valid and invalid) from each other, yet they are not unconnected. There is a relation between truth and falsity of the premisses and conclusion, on the one hand, and validity or invalidity of an argument, on the other hand. In fact, the entire study of logic is intended to explore the relationship between truth and falsity of propositions, and validity and invalidity of arguments. **Generally, it is believed that a valid argument has a true conclusion and invalid argument has false conclusion. But it is wrong.** Thinking of such kind is source of serious errors in logic. The true conclusion does not necessarily mean the argument is valid. Similarly, the false conclusion does not necessarily mean the argument is invalid. A valid argument can have a false conclusion or invalid argument can have true conclusion. But valid arguments having a false conclusion must have at least one false premiss. **If all the premisses are true and the conclusion is false, then the argument is definitely invalid. In fact, the chief characteristic of deductive logic is that it is impossible to have all true premisses and a false conclusion.** A deductive argument takes the form. "If you accept these premisses as true, then you must accept this conclusion as true as well".

Let us now examine the various situations in which the truth and falsity of premisses and conclusion make the argument valid or invalid.

Consider a situation in which all propositions, premisses as well as conclusion, are true. In certain cases they yield a valid argument and in some other an invalid argument depending on the arrangement of premisses and conclusion. For example :

All human beings are mortal.

All professors are human beings.

Therefore, all professors are mortal,

is a valid argument having all true premisses and a true conclusion.

All Presidents of India are Indian citizens.

Mr. Pranab Mukherjee is President of India.

Therefore Mr. Pranab Mukherjee is Indian citizen.

But the arguments having all true premisses and true conclusion can be invalid also depending on the form of the argument. See the following examples.

All cats are mammals.

All cats are rat-eaters.

Therefore, some rat-eaters are mammals,

is invalid in spite of the fact that all premisses and conclusion are true. Take another example:

Similarly:

All professors are mortal.

All income tax payers are mortal.

Therefore some income tax payers are professors.

is invalid argument in spite of the fact that all premisses and conclusion are true.

On the other hand, all false propositions (premisses as well as conclusions) may make an argument valid. For example:

All vegetarians can fly.

All cats are vegetarians.

Therefore, all cats can fly,

is valid argument in spite of the fact the premisses and the conclusion are all false.

But there are invalid arguments having all false premisses (or at least one false premiss) and false conclusion.

All Presidents of India are industrialists.

All MPs are Presidents of India.

Therefore, all MPs are industrialists.

Take yet another example:

All Indians are scientists.

Mr Barack Obama is an Indian.

Therefore, Mr Barack Obama is a scientist.

See some more examples:

All cats are wild creatures.

All horses are wild creatures.

Therefore, all horses are cats,

All Indians are scientists

All Indians are Hindus.

Therefore, all Hindus are scientists.

All Presidents of India are industrialists.

All MPs are industrialists.

Therefore, all MPs are Presidents of India.

are invalid having all false propositions.[4]

The combination of false premisses and true conclusion may make an argument valid or invalid depending on the arrangement of premisses and conclusion. For example:

4. Why and how the argument is invalid is discussed in chapter 7.

All bricks are combustible.
No paper is combustible.
Therefore, no paper is brick,

is valid argument having false premisses but a true conclusion. Similarly,

No living creatures need air to breathe.
All stones are living creatures.
Therefore, no stone needs air to breathe,

is valid though both the premisses are false, and the conclusion is true.

All Presidents of India are below forty years of age.
Sachin Tendulkar is President of India.
Therefore, Sachin Tendulkar is below forty years of age.

But look at the following examples where all premisses are false but conclusion is true, and yet the arguments are invalid.

All literate beings are women.
All Indian Prime Ministers are women.
Therefore, all Indian Prime Ministers are literates,

Similarly the following examples are invalid having all false premisses and true conclusion.

All Presidents of India were industrialists.
Mr. Abdul Kalam is an industrialist.
Therefore, Mr. Abdul Kalam was President of India

All scientists are Indians
Isaac Newton was Indian
Therefore, Isaac Newton was scientist

If all the premisses are true and the conclusion is false, then a deductive argument is bound to be invalid. In fact, the chief characteristic of deductive reasoning is that it is impossible to have all true premisses and a false conclusion. A true proposition or a set of all true propositions can imply only true propositions.[5] For example the following arguments are invalid:

All cows are four-legged creatures.
All horses are four-legged creatures.

Therefore, all horses are cows,

All Presidents of India are Indian citizens
Anna Hazare is an Indian citizen

Therefore, Anna Hazare is President of India

All professors are mortal
All income tax payers are mortal.

Therefore, all income tax payers are professors.

Why all true premisses and false conclusions make the argument invalid? There is a reason. In the formal logic the conclusion is already contained in the premisses. The premisses inherit the conclusion in the implicit form. The conclusion does not go beyond the premisses. Thus, if the premisses are true, the conclusion must necessarily be true, for the conclusion says nothing new or different from the premisses. To have all true premisses and false conclusion means to contradict oneself. We accept the truth of certain facts in the premisses and in the conclusion we deny the same thing. How can this be possible? It is inconsistent to assert and deny the same thing. No one, specially the logician, must not contradict himself. Thus, "an argument is valid only if it would be inconsistent (or self-contradictory) to assert the premisses while denying the conclusion".[6]

From the above discussion it is absolutely clear that the relationship between truth and falsity of propositions on the one hand, and validity and invalidity of the argument on the other hand, is of 'peculiar type'. In the following chapters you will learn this relationship in detail.

---

5. W.V. Quine, *Methods of Logic,* p. 4.
6. P.F. Strawson, op.cit. p. 2.

Deduction and Induction

There are two types of relationships necessary and probable between premisses and conclusion. Consequently, there are two types of reasoning and two types of logic: deductive and inductive. Though the nature of reasoning in both of them is different, their aim is none the less same. **Both deductive and inductive logic provide methods and criteria to differentiate correct reasoning from incorrect ones.**

The relationship between the premisses and the conclusion in deductive reasoning is of implication and 'entailment'. The implicative and 'entailment' relationship justifies the assertion that the conclusion necessarily follows from the premisses in accordance with the logical principles. This is because the conclusion is already inherited in the premisses. For instance in the argument.

All men are mortal.
Socrates is a man.
Therefore, Socrates is mortal.

The conclusion "Socrates is mortal" is already inherited in the premisses "All men are mortal" and "Socrates is a man". The conclusion is present in the premisses in the implicit form. The reasoning makes the implicit form of the conclusion explicit. The conclusion, thus, provides no new information.

Besides, the set of premisses "All men are mortal" and "Socrates is a man" are *conclusive* ground for the conclusion "Socrates is mortal". Conclusive ground means complete evidence, sufficient and total evidences to support the conclusion. Only deductive logic has the privilege of supporting the conclusion with conclusive evidences. In the above-cited example, the conclusion "Socrates is mortal" follows necessarily from the premisses "All men are mortal" and "Socrates is a man". Any addition to already given set of premisses, for instance "Socrates was a philosopher", "He was a Greek", "He was a teacher of famous philosopher Plato", etc. makes no difference to the conclusion "Socrates is mortal". The given two premisses "All men are mortal" and "Socrates is a man" are sufficient and enough to imply the conclusion "Socrates is mortal". In this sense and only in this sense evidences in deductive reasoning are conclusive and complete.

As we have seen the conclusion is already inherited in the premisses, it is impossible then for a valid deductive argument to have all true premisses and a false conclusion. All true premisses implying false conclusion means to contradict oneself. Since the conclusion is already present in the premisses and all premisses are true, then how can the conclusion be false without 'contradictory oneself'.

But very often the conclusion of an argument does not stand to the premisses in so necessary a logical relation as that of being implied or entailed by the premisses. Most of the reasoning that we do in everyday life is non-deductive (inductive). Doctors use non-deductive reasoning in diagnosing the probable causes of a patient's symptoms. Legal scholars often use non-deductive methods to determine what law governs in a particular case. Non-deductive or inductive arguments are tentative, provisional and probable.

There is nothing contradictory in accepting all true premisses and a false conclusion in non-deductive arguments. For instance in the following example.

Professor X is a writer and he is rich.
Professor Y is a writer and he is rich.
Professor Z is a writer and he is rich.

Therefore, all professors who are writers are rich,

All the premisses are true but the conclusion is false, and still it is not contradictory to accept the truth of the premisses and falsity of the conclusion. Thus the chief characteristic of deductive logic that it is impossible to have all true premisses and false conclusion is **not** applicable to the arguments of inductive reasoning.

Moreover, in the inductive reasoning the evidences do not conclusively support the conclusion. The evidences may be very weighty and strong yet they are inconclusive ground for the conclusion. They (evidences) do not imply the conclusion with utmost certainty. That is why, the conclusions in inductive reasoning are merely probable. Look at this example:

Crow X is black.
Crow Y is black.
Crow Z is black.
___
Therefore, probably all crows are black.

Here one can never be sure that all crows are black. It is possible that in future one may come across a crow which is of non-black colour. Since one cannot conceptually rule out the possibility of non-black coloured crow, the conclusion "All crows are black" is merely probable. This means the conclusion and the premisses are not related by strict implicative relation in inductive arguments. The evidences may be very strong in favour of a certain conclusion still the conclusion is not as certain as we find in deductive reasoning. The conclusions of experimental sciences have very high degree of probability but they still are not certain in the strict sense of the term. The strength of the conclusions of inductive reasoning vary in degrees: some conclusions are highly probable whereas some others are less probable. Evidences also vary in their strength. Evidences in some cases are very strong, 'overwhelming' while in other cases they may be merely 'slender' or 'poor'. The evidences (premisses) only support the conclusion and do not 'entail it'. That is why the evidences in inductive inferences (reasoning) are inconclusive and incomplete.

An inductive argument is neither true nor false; also it is neither valid nor invalid either. An inductive argument is characterized or evaluated as sound or unsound, good or bad, right or wrong, appealing or non-appealing, convincing or unconvincing, etc. The relative notions which carry degrees of changeability as good/better, convincing/not so convincing, appealing/not so appealing characterize inductive arguments. Inductive arguments do not differ among themselves in kinds; they differ only in degrees. No inductive argument is totally valid or invalid: it can only be better or worse. But in deductive arguments there is a clear polarization. They differ in kinds, and not in degrees. A deductive argument is either valid or invalid. The phrase 'moderately valid' is not for deductive arguments whereas it can be applied to inductive reasoning very comfortably.

The basic principle behind every deductive argument is that conclusion can never be wider than the sum total of the premisses. In a valid deductive argument a conclusion is either equal or less than the premisses whereas the conclusion in a sound inductive argument can be more, less or equal to the premisses.

Deductive logic like mathematics is a formal science. The 'form' of an argument alone decides the validity of an argument; the matter has absolutely no role in determining the validity of an argument. The 'pure form' of an argument is ideal for the deductive logicians and they are interested only in that because validity of an argument depends on it.

Thus, while form is the only deciding factor in assessing the validity of a deductive argument, it is both form and matter which evaluate inductive arguments. The logical form of an inductive argument is as follows:

All observed crows are black.

Therefore, all crows are black.

All observed Ms are Ns.

Therefore, all Ms are Ns.

The above argumental form, however, may not be true for all arbitrary values of M and N unlike the case of deductive argument.

A deductive logician never questions the status of the premisses; he does not bother whether the given premisses are actually true or false. The premisses are 'given' to him and he takes for granted their truth value and accept them as they are. The job of a deductive logician is merely to examine what necessarily follows from the 'given' set of premisses. In the case of inductive reasoning, however, the job of a logician is not that simple. The premisses are not 'given' to him. The inductive logician hunts and collects the premisses which are in the form of evidences and data. The evidences are actually experienced events which are witnessed by the arguer or by some other being. After collecting sufficient number of data or evidences, the arguer establishes conclusion. For instance, from the evidences that all the crows observed so far are black, one establishes that "All crows are black". But the conclusion is merely **established** and **not entailed.** Entailment relation is a strict and necessary relation which is not applicable to any of the inductive inferences.

In other words, it is 'reasonable' and 'not rational' to establish a conclusion on the basis of collected data. It is only reasonable to draw the conclusion "All crows are black" on the basis of "All *observed* crows are black". In logic 'being rational' means being 'formally valid' whereas being reasonable means acceptably sound. Non-deductive arguments (inductive arguments) can at best be reasonably sound and not rationally valid.

Thus, the job of an inductive logician is twofold: first to collect the *data* (premisses) and second, to establish a reasonably acceptable conclusion on the basis of collected data. The deductive logician, on the other hand, has only one task, that of examining what follows necessarily from a given set of premisses.

It is, however, very wrong to consider deduction and induction as opposed reasonings. They are not to be considered as contradictory to each other but rather as complementary and supplementary to one another. The conclusion of inductive reasoning may serve as the premiss for deductive reasoning. The relation between deductive and inductive reasoning is more like a relay race. Deduction begins where induction ends. They differ only in their 'starting points'.

Just as deductive logic has affinity with mathematics, inductive logic has affinity with the methods employed by the scientists. A question may arise; why a logician is interested in the scientific methods? A logician is interested in the scientific methods and scientific methodology because a scientist like a logician is concerned with the evidences which support the conclusion.

Exercises

1. "Logic is a science of valid reasoning". Explain.
2. Differentiate between truth and validity. Does logic deal with truth or validity or both? Explain with examples.
3. Can a valid argument have false conclusion? If yes, explain how?
4. All true premisses and a false conclusion always make any deductive argument invalid. Do you agree with this? Support your answer with examples.
5. What is meant by *form* of an argument? Are logicians concerned with form or with content or with both? Explain.
6. Do you think 'form' of an argument and its validity are related? If yes, then explain how?
7. Explain and illustrate the similarities and dissimilarities between an argument and an explanation.
8. Explain with examples the difference between deductive and inductive argument.
9. Explain very briefly the following terms:
    1. Premiss and conclusion
    2. Argument
    3. Explanation
    4. Form of an argument
    5. Validity of an argument
    6. Truth and falsity of a proposition
    7. Deduction and Induction.

Chapter 2

Functions and Uses of Language

LANGUAGE is an important vehicle through which ideas and concepts are transmitted. It is a primary source, a common platform and an indispensable medium of social interaction. The study of language is an inquiry into the human minds and language is considered 'the best mirror of the human minds'. Language has a profound influence on human development and use and misuse of language have been fundamental factors in shaping human history. A question may arise: why is a logician interested in the study of language? The answer is simple. Language is both 'aid and obstacle in reasoning'. Logic is study of arguments, and arguments are expressed through language. As the chief aim of logician is to determine the validity/invalidity of arguments, the validity of arguments depends on the correct form of the arguments. The correct form of arguments, in turn, requires clear and precise use of language. Incorrect use of language, on the other hand, leads to fallacious reasoning. Thus, the study of language is all the more important to a logician because the purpose of logic is to improve our critical thinking. To think critically is to recognize, analyse, construct and evaluate arguments.

Language Makes Thinking Possible

It is an established fact that there is a close relation between language and thinking. "Language makes thought possible. Learning a language is not just learning a new way to put our thoughts into words; it is also learning a new way to think."[1] Without words or symbols we cannot think. Our thinking becomes

---

1. Gilbert Harman, *Thought*, pp. 84-85.

intelligible only in the matrix of language. Even in Soliloquy where one talks to one's own self, the use of language is indispensable. An expressive summary of this is found in Shelley's remark. "He gave men speech, and speech created thought . . . .".[2] Language and thought are interdependent. But the thinking in which the logicians are interested in is 'reasoned thinking' which takes place as we work out problems, tell stories, plan strategies, and so on. It has been, called 'rational', 'direct', 'logical' or 'prepositional thinking'. It involves elements that are both deductive (when we solve problems by using a given set of rules as in arithmetical task) and inductive (when one solves problems on the basis of data placed before us, as in working out a travel route). Language seems to be very important for this kind of thinking. The formal properties of language, such as word order and sentence sequencing, constitute the medium in which our connected thought can be presented and organized.[3]

It is very important for a student of logic to learn what conclusion follows from a given set of propositions (premisses). He should know how to organize his thoughts in the sequence of given facts (the basis, the premisses) and the inferred facts (conclusion).[4]

Various Functions of Language

Language serves numerous functions for human beings. We use language in our everyday life to communicate information, describe objects, to greet people, to let others know our requirements, to express our feelings, to request, to give instructions, to sing, to crack jokes, and many more things. There are 'countless' uses of language. Ludwig Wittgenstein, a famous twentieth-century linguistic philosopher, has described language

2. Cf. David Crystal, *The Cambridge Encyclopedia of Language* (second edition) p. 14.
3. Ibid.
4. Cf. Noam Chomsky, *Knowledge of Language (Its Nature, Origin and Use)*, p. xxvi.

as a 'tool', as an 'instrument'. Using language is like playing games, 'language-games'.[5] Language-games are not part of any theory about language, but is one way of looking at language as a phenomenon.

While studying language it is important to analyse the tasks performed by language and kinds of sentences used in performing these tasks. In ordinary discourse, language serves multiple functions, and in determining its specific use one must consider its context and purpose of the speaker. The grammarians divide the uses of language into such classes as directive, expressive, evaluative, cognitive, ceremonial, and so on. But three functions of language need special mention. Identifying these three functions is simple but their awareness is important to understand complexity of language. These three functions are:

(i) Informative function

(ii) Expressive function

(iii) Directive function

INFORMATIVE FUNCTION

The first basic function of language is to inform, to report and to describe facts. We communicate our beliefs and opinions with others which may be true or false. See the following examples:

"Socrates was a Greek philosopher".
"New Delhi is capital of India".
"Shakespeare was the author of *King Lear*".
"Mercury rises with heat".
"Two plus two is four".

All the above statements are informative and their purpose is to state 'what the facts are.' We may believe or disbelieve, assert or deny them. The information provided may be correct or incorrect. The main characteristics of these statements are that they declare whether facts exist or not. They are dichotomical statements true or false.

---

5. Ludwig Wittgenstein, *Philosophical Investigations,* tr. G.E.M. Anscombe, Oxford: Basil Blackwell; New York: Macmillan, 1958.

Logicians and scientists are concerned exclusively with this type of statements. A scientific statement is exact and precise and it carries truth-values, true and false. However, a scientific statement cannot be both true and false at the same time; it also cannot be neither true nor false at the same time. Exactitude is the characteristic of the scientific statements and only informative use of language makes such statements with exactitude. Like scientist a logician is also concerned with precise use of language in affirming or denying propositions, formulating arguments,and evaluating them. The criterion of truth and falsity is attached to them. Logicians and scientists thus are interested exclusively in this function of language.

EXPRESSIVE FUNCTION

The expressive use of language employs words, phrases, or even sentences to show the feelings, emotions, attitudes, and dispositions of the speaker. Through language we express our joys and sorrows, pleasure and pain. A player in a match expresses his pleasure when he utters "We have won"! See the following examples:

"Oh! what a beautiful rainbow"
"Cricket is a great play"!
"The portraits are beautiful"!
"Oh! What a relief"!
"Fantastic"!
"Oh! That's great"!
"Terrific"!
"Oh! My God"!
"You Bravo"!

These statements express feelings and emotions. Expressive language can be used effectively to arouse feelings of love, anger, hate, etc. in the minds of listeners. Lyrical poetry is very good example of expressive function of language. Poems are not meant to report any information but to express the feelings that the poet feels keenly about. No criteria of truth or falsity are applied to emotions or feelings because they are neither true nor false. Language used to express emotions is called 'emotive language'

DIRECTIVE FUNCTION

Language is also used to get a particular work done. Sentences and words cause overt actions. By means of language one can command, direct, request or suggest others to do some work. One can compel others to perform or to prevent them to do a certain action. See the following examples:

"Close the door".
"Please give me your pen".
"I suggest you to take up this study course material".
"Is tomorrow a holiday"?
"Right turn"!
"Please pass this tray".
"When do the classes begin"?
"Attention".
"Brush your teeth twice a day".
"Come here"!

No one asks whether these statements are true or false because the criterion of truth/falsity is not applied to them. Similarly language expressing emotions is subjective and likely to be used differently by different people.

Besides communicating, reporting, describing, commanding, language serves other functions also, for instance ceremonial and performative functions. Though it is true that ceremonial discourse can "always be regarded as a mixture of expressive and directive discourse, rather than as a separate kind that is unique"[6] yet it needs to be mentioned here separately. To greet a friend using words or phrases like 'Hey', 'Hello', 'Good morning', 'How are you', etc. are some of the illustrations of the ceremonial discourses. Here we refer to phrases or sentences "ranging from trivial words of greeting to the verbal rituals performed on holy

---

6. I.M. Copi, *Introduction to Logic* (ninth edition) p. 84.

days in houses of worship".[7] Ceremonial phrases are important for "goodwill and sociability". Sentences of this kind are, usually, automatically produced and are of stereotyped structure. The most common linguistic expression of emotion consists of conventional words or phrases such as 'Gosh', "What a sight"! The ritual exchanges about health or the weather is not to communicate ideas but to maintain 'comfortable relationship between people'.[8] Ceremonial function thus can hardly be informative for those who use it. A performative expression, on the other hand, is the one that is used to accomplish some social acts, in contrast to reporting, evaluating, reacting to it, etc. For instance, while performing marriages the priest's discourses are performative in nature. Casting a vote is another example of performative function. Yet another example of this category is party saying "I accept the offer" or "I accept the proposal".

By this time you must have noticed that language is very flexible and it may serve many functions simultaneously. For example, a traveller tells his friend "The train leaves in ten minutes". Such a statement is not only informative but is designed to influence the action of the friend as well. Any ordinary communication exemplifies all the three basic functions of language to a greater or lesser extent. This 'mixed use' of language recognizes that a given expression may have multiple uses in a given context. For example: "This building is on fire"! indicates many functions at the same time. It is informative, expressive as well as directive simultaneously.

The three basic functions of language (informative, expressive and directive) thus are not mutually exclusive. They are overlapping functions and a statement which is used informatively can also be used expressively, or what can be used directively, can also be used expressively, and so on. The descriptive purpose in language may come in conjunction with

7. I.M. Copi, *Introduction to Logic* (ninth edition) p. 84.

8. David Crystal, op. cit., p. 10.

other purposes of discourse as well. However, the logician's chief concern would be to identify the informative discourse only. A student of logic should be able to separate it from its expressive, directive, ceremonial or performative uses.

Arguments sometimes became fallacious because the meanings of the terms and sentences are not properly known. Fallacies such as those of *Relevance* (which provide a weak link between premisses and conclusion) or of *Ambiguity* (which occur because of the use of expressive language) make arguments invalid. Since logic is concerned with what is inferred and on what ground it is inferred, the logician aspires only for emotionally neutral language.

Emotively (Emotionally) Neutral Language

In examining the validity of deductive arguments, it is extremely important to use emotively neutral language. Although it is not always easy to achieve emotively neutral language in every instance — because language has various functions and it fulfils many purposes — it is important to separate emotively neutral language from its other uses, because it alone decides the validity or invalidity of an argument. Emotions are subjective and they vary from person to person. Words and sentences are powerful tools to influence the thoughts of the listeners. Emotionally charged language is purposely used to persuade someone to accept other's viewpoints. Words and sentences are wrapped up in emotions since man is an emotional being. Usually each one of us constructs normal arguments in a non-logical form — and there is nothing intrinsically wrong with it — but it hinders in the correct understanding and evaluation of an argument. If one wants to argue well and wants to evaluate the arguments of others, one needs to know how to use emotionally neutral language. For instance, someone asks rights for Dalits on the grounds of the atrocities done to them in the past, then he is not arguing in a logically correct way. This is simply getting emotional, using emotive words and mobilizing the mob on this basis. As per the demand of logic, equal rights should be asked for Dalits on the basis of their being human beings. By virtue of this, they have an equal right to live like other individuals in the society. Such an argument would be logically as well as principle-wise correct.

Agreement and Disagreement

You have seen language is extremely important for us logically as well as non-logically, but at the same time it is also true that the use of language is one of the major sources of disputes among people. The emotionally inclined language can create some serious disputes and disagreements. The unfortunate thing is that when people disagree they often do not know what they disagree about.

There are two types of disagreements: disagreements over facts and disagreement in the evaluation over those facts. First type of disagreement generally is called disagreement in belief, while second type of disagreement is known as disagreement in attitude. Here are some examples of disagreement in belief. People disagree whether euthanasia should be legalized. They disagree whether alternative healing methods like Reiki or naturopathy actually help in curing people or they are merely pseudo-sciences. They disagree whether walking actually helps in losing one's weight, and people disagree whether meditation really helps a person in relieving tension and getting peace. Take yet another example: Ram says "Sohan died of brain haemorrhage." Gopal says "No, he died of heart attack." These and other such disagreements are mainly due to different and sometimes mutually incompatible beliefs. The disagreements in belief are *factual* differences which can be removed by resorting to mutually agreeable facts, taking help of consulting authorities, using reference books, making unbiased observations of the states of affairs, etc. Rephrasing the disputes in the emotionally neutral language is also one of the effective devices in solving the disagreement in belief.

The disagreement in attitude, on the other hand, is of evaluation — it is associated with judging and assessing a state of affair. They disagree on the issue whether a particular phenomenon or state of affairs is good or bad, right or wrong, acceptable or unacceptable, desirable or undesirable. Disagreement in attitude comes about by our approval or disapproval about the matter of issue. For instance, though homosexual marriages have got legal sanction, yet people may approve or disapprove of them, considering them either good or bad. Similarly in the case of 'live-in' relationships, there are divergent attitudes which can result in serious debates in a society. However, the disagreement in attitude sometimes can be resolved by using 'methods of rhetoric and persuasion.' There are also certatin situations when people either disagree completely or when they agree on certain points but disagree over others. Combining the agreement and disagreement in belief and attitude, we have four possible combinations:

1. Agreement in belief and agreement in attitude. Both the parties here agree over facts as well as in attitude. For instance, people agree on the issue of the right to education to all the children up to fourteen years of age in India. In attitude also they agree that it is a healthy development both for the child as well as for the society. There are no disputes in such cases.
2. Agreement in belief but disagreement in attitude. For example both the sides agree to the provision made for the 'right to food' for the Below Poverty Line (BPL) people in the Budget of 2009. They will get 25 kg of wheat or rice at the rate of two rupees per kilo per family. Yet they may disagree in attitude. One may say it is good to help poor whereas another may call it a political gimmick.
3. Disagreement in belief but agreement in attitude. For example there are two political parties having the attitude of hatred towards terrorism; both want to abolish it. But they have different beliefs for combating terrorism. Party

A feels that implementation of stringent laws such as TADA or POTA is the only justified means to root out terrorism whereas party B believes that such draconian laws would propagate rather than mitigate terrorism. And other strategies such as strengthening intelligence, negotiations and reformative methods should be used to combat terrorism. Euthanasia is another example which explains this kind of disagreement. People are divided in their beliefs over 'mercy killing' getting a legal sanction though everyone agrees in attitude that the patients should not suffer endlessly.

4. No agreement at all. People may disagree in belief as well as in attitude. For instance, there are divergent views among members of political parties over the bill for reservation for women in Parliament. Those members who have the attitude of chauvinism and feel that Indian society is male-dominated are of the belief that the reservation for women should be limited to a bare minimum extent, whereas those who have the attitude of giving equal status to women are of the belief that reservation for women should be equivalent to that of men.

The aforementioned instances help us to evaluate and explore the connection between belief and attitude. At times our beliefs are an outcome of our attitude and vice versa, while there are also cases in which belief and attitude are diametrically opposed to each other. Besides, it cannot be doubted that there is a very thin line to demarcate beween belief and attitude. Quite often in day-to-day life we maintain that our belief is our attitude or our attitude is what we believe in.

However, most of our disagreements can be easily resolved because they are not of the same magnitude. Some of the disagreements may be superfluous and can be resolved by reframing them in an emotionally neutral language or through 'persuasive' methods such as negotiation, showing valid proofs, consulting authorities, etc. Some differences may be very sharp and deep. None the less it is very important to know what we disagree about.

Exercises

1. Explain basic functions of language.
2. Logicians are interested only in informative function of language. Do you agree? Support your answer with suitable examples.
3. State the characteristics of the use of 'emotional language'. Is it of any use to a logician? Discuss.
4. Explain the notions of agreements and disagreements in brief, with suitable examples.
5. Explain the phrase 'agreements and disagreements in attitude'.
6. What is the difference between 'disagreements in belief' and 'disagreements in attitude'? Support your answer with suitable examples.
7. Write a short note on Emotively (or Emotionally) Neutral Language.

Chapter 3 – Section A

Proposition
Traditional Account

A PROPOSITION is a unit of reasoning in logic. Both premisses and conclusion of an argument are propositions. A proposition is a sentence, a meaningful arrangement of words. It has a subject, a predicate and a copula. Every sentence, however, is not always a proposition. Informative, indicative or factual sentences alone are propositions. Interrogative, exclamatory, emotive, or imperative sentences are not propositions.

A proposition is a sentence which is either true or false, asserted or not asserted, believed or disbelieved, supposed or doubted. Whereas factual or indicative sentences are true or false, the imperative, exclamatory or interrogative sentences are neither of them. For example, when one utters "What a beautiful rainbow!" no one expects it to be true or false. The uttered sentence is merely an expression of a feeling. Similarly, if the father orders the child to close the TV, the uttered sentences do not carry any true value. It is an order to be obeyed. Questions may be asked, commands given, and exclamations uttered, but none of them can be affirmed, denied or judged to be either true or false.

A proposition is true when it describes the facts correctly; and a proposition is false when it does not describe the facts correctly. One may believe a sentence to be either true or false. In this capacity the believed or disbelieved sentences become propositions, for they carry truth values. Mythical statements too are propositions because they are believed to be either true or false. "Ram has killed Ravan" is a proposition, for it is believed to be true. "Padmani was a beautiful lady" is a proposition, for it is believed to be true, but "P is beautiful" is not a proposition because it is neither true nor false.

A proposition which is always true is called *tautology* in logic. For example, "The sum of all angles of a triangle is equivalent to 180°", "Cats are mammals", "No man is immortal", etc. are tautologous propositions. A proposition which is always false is called *contradictory* or *self-contradictory*. For instance, "All men are immortal", "All circles are polygon" are self-contradictory propositions. However, when a proposition is true in some cases and false in some other cases, it is called *contingent*. For instance, the proposition "It is raining" is true just now but it may be false some other time.

Traditional Classification of Propositions

Traditional logicians[1] have divided the propositions into two groups, categorical and conditional. A proposition is either categorical or conditional. The modern logicians,[2] however,

Traditional classification of propositions

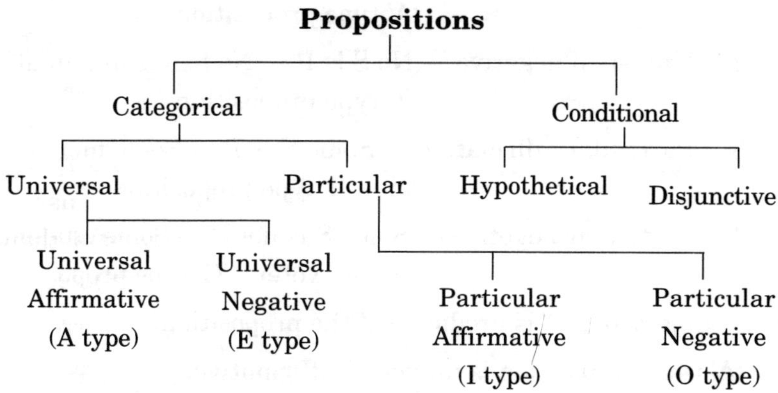

1. The ancient Greek philosopher Aristotle was the founder of logic as the science. He was one of the first scholars to carry out a systematic study of the propositions and arguments.
2. Modern logic extends far beyond the work of traditional Aristotelian logic. Modern logicians unlike the traditional logicians have used mathematical methods and techniques to test the validity of arguments. Some of the leading modern logicians are British mathematicians such →

classified them differently. Let us first examine the traditional classification of propositions.

Categorical Propositions

Categorical propositions are stated without any condition. Here the predicate is either assigned or denied to the subject without any condition. For instance, "All men are mortal", "This chair is round", "Some students are not scholarship holders" are categorical propositions. A conditional proposition, on the other hand, is that in which a predicate is assigned or denied to subject on certain conditions. For instance, "If we get tickets, then we shall go for movie", "Sita will not get job unless she hunts for it", "If Ram is intelligent then he will qualify the test", "Either I will go to the library or attend the conference"are conditional propositions.

Aristotle and other classical logicians divided the categorical propositions into four types:

1. Universal affirmative — All S is P — All men are mortal. 'A' type proposition
2. Universal negative — No S is P — No fish is mammal. 'E' type proposition
3. Particular affirmative — Some S is P — Some men are wise. 'I' type proposition
4. Particular negative — Some S is not P — Some students are not voters. 'O' type proposition

'S' is subject and 'P' is predicate of the proposition

'A' type proposition is universal affirmative.
'E' type proposition is universal negative.
'I' type proposition is particular affirmative.
'O' type proposition is particular negative.

→ as George Boole, Alfred North Whitehead and British Philosopher Bertrand Russell. Today, logic is used mainly to test the validity of all kinds of arguments. It also has important uses in working with such devices as computers and electric switching circuits.

All these propositions A, E, I, O have only one form that is 'subject predicate form'. The traditional logicians have recognized only one form for the categorical propositions. There are three constituents of a categorical proposition — subject, predicate and copula. In a proposition "All S is P", 'S' is subject, 'P' is predicate and 'is' is copula. Both 'S' and 'P' are terms and they represent classes.

Quantity and Quality

The traditional logicians have introduced two more notions for the categorical propositions. They are quantity and quality.

Quantity of a proposition is related to the generalization of the subject of a proposition. The generalization can be unrestricted or restricted. Hence, there are two quantities — universal and particular. Subject of a universal proposition indicates unrestricted generalization, and in a particular proposition subject indicates restricted generalization. For instance, in the proposition, "All crows are black", the subject term 'crows' denotes the entire class of crows. In the proposition, "All men are mortal", since the entire class of 'man' is taken into consideration, the quantity of the proposition is universal. In the proposition "No fish is mammal", again the quantity is universal. Here the entire class of fish is excluded from the entire class of mammals. However, when the subject of a proposition indicates only some members of a class, the quantity of the proposition is particular. For instance, in the proposition "Some students are scholarship holders", the quantity is particular and similarly in the proposition, "Some men are not happy beings", the quantity is particular.

Quality of a proposition means whether the predicate is assigned or denied to the subject. There are two qualities which a proposition can have, affirmative or negative. If a predicate is assigned to subject, then quality of the proposition is affirmative. For instance, in the proposition, "All flowers are beautiful", the predicate 'beautiful' is assigned to the subject 'flowers'. If a predicate is denied to the subject, then quality of the proposition is negative. For instance, in the proposition "Some men are not wise", predicate 'wise' is denied to the subject 'men'. However, a negative term like 'immortal', 'unwise', etc. do not make a proposition negative. It is negative copula which makes a proposition negative. For example, "Some men are unwise", is an affirmative proposition with a negative predicate whereas "Some men are not wise", is a negative proposition.

Quantity and quality together give four types of propositions:

1. Universal affirmative
2. Universal negative
3. Particular affirmative
4. Particular negative

In 'A' proposition, "All men are mortal", quantity is universal and quality is affirmative. In 'E' proposition, "No fish is mammal", quantity is universal and quality is negative. In 'I' proposition, "Some students are hardworking", quantity is particular and quality is affirmative. And in 'O' proposition, "Some men are not wise", quantity is particular and quality is negative.

A singular proposition, in the traditional classification of proposition, is included under universal proposition. In singular proposition subject is either a proper noun or refers to specific person or object. For example, "Socrates was a Greek philosopher", "This is a girl's college", "New Delhi is capital of India", are few instances of singular propositions. No independent status is given to such propositions by the traditional logicians; these propositions are bracketed with universal propositions. "Socrates was a Greek philosopher", is universal affirmative proposition whereas "Socrates was not an Indian", is universal negative proposition. This was, however, challenged and criticized by the modern logicians which you will study later in this chapter.

Why were the singular propositions treated as universal propositions by the classical thinkers? It is because in spite of the fact that the subject term of the singular proposition is a 'specific individual or object', it represents a class, a unit class[3] (one-membered class)[4]. There is only one member in the class referred by the subject Socrates in the proposition "Socrates was a Greek philosopher". Since the predicate in this proposition is assigned to that very one member of the class, it becomes 'A' proposition. "Socrates was not an Indian", is 'E' proposition for the similar reason. The predicate 'an Indian', is denied to the subject 'Socrates', which incidentally is only one-membered class.

Traditionally all the categorical propositions are divided into four groups whose standard logical form is as follows:

All S is P - A
No S is P - E
Some S is P - I
Some S is not P - O

All the simple, singular, unconditional categorical propositions are one of the above four types.

Reduction of the Sentences into Standard Logical Form Propositions

In our ordinary life and also in various branches of sciences, sentences are not always in this neat and formal logical form. For instance sentences like:

"All roses are not red".
"An elephant is a vegetarian animal".
"Many students are not interested in the formal education".

3. "Woman Prime Minister of India up to year 1982" is an example of unit class. Since there is one member in the class of Woman Prime Minister of India, it is called unit class.
4. Cf. Irving M. Copi and Cohen Carl, *Introduction to Logic* (Ninth Edition), p. 278.

are not in the standard logical form. They are to be translated into the standard logical form propositions. The above propositions are translated as :

"Some roses are not red things".

"All elephants are vegetarian animals".

"Some students are not interested in the formal education".

respectively. The translation or the reduction of non-standard form sentences into standard form propositions is important because all the methods and techniques to determine the validity of arguments are in terms of standard form propositions. There are various devices to reduce a non-standard form sentences into standard form proposition. However, the meaning of the proposition should not be lost in this process. This is very important. In fact, the meaning of the proposition helps in the reduction and translation. Some of the devices and techniques are as follows:

Device 1. Both subject and predicate of a standard form categorical proposition are substantive nouns. If either of them (subject or predicate) is not noun, then it has to be translated into appropriate noun.

The proposition "Some roses are beautiful", is translated as "Some roses are beautiful things".

"All cats eat meat", becomes "All cats are meat eaters".

"All chairs are meant for sitting", is reduced as "All chairs are things meant for sitting".

"Ram plays football", is translated as "Ram is football player".

"Violence breeds violence", becomes "All acts of violence are violence breeders".

The above examples show that if predicate is a verb or an adjective, then it should be replaced by substantive noun. In a standard form categorical proposition there should be one subject term (noun) and one predicate term (noun), and a copula to join them. Both subject and predicate should necessarily be substantive noun. It is because both subject and predicate represent classes and only substantive nouns can do that.

Device 2. Propositions like:

"All that glitters is not gold".
"Not all roses are red".
"Every student is not scholarship holder".
"Not every inexplicable event is miraculous event".

are not universal negative propositions. They deceptively suggest that they are universal negative, but their meaning indicates that they are only particular negative propositions. After translation the above propositions become:

"Something that glitters is not gold".
"Some roses are not red things".
"Some students are not scholarship holders".
"Some inexplicable events are not miraculous events".

respectively.

Words like 'hardly', 'rarely', 'seldom', 'scarcely', 'few' and 'little', 'Not always', 'not everywhere', 'sometimes not' are indicators of particular negative propositions. But the words like 'never', 'nowhere', 'under no circumstance' indicate universal negative propositions.

Device 3. There are propositions having words like, 'only', 'none but', etc. For example:

"Only policemen are indispensable".
"None but scholarship holders are invited for the discussion".

can be translated into universal affirmative 'A' propositions provided subject term and predicate term interchange their places. The above propositions are reduced as follows:

"All those who are indispensable are policemen".
"All those who are invited for the discussion are scholarship holders".

Though this type of reduction is quite popular but there are other ways also in which 'only', 'none but' propositions can be translated. The proposition, "Only policemen are indispensable", can also be translated into 'E' proposition as, "No non-policemen are indispensable", and "None but scholarship holders are invited for the discussion", can be reduced as "No non-scholarship holders are invited for the discussion".

But proposition like "Only some students are hard-working", is translated differently from what we have done above. Such translations you will find in device number 9.

Device 4. There are propositions having no quantifiers at all. For instance:

"Children are naughty".

"Students are present".

"There are honest politicians".

"Flowers are beautiful".

The meaning of these propositions reveal their quantity. The above propositions are translated as follows:

"All children are naughty".

"Some students are persons who are present here".

"Some politicians are honest beings".

"All flowers are beautiful things".

Device 5. There are words which indicate universal quantity such as 'each', 'any', 'every', 'always', 'everywhere', 'in every instances', 'who', 'whatsoever', etc. For instance the propositions:

"Any person is free to be a member of this Library".

"Every man loves children".

"Women always are delicate".

"Each application was checked".

are translated as :

"All persons are eligible to be the member of this Library".

"All men are children lovers".

"All women are delicate beings".

"All applications are things checked". respectively.

Device 6. But the quantity of the propositions having words like, 'a' or 'an' is determined by the context in which they occur. For instance, proposition like. "A snake is reptile", has different quantity from the proposition "A snake was killed by the gardener yesterday". Whereas, the former suggests universal affirmative proposition, "All snakes are reptile creatures", the latter is a particular affirmative proposition, "Some snake was a creature killed by the gardener yesterday". Similarly, the proposition "A policeman is a government employee", is universal affirmative proposition but the proposition "A policeman is at the gate", is particular affirmative proposition.

Device 7. Words like, 'a few', 'most', 'majority', 'many', 'most of them', 'several', 'sometimes', 'generally', 'usually', 'occasionally', 'once', etc. suggest particularity of the propositions. For example:

"Many doctors are not greedy persons", is reduced into 'O' proposition "Some doctors are not greedy persons".

"Most politicians are liars", is 'I' proposition and its standard logical form is "Some politicians are liars".

Device 8. There are propositions in which all the components of the proposition such as subject term, predicate term, quality, quantity are present but they are not arranged in proper order. For instance:

"Tall buildings are all expensive".

"Insects are sometimes poisonous".

"Birds all have wings".

"Happy are those who know their limitations".

are translated as follows :

"All tall buildings are expensive things".

"Some insects are poisonous creatures".

"All birds are winged creatures".

"All those who know their limitations are happy beings" respectively.

Device 9. The propositions containing words like 'except', 'alone', 'all but a few', 'only some' are not simple propositions. They are rather compound propositions. They mean two propositions simultaneously. Therefore, they are translated differently. Propositions like "All except children are allowed in the hall" means "All non-children (adults) are allowed in the hall" and "No child is allowed in the hall",[5] "Man alone is rational animal", is translated as the combination of two propositions. "All men are rational animals" and "No non-man is rational animal". The proposition "Only some students of this institution are Indian citizens", is translated as "Some students of this institution are Indian citizens" and "Some students of this institution are not Indian citizens".

Device 10. Sometimes a sentence has a negative predicate. It has to be translated in a proposition having a positive predicate. For example, the sentence "Some employees are non-residents", will be translated as "Some employees are not residents". Take another example "All fish are non-mammals", will be translated as "No fish is mammal". The negative predicate is changed into affirmative predicate by using obversion which is one of the important forms of immediate inference about which you will learn in chapter 6.

Device 11. Some sentences are stated in interrogative form. But their meanings reveal that some of them are universal affirmative propositions while some others are universal negative propositions. For example sentences like:

1. "Is there a mother who does not love her children?"*
2. "Is there a man who is perfect?"

Are translated as:

5. Cf. Irving M. Copi and Carl Cohen, op.cit., p. 283.

* This was suggested to me by my colleague Dr Rajib Roy, Associate Professor, Philosophy Dept, K.M. College, University of Delhi, Delhi.

1. "All mothers love their children."
2. "No man is perfect."

respectively.

We have discussed various devices for translating the non-standard form sentences into standard logical form. They, however, are by no means exhaustive. There may be sentences which are not covered by any of the above devices, but in order to reduce such propositions into standard form, their meaning is the only guide.

Exercises

1. Reduce the following sentences into standard logical form propositions:
    1. Every citizen is a voter.
    2. All roses are not red.
    3. Birds have wings.
    4. Cats are mammals.
    5. A politician is hardly honest.
    6. All old people are not wise.
    7. Only mathematicians are good logicians.
    8. Contractors are never dependable.
    9. A few doctors are registered.
    10. Few leaders are honest.
    11. Good logicians are generally good mathematicians.
    12. Many politicians are not socialists.
    13. Many birds build nests.
    14. Children are rarely dishonest.
    15. Policemen are not allowed in the religious institutions.
    16. Every student of this class is a voter in the general election.
    17. Only children are allowed to play in this park.

18. Boys are not allowed in this college.
19. Some good books are seldom read.
20. Usually children are emotional beings.

2. Reduce the following sentences into their standard form propositions:
    1. Soldiers are patriots.
    2. Not all good speakers are good writers.
    3. Only ladies are allowed in this bus.
    4. Scientists are all genius.
    5. None but brave win medals.
    6. Wars are sometimes necessary.
    7. Every man cannot be a leader.
    8. Only man is rational animal.
    9. Psychopath can never be trusted.
    10. A few cars are expansive.
    11. Few employees are hard-working.
    12. Not all politicians are statesmen.
    13. Artists usually are not rich.
    14. Honesty is no where valued.
    15. Under no circumstances, a lion will eat grass.
    16. Selfishness is condemned everywhere.
    17. Every dog has his day.
    18. Easy come, easy go.
    19. Mango is a delicious fruit.
    20. Not even a single match was won by official team.
3. What is a proposition? Explain the relation between a sentence and a proposition? Is it true to say that a proposition is sub-set of a larger set of a sentence?
4. Give brief account of traditional classification of propositions.

5. Explain with examples the notions of 'quantity' and 'quality' of propositions.
6. State the 'quantity' and 'quality' of the following propositions:
    1. All children are innocent beings.
    2. No saint is cheater.
    3. Some students are scholarship holders.
    4. Some roses are not red things.

Chapter 3 – Section B

Modern Logicians' Treatment of Categorical Propositions

THOUGH modern logicians[1] have accepted the traditional account of proposition in general, yet their treatment and classification of the propositions is different from that of the traditional thinkers. The existential import of the propositions is the main cause of this difference. Before knowing the modern logicians' treatment and classification of the propositions, we must know about the existential import of the propositions.

Existential Import

A proposition is supposed to have existential import if it assumes and accepts the existence of objects or things. For example "This table is round" has existential import, for it accepts the existence of 'table'. "That student is scholarship holder" has existential import, for it accepts the existence of a 'student'. "All men are mortal" has existential import since it accepts the existence of 'man'. "Some voters are women" accepts the existence of at least one 'voter', hence it has existential import. But not all propositions have existential import. For example "All unicorns breathe air" does not have existential import because there is no real existence of 'unicorn'.

A proposition is said to have existential import if its subject term denotes 'actually existing things'. The proposition mentioned above "All unicorns breathe air" does not have existential import

1. Modern logic originated in the first half of the ninteenth century. George Boole was one of its founder members. The other prominent logicians were B. Russell and A.N. Whitehead.

because there is actually no real existence of 'unicorn'. The problem of existential import has stirred a new controversy among the logicians specially between traditional logicians (Aristotle) and modern logicians (George Boole). Whereas Aristotle held the view that the class of subject term of any proposition (A, E, I, O or singular) assumes and accepts that there are members in the class of subject term and hence have existential impact, George Boole holds the view that only particular propositions (I, O and singular) have existential import. Particular affirmative 'I' proposition "Some students are scholarship holders" is analysed as "There exists at least one student who is scholarship holder". Similarly particularly negative 'O' proposition "Some cats are not black" is analysed as "There exists at least one cat which is not black". For him (George Boole) the universal propositions do not assume the existence of members in the class of subject term and thus they do not have existential import. This standpoint of modern logicians has led to the criticism of Aristotelian logic. Consequently some of the argument forms which were valid in Aristotelien logic have become invalid in the modern logic in the context of existential import.

Let us see the following illustration:

Proposition	Aristotle's view	Boole's view
1. All men are mortal.	implies the existence of subject term 'man'.	does not imply the existence of subject term 'man'.
2. All skyflowers are red.	does not imply the existence of subject term 'skyflower' because there is no actual existence of 'skyflower'.	does not imply the existence of subject term 'skyflower'.
3. No child is voter.	implies the existence of the subject term 'child'.	does not imply the existence of subject term 'child'.
4. No mountains made of gold are situated in India.	does not imply the existence of subject term 'mountains made of gold' because there is no actual existence of 'mountains made of gold'.	does not imply the existence of 'mountains made of gold.
5. Some students are voters.	implies the existence of 'student'.	implies the existence of 'student'.
6. Some cats are not black.	implies the existence of 'cat'.	implies the existence of 'cat'.

The above illustration makes it clear that Aristotle and traditional logicians do not have a fixed or rigid standpoint regarding existential import of universal propositions. Whenever the class of subject term of universal propositions refers to actually existing object or thing there the proposition has existential import otherwise not. But the modern logicians specially George Boole is very specific and "neutral about existence" of the members of the class of subject term of universal propositions. He appears to be more logical and consistent. The analysis of universal propositions make it very clear that the propositions can be meaningful even without referring to the actual existence of things or objects.

Universal affirmative 'A' proposition "All men are mortal" is interpreted to mean "If there is a man, then he is mortal." Similarly "No child is voter" is interpreted to mean "If there is a child, then he is not voter". When I say "All men are mortal" I mean to accept that an inseparable relationship holds between 'man' and 'mortal'. I am not here accepting or assuming that there is an entity called 'man'.

The meaning of the proposition does not depend on the assumption that class of 'man' have members rather it depends on the acceptance of a relation between subject term and predicate term. Similarly universal negative 'E' proposition "No child is voter" means to accept only that 'children' and 'voter' do not common member. According to modern logicians all universal propositions irrespective of whether there are members in the class of subject term or not, they only highlight internal inseparable relation between subject term and predicate term. They are conditional (hypothetical) propositions which do not assume the existence of entities. The meaningfulness of universal propositions does not depend on the existence of members in the class of subject term but depend on their inseparable relationship. Since the traditional logicians do not have one definite stand regarding the existence of members of subject of universal propositions, there are two options before them. First they may make 'restricted' use of existential import for the universal propositions. It means only those universal propositions are referred to have existential import where there are members in the class of subject term as shown in example no. 1 and 3 in the illustrated example. Secondly to accept existential import for all propositions, universal, particular and singular. This is popularly known as 'blanket presupposition' of existential import for propositions.

But unfortunately both the options are unacceptable. The first will 'restrict' the use of logical rules only to those universal propositions where subject term have members. Universal propositions having empty subject terms will not be covered. This will make logic also 'restricted'. But sometimes in our daily life, in sciences and in executing legal rules, we want universal propositions having subject term as empty classes. For example when it is said "All those found guilty betting for IPL will be jailed" it means we want to keep the class of "those betting in IPL" empty.

If we grant 'blanket presupposition' of existential import for all the propositions (irrespective of whether they are universal or particular) then the law of contradiction cannot be accepted. The law of contradiction states that the two contradictory propositions 'A' and 'O' or 'E' and 'I' both cannot be true at the same time and also cannot be false at the same time. For example if "All voters are citizens" is true then its contradictory proposition "some voters are not citizens" is definitely false. If "All women are literate" is false then "some women are not literate" is true. Two contradictory propositions can neither be true together nor can they be false together. But if we grant existential import to all the propositions then there can be a situation where contradictory propositions 'A' and 'O' and 'E' and 'I' will be false together. For example "All unicorns are red" and "some unicorns are not red" both will be false at the same time if there is actually no entity called 'unicorn'. If two propositions can be false at the same time then they are no longer contradictory propositions. The second option of 'blanket presupposition' of existential import for all propositions is even more harmful than the first one.

Thus it is more logical and consistent to accept the modern logicians' views that only particular propositions have existential import.

In the following discussions you will see how the existential import of the propositions influenced George Boole's and John Venn's[2] formulations of the categorical propositions. While Boole had formulated A, E, I and O propositions in terms *of empty classes,* Venn represented them through diagrams. But in their treatment of the categorical propositions, there is a presumption that universal propositions do not imply the existence of members in the class of subject term whereas the particular propositions imply the existence of members in the class of subject term.

Boolean Analysis of Categorical Propositions

Boolean interpretation of categorical propositions depends on the empty classes. A class is either empty or has members. Universal propositions are equated to empty class (zero) and particular propositions are not equal to empty class.

Proposition "All S is P" means no member of class 'S' is outside the class 'P'. In other words the class having members of 'S' but not of 'P' is empty. The proposition "All S is P" is symbolized as:

$S\bar{P} = 0$

$\bar{P}$ means not P

"All scientists are philosophers" in Boolean formulation is expressed as:

$S\bar{P} = 0$

S - scientists
P- philosophers
$\bar{P}$ - non-philosophers

The proposition "All scientists are philosophers" means there is no scientist who is non-philosopher. Hence the class of non-philosopher scientists is empty.

Proposition 'E', "No S is P" means there is nothing common between 'S' and 'P'. In other words, there is not even a single member common between the classes of S and P.

2. John Venn (1834–1923) was a famous British logician who invented mechanical method of diagrams to express the categorical propositions.

$SP = 0$

"No socialists are pacifists", means there is not even a single socialist who is pacifist. Hence, it is expressed as

$SP = 0$

S = socialists
P = pacifists

'I' proposition "Some S is P" indicates there exists a class which has members of both the classes S and P.

$SP \neq 0$

"Some students are politicians", means there are students who are politicians. This means there are members in the class of student politicians. Hence,

$SP \neq 0$

S - student
P - politician

The 'O' proposition "Some S is not P", indicates there exists a class which has members of both S and non-P.

$S\bar{P} \neq 0$

"Some socialists are not public figure", means there are students who are non-public figures. Hence, it is symbolized as :

S - socialists
P - public figure
$\bar{P}$ - non-public figure

John Venn's Diagrams

John Venn's diagrams is yet another method of expressing categorical propositions in modern logic. Earlier Euler (1707-83), a Swiss mathematician, used diagrams in the areas of calculus, geometry, algebra and number theory. Venn used circles to express categorical propositions and later, the validity of arguments were also tested by drawing circles.

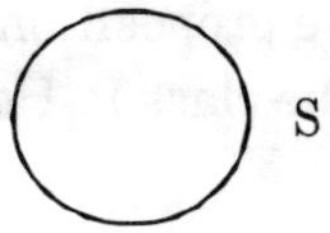

The circle represents class S

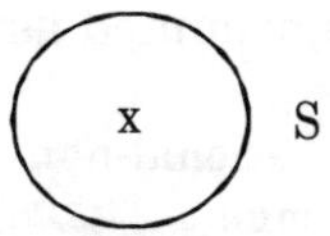

The circle shows the class S is not empty. It has members, say x

$S \neq 0$

The shaded circle shows the class S is empty. There is no member in the class S

$S = 0$

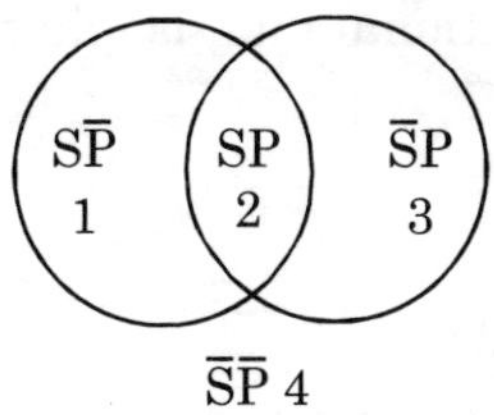

Number 1 segment of the circle represents that portion which has members of class S but not class P. Number 2 stands for the overlapping circles which has members of both the classes S and P. Number 3 represents that segment of circle which has members of P but not of S. Number 4 represents a class having members neither of S nor of P.

In each of the categorical propositions since there are two terms, subject and predicate, so there are two classes and two circles. Let us see how the categorical propositions are diagrammed through circles.

"All S is P", universal affirmative, 'A' type proposition is shown through the diagrams as follows:

The shaded portion $S\bar{P}$ is shown empty. The proposition "All S is P" means no member of class S is outside the class P. Hence,

$S\bar{P} = 0$

For example: "All men are rational", is diagrammed as:

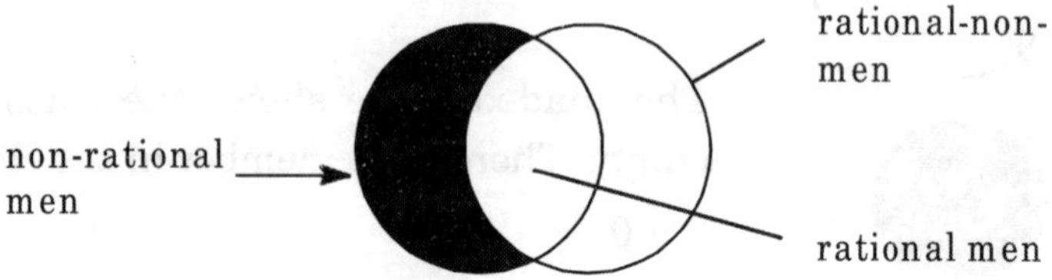

The class of non-rational man is empty.

$M\bar{R} = 0$

M - class of men

R - class of rationals

'E' proposition "No S is P", is diagrammed as:

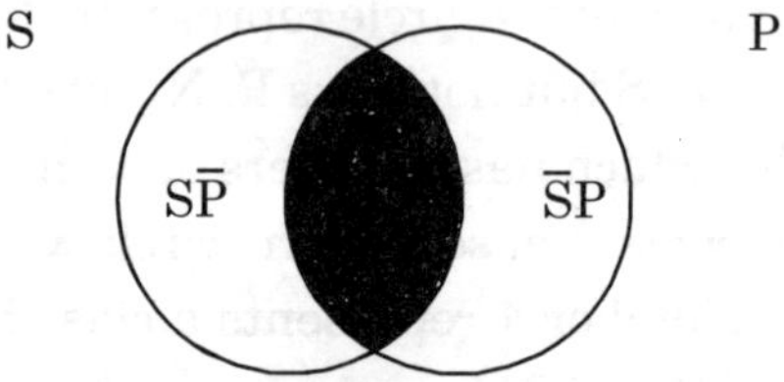

'E' proposition states nothing is common between S and P. Both the classes are mutually exclusive. Hence,

SP = 0

"No fish is mammal", is diagrammed as:

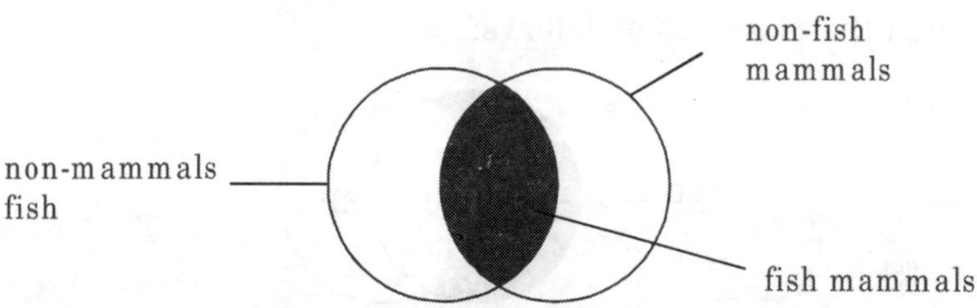

The class of fish mammal is empty.

FM = 0

F - fish
M - mammal

'I' proposition "Some S is P", is shown as:

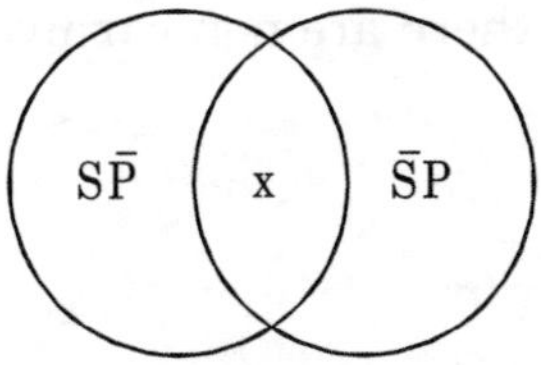

'I' proposition shows there are common members in the classes of S and P. The class SP is not empty. It has members say x

SP ≠ 0

"Some philosophers are religious leaders" is diagrammed as:

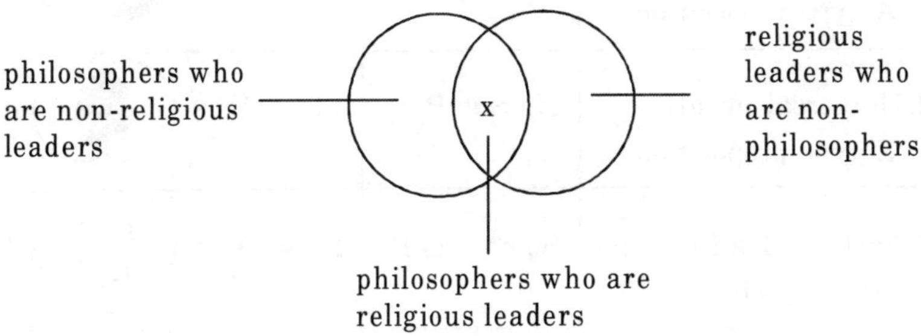

P - philosophers

R - religious leaders

PR ≠ 0

'O' proposition "Some S is not P", indicates there are members in the class S which do not share the characteristics of the class P.

$S\bar{P} \neq 0$

"Some animals are not carnivorous", is diagrammed as:

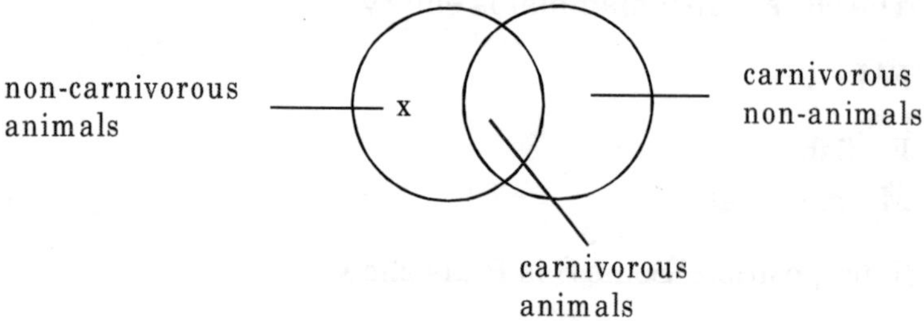

The proposition says there are non-carnivorous animals.

Hence, $A\bar{C} \neq O$

A - animals

C - carnivorous

Let us now compare all the three different formulations of the categorical propositions.

Proposition	*Traditional*	*Boolean*	*Venn*
1. Universal affirmative 'A' type proposition	All S is P	$S\bar{P} = O$	S 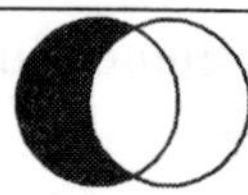 P
2. Universal negative 'E' type proposition	No S is P	$SP = O$	S 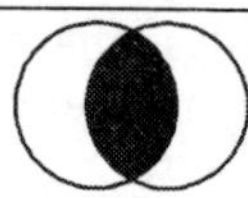 P
3. Particular affirmative 'I' type proposition	Some S is P	$SP \neq O$	S 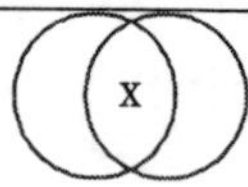 P
4. Particular negative 'O' type proposition	Some S is not P	$S\bar{P} \neq O$	S 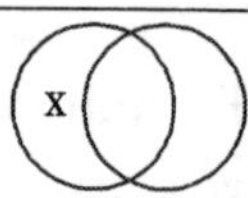 P

Modern Classification of Propositions

Modern logicians classified propositions as follows:

1. Categorical Propositions
   (i) Singular (Simple)
   (ii) General

2. Compound Propositions

CATEGORICAL PROPOSITIONS

Both singular and general propositions are categorical propositions. A categorical proposition is singular when its subject term is one specific individual or object. A categorical proposition is general when the subject term represents either some or all the members of a class.

Singular Proposition

A singular proposition has a singular or a proper noun as its subject. The subject can also be uniquely referred to as individual object. For instance, "That chair is comfortable", "Ram is student of this college", "New Delhi is one of the crowded cities of India" are instances of singular propositions.

You have already seen earlier, the traditional logicians had never assigned any separate status to the singular propositions. They had included them under the universal propositions. But the modern logicians do not agree with them. They differentiate singular propositions from universal propositions because of the existential import. Whereas former are existentially loaded, the latter are existentially negative.

The singular propositions share the unrestricted generality (distribution) with universal propositions ('A' and 'E') but not the existential import. Similarly the singular propositions share the existential import with the particular propositions ('I' and 'O') but not their restricted generality (distribution). Therefore, the singular propositions are neither universal nor particular. They are unique and have separate status.

General Proposition

The subject of a general proposition refers either to all the members of a class or to some members of a class. There are two types of generalizations, universal and particular, unrestricted and restricted. 'A' and 'E' are the universal propositions and 'I' and 'O' are particular propositions. Since you had already studied about them (they were discussed under the traditional classification of propositions), we will not discuss them here any more.

Besides the difference of generality between universal and singular propositions, there is yet another major difference between the modern and the traditional logicians' treatment of the categorical propositions. As you have already seen the traditional logicians have recognized only **one form, 'subject predicate form'** (the form which ascribes a predicate to a subject) for the categorical propositions. Propositions like:

(i) Gita is a hardworking student.

(ii) Gita is daughter of Mr X.

(iii) Gita is older than Mohan.

were treated as similar by them. They thought all the above propositions have one form, that is, subject predicate form. But the modern logicians differ. They are of the opinion that while the first proposition "Gita is hardworking student" has subject predicate form, the other two are relational propositions. The relational propositions can never be reduced to the 'subject predicate form' propositions. The propositions "stating that two things have a certain relation have a different form from subject-predicate propositions, and the failure to perceive this difference or to allow for it has been the source of many errors in traditional metaphysics"[3]. The modern logicians thus extended the treatment of categorical propositions far beyond the traditional thinkers. Along with 'subject predicate form' of the proposition, they recognized the relational form of categorical propositions also.

COMPOUND PROPOSITIONS

A compound proposition is constituted by two or more categorical propositions (singular or general). Basically three types of compound propositions are recognized. They are :

3. B. Russell, "Logic as the Essence of Philosophy" in *Essays in Logic,* ed. Ronald Jager, p. 127.

(i) Conjunctive

(ii) Disjunctive

(iii) Hypothetical

Conjunctive Proposition

Two categorical propositions when joined by 'and', makes conjunctive compound proposition. For instance, "Ram is intelligent boy and he is hardworking". "She is dark and pretty".

Disjunctive Proposition

Two categorical propositions when joined by the relation of 'either or', then it is called disjunctive proposition. For instance, "Either he is sick or he is out of station", "Either it rains or we shall not go for picnic", etc.

Hypothetical Proposition

Two categorical propositions when joined by 'if then' relation, then it produces a hypothetical proposition. For instance, "If I get admission, then I will complete the course in a year", etc.

Modern Classification of Proposition

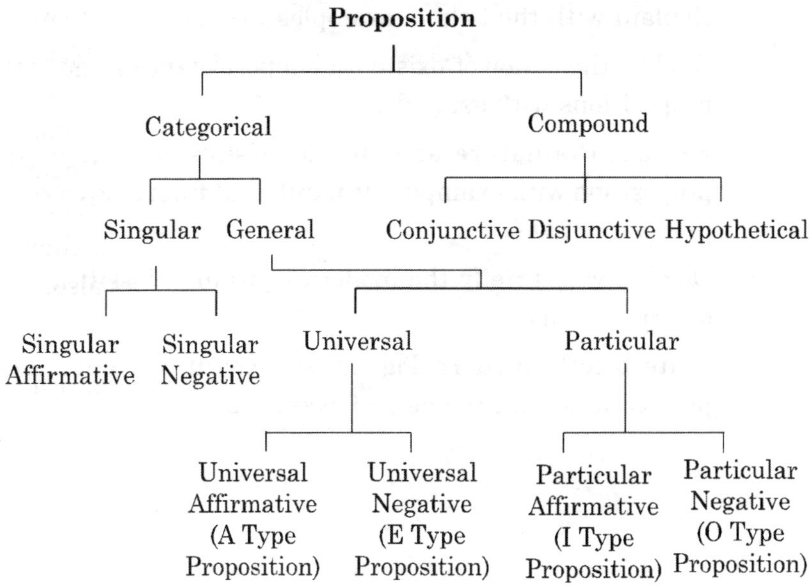

Exercises

1. Represent the following propositions through Venn diagrams:
    1. All squares are polygons.
    2. No egg is square.
    3. Some cars are expensive items.
    4. Some politicians are not sinners.
    5. All learned are fortunate beings.
    6. No circle is polygon.
    7. Some communists are God-fearing.
    8. Some famous leaders are not degree holders.
    9. All sailors are patriots.
    10. No soldier is coward.
2. Formulate the above propositions — in terms of George Boole's 'empty classes'.
3. What is the basic differene between George Boole's and John Venn's formulation of categorical propositions? Explain with the help of examples.
4. Explain the notion of 'existential import' of the categorical propositions with examples.
5. Explain the nature and characteristics of a singular proposition with examples. Is it different from a universal proposition? Discuss.
6. Discuss very briefly the modern logicians' classification of propositions.
7. State briefly modern logicians' account of compound propositions with the help of examples.

Chapter 4

Terms

A PROPOSITION is a statement in which something is said about something else either affirmatively or negatively. The thing about which something is said is subject of the proposition and that which is said about the subject is predicate. In the proposition "Ram is a hard-working boy", 'Ram' is subject term and 'a hard-working boy' is predicate term.

Both subject and predicate of a proposition are called terms. A term is a word or group of words which is either a subject or a predicate of a proposition. If a word or a group of words are neither a subject nor a predicate of a proposition, then it is not a term. In the propositions, "All men are mortal", 'men' and 'mortal' are terms but 'all' and 'are' are merely words for they are neither subject nor predicate of the proposition. Thus, whereas all terms are words, all words may not be terms.

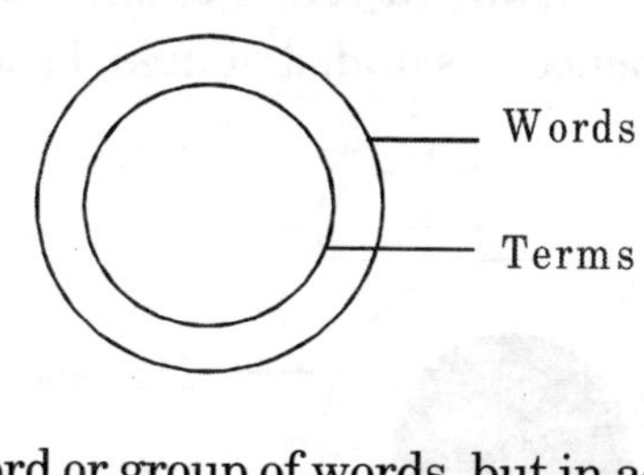

A term is a word or group of words, but in addition to that it is:

(i) either a subject or a predicate of a proposition, and

(ii) it must have a definite meaning of its own.

The word 'term' comes from the Latin word *terminus*, a limit or boundary. Terms limit the movement of the thought. Proposition is a unit of reasoning and terms are its constituents. In each categorical proposition A, E, I and O, there are two terms, subject and predicate.

Three important aspects of a term are discussed here :

1. Distribution of terms
2. Denotation and Connotation of terms
3. Types of terms

Distribution of Terms

A term is said to be distributed if it refers to all the members of a class. For example, in the proposition, "All cats are mammals", the term 'cat' is distributed for it refers to all the members of the class cat. If, on the other hand, a term refers to some or few members of a class, then it is called undistributed term. In the proposition, "Some cats are black", the term 'cat' is undistributed, for it refers to only some members of the class 'cat'. In other words, **a term is distributed when it includes or excludes all the members of a class,** and if a term includes or excludes only some members of a class, then it is undistributed.

In a universal affirmative proposition, say "All S is P", subject term S is always distributed but predicate term P is undistributed. In the proposition "All men are mortal", the term 'men' refers to all men and hence it is distributed, whereas the term 'mortal' does not refer to all mortals (it refers to only some mortals, that is, human beings), hence it is undistributed. Look at the following diagram :

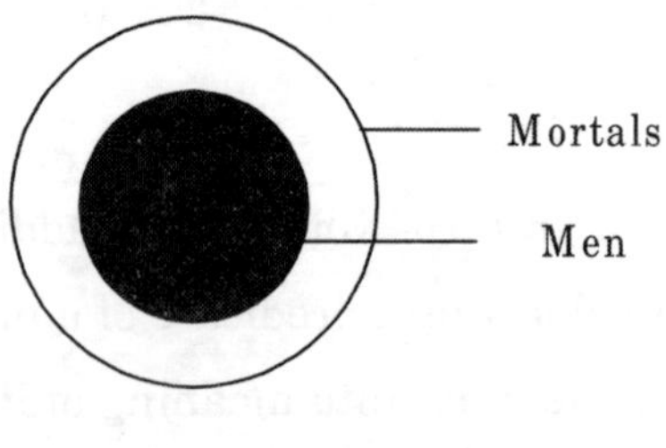

Whereas the class of men is in the preview of the class of mortals, the class of mortals is not in the preview of the class of men.

In a universal negative 'E' proposition, "No S is P", both subject and predicate terms are distributed. In the proposition, "No men are immortal", all members of the class 'men' are excluded from all members of the class 'immortals'. Therefore, both subject and predicate terms are distributed in 'E' proposition.

In a particular affirmative, 'I' proposition, say "Some S is P", none of the terms is distributed. In the proposition, "Some students are voters in the general election", the subject term 'students' indicates 'some' students, thus the subject term is undistributed. The predicate term "voters in the general election" also does not refer to all the members of the class of voters in the general election (there are voters in the general election who are not students). Thus, both subject and predicate terms are undistributed in 'I' proposition.

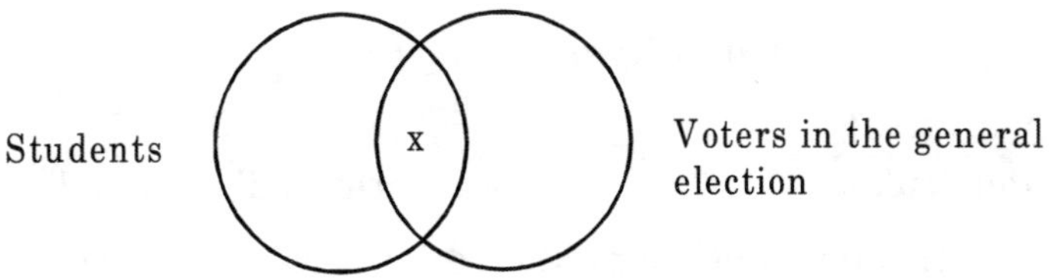

In a particular negative, 'O' proposition, "Some S is not P", subject term is undistributed but predicate term is distributed. "Some students are not scholarship holders" distributes its predicate term 'scholarship holders' but not the subject term 'students'. The subject term 'students' here refers only to part of students, so the subject term in 'O' proposition is undistributed but the predicate term 'scholarship holders' is distributed. The meaning of the proposition states that the entire class of 'scholarship holders' is excluded from some students. Hence, the predicate term is distributed in the 'O' proposition.

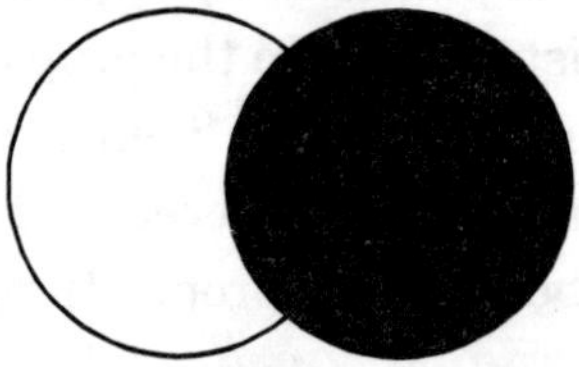

The position of distributed and undistributed terms in the four categorical propositions is as follows:

Proposition	*Subject*	*Predicate*
A	Distributed	Undistributed
E	Distributed	Distributed
I	Undistributed	Undistributed
O	Undistributed	Distributed

The quantity of a proposition determines whether a subject term is distributed or not. If quantity of the proposition is universal as in 'A' and 'E' propositions, then subject term is distributed. If quantity of the proposition is particular as in 'I' and 'O' propositions, then the subject term is undistributed.

Quantity of a Proposition

Universal	Subject term distributed
Particular	Subject term undistributed

To determine whether predicate term is distributed or not, one looks to the quality of a proposition. In affirmative propositions ('A' and 'I'), predicate term is always undistributed whereas in negative propositions ('E' and 'O') predicate term is always distributed.

Quality of a Proposition

Affirmative	Predicate term undistributed
Negative	Predicate term distributed

The validity of deductive reasoning is partially decided by the distribution of terms. You will learn more about this in chapters 6 and 7.

Denotation and Connotation of Terms

The aim of a logician is to identify fallacies which arise in the reasoning, and to suggest their remedies. Fallacies in reasoning may arise from various sources. The wrong use of language is one of them. Sometimes the meaning of terms is not known or merely half known and in that case their use in reasoning may make it fallacious. In order to keep our reasoning straight, the meaning of the terms used in the reasoning should be absolutely clear. The ambiguous or vague terms must not be used in the propositions. The logicians have suggested two different techniques for making the meanings of terms clear. They are denotative and connotative techniques. Let us first see what is denotation and what is connotation of a term.

Denotation of a term is the object or thing referred by the term. For example, the denotation of the term 'man' is Gita, Mohan, Kamala, etc. The denotation of the term 'poet' is Wordsworth, Keats, Mahadevi Verma, etc.

Connotation of a term is the set of qualities and characteristics possessed by the objects or things referred by the term. For example, the connotation of the term 'man' is mortality and rationality. Connotation means those common characteristics which are possessed by all the members denoted by the term. Mortality and rationality are two characteristics possessed by all men. Other characteristics like being educated, Indian, employed, tall, etc. are not possessed by every man and, therefore, are not essential. So the connotation of a term refers only to those qualities which are minimum but absolutely indispensable for the meaningfulness of a term.

Denotation of a term refers to the objects or things which possess the qualities. Connotation refers to the set of characteristics essentially possessed by every object denoted by the term. Denotation denotes the objects, connotation connotes the characteristics.

The concept of denotation and connotation can be made clearer in the context of 'class'. The class of 'man', for instance, has twofold aspects. The members belonging to the class say, x, y, z, etc. are denotation of the term 'man'. The class characteristics 'mortality' and 'rationality' possessed by every member of the class man, is the connotation of the term 'man'. The members of the class are the denotation and characteristics possessed by them is connotation.

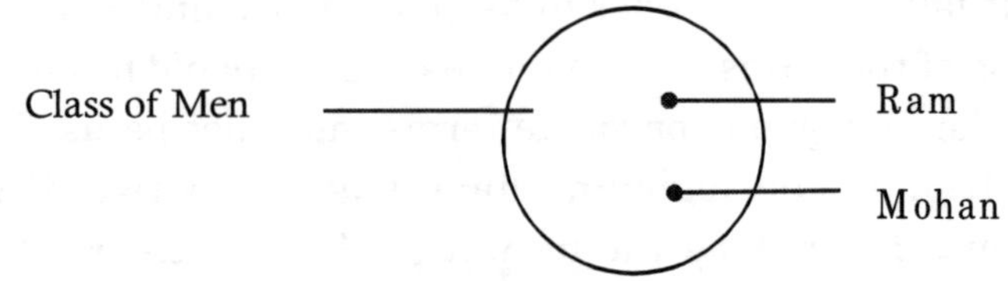

Hence, a class carries twofold meaning, denotative and connotative. Denotative meaning of a term is referential or extensional, for it refers to members of the class. Denotation fixes the boundary of the term and hence, indicates the extent to which the term is applicable.

Connotative meaning of a term is intentional which means the intended and indicated characteristics of a term.

Generally three types of connotations[1] are recognized. They are

(i) Subjective
(ii) Objective
(iii) Conventional

A logician, however, is interested only in conventional connotation. Neither subjective nor objective connotation is of any use to him.

(i) Subjective Connotation: Sometimes a term refers to a set of characteristics which differs from one group of people to another. In that case there is no common or fixed connotation of the term. For example, the term, 'married woman in white clothes' connotes a figure of sorry woman

1. Cf. Irving M. Copi, *Introduction to Logic* (sixth edition), p. 155.

in India (widowhood) whereas the same term connotes a figure of happy woman in Western countries (wedding dress). Such connotations are subjective and are of no use to a logician who is interested in that kind of connotation which is relatively fixed and common for all.

(ii) Objective Connotation: The connotation of a term when it refers to all the characteristics of the object or thing, known and unknown, then it is called objective connotation. A human being, however, can never be sure whether the characteristics he knows are all or merely few. Only an omniscient or super being can claim to know *all* the characteristics referred by a term. We know the term 'man' has two characteristics, mortality and rationality, and the other essential characteristics of the term 'man', if at all they are there, are still unknown to us. Therefore, a logician is not interested in objective connotation either. He is interested only in the conventional connotation.

(iii) Conventional Connotation: The conventional connotation of a term is the set of all the known common characteristics possessed by all the members denoted by the term. Accepted and agreed set of qualities of a term saves us from the defects of subjective as well as objective connotations. In a way conventional connotation is a middle path between them. It is not wrong to say that conventional connotation is a definition of a term, and definition is common for all. If a set of characteristics of a term changes, so also definition of the term.

RELATION BETWEEN CONNOTATION AND DENOTATION

Though theoretically connotation and denotation of a term can be discussed separately yet they are inseparably related. The relation between them is of inverse variable which means if connotation increases, denotation decreases and if connotation decreases, denotation increases. An example is illustrated here for the better understanding of this relationship.

Connotation	*Corresponding denotation*
(i) Mortality	All living beings (men, animals and plants)
(ii) Mortality + Rationality	Only human beings
(iii) Mortality + Rationality + Indian	Indian men and women
(iv) Mortality + Rationality + Indian + Educated	Only educated Indians are members of the new class

The above illustration shows that with the increase in qualities (connotation), the members (denotation) decreases. Similarly, with the decrease in the connotation, denotation increases. The lesser the qualities, more are the members referred by the term.

However, it is the connotation which determines denotation, and not the other way round. The set of characteristics fixes the members in a class. The denotation, the things or the objects do not fix the qualities very satisfactorily. It is not appropriate to say that with the increase in denotation, connotation decreases always or with the decrease in denotation connotation increases. The trouble may arise in those situations where with the increase of denotation we expect connotation to decrease or with the decrease in denotation we expect connotation to increase. Let us see the following example.

With the increase in man's population can we say the connotation, the essential characteristics of the term 'man', mortality and rationality have decreased? Certainly not. The connotation of the term 'man' (rationality and mortality) remains the same. Thus, with the increase or decrease of denotation, the connotation either remains where it is or if at all it (connotation) changes, it will change in opposite direction.

Though both connotation and denotation of a term are inseparable aspects of a term, yet it is connotation which is more basic and fundamental. Through connotation, it is easier to locate appropriate denotation. But by starting with denotation, connotation is not so accurately determined.

There are terms which have both connotation and denotation. General terms and common nouns are examples of such terms, and they are called 'Connotative Terms'.

However, some terms, for example, singular terms and proper nouns have proper references but not proper connotation. In such cases connotation is either incomplete or ambiguous. For example, the term 'Ram' has a suitable reference (denotation) but the meaning of the term 'Ram' may mean a student who is my friend, or a legendary figure in Indian mythology or an employee. The connotation of the term 'Ram' is ambiguous in the sense that it can be used differently in different context. Unless further information is provided, the meaning of the term 'Ram' is merely half. The singular terms are like variables. They keep changing their values according to the context in which they occur. "The singular term 'Jones' is ambiguous in that it might be used in different contexts to name any of various persons. . ."[2]."

But there are some terms which have proper connotation but not proper denotation. For instance, the term 'square round' (being a non-existent reality) does not have reference, though the term has definite connotation. There are null classes, empty classes, where denotation is zero.

The terms which do not have both connotation and denotation (either proper connotation is missing or a proper denotation is not there) are called 'non-connotative' terms by J.S. Mill. Common nouns and general terms are connotative terms whereas proper nouns, abstract terms, singular terms are non-connotative.

Types of Terms

Logicians have classified terms into various groups. Broadly terms are classified as:

2. W.V. Quine, *Methods of Logic* (third edition), p. 217.

(i) Singular and General Terms

(ii) Concrete and Abstract Terms

(iii) Positive and Negative Terms

(iv) Collective and Distributive Terms

SINGULAR AND GENERAL TERMS

A singular term refers to one single, or specific person, object or thing. For instance, Socrates, New Delhi, this book, that man, etc. According to Quine, "a term is singular if it purports to name an object (one and only one), and otherwise general"[3]. 'I' and 'thou' are also singular terms. A general term, on the other hand, is used as common noun. For instance, in the proposition "Man is mortal", the term 'man' is used as common or general term. All common nouns when used as terms in propositions are general terms. For instance, school, student, college, pen, cat, etc. are general terms. In logic general terms are also known as classes.

Singular terms are of two types:

(i) Proper names or nouns

(ii) Specifically or uniquely described term.

Singular terms which are proper nouns can be easily recognized. All proper nouns or names when used in propositions either as a subject or as a predicate are called singular terms, for example, India, Sita, University of Delhi, etc.

Specifically and uniquely descriptive terms are those which though not proper names yet have a unique reference. Uniquely descriptive term refers to single person or object. For example, "Women Prime Minister of India up to 1982" has a unique reference; it refers to a single person Mrs Indira Gandhi. Hence the term "Woman Prime Minister of India up to 1982" is a singular term.

3. W.V. Quine, op. cit. (third edition), p. 218.

CONCRETE AND ABSTRACT

Terms that denote things, objects, persons and articles are concrete, for example, chair, pen, book, crow, man, etc. Abstract terms, on the other hand, refer to abstract entities, characteristics or attributes in themselves. "Concrete terms are those which purport to refer to individuals, physical objects, events; abstract terms are those which purport to refer to abstract objects, e.g. to numbers, classes, attributes"[4]. For instance, happiness is an abstract term but happy is not abstract term. An abstract term is not simply the name of a quality but a quality considered by itself. Adjectives are not abstract terms because an adjective refers to quality as qualifying objects. For example, in the proposition "Trees are green", 'green' is not an abstract term, for it refers to quality of greenness as qualifying trees. So 'greenness' is abstract term whereas" 'green' is merely an adjective. It should be recalled that both subject and predicate terms are nouns. If either of the terms is not noun, then it is to be changed into appropriate noun. The above proposition. "Trees are green", is reduced to "Trees are green objects". Both subject term 'trees' and predicate term 'green objects' are concrete terms.

J.S. Mill points out that concrete terms and abstract terms usually go in pairs. For example, happy – happiness, triangle – triangularity, man-manhood, strong – strength, etc. However, the distinction between concrete and abstract term is not absolute. The same term can be used as concrete term in one context and abstract in another context. For example, in the proposition, "Cricket team got hostile" the term 'cricket' is used as concrete term whereas in the proposition "Cricket team teaches discipline" the term 'cricket' is used as an abstract term. Similarly in the proposition, "I have faith in honesty", the term 'honesty' is used as concrete term, whereas in the proposition, "Honesty is virtue" the term 'honesty' is used as an abstract term.

4. W.V. Quine, op. cit. (third edition), p. 217.

POSITIVE AND NEGATIVE TERMS

A positive term is one which posits or affirms the presence of an attribute. For instance, wise, true, happy, voters, citizens, etc. are positive terms. Negative terms deny the presence of an attribute like unwise, unhappy, immortal, bald, orphan, etc. Negative terms are not to be confused with negative propositions. For example, "Some men are not wise" is a negative proposition, whereas "Some men are unwise" is affirmative proposition with a negative predicate.

The distinction between positive and negative term becomes extremely important in the context of contradictory and contrary terms.

Two terms are contradictory if they are mutually exclusive and collectively exhaustive. For instance, equal and unequal pairs of terms exhaust the entire class of relation and, hence are contradictory. The universe of discourse (the field of reference) is exhausted by them. Equal or unequal, black and non-black, white and non-white are examples of contradictory terms.

One easy way to make pair of contradictory terms is by prefixing 'non' or 'not' to a term such as happy and non-happy, black and non-black, Indian and non-Indian, voters and non-voters. It is very difficult, however, to find pair of contradictory terms in our practical life. In the formal sciences, however, they are easily available.

Contrary terms just as contradictory terms cannot coexist and are incompatible, yet contrary terms do not exhaust entire universe of discourse. **A pair of terms are contrary when they are mutually exclusive but not exhaustive.** Black and white colours are exclusive but do not exhaust the field of colours. There are colours which are neither black nor white. It could be red, blue, green or yellow. Black is not white colour but both black and white do not cover or exhaust the entire field of colours.

Contradictory Terms
(White, non-white)

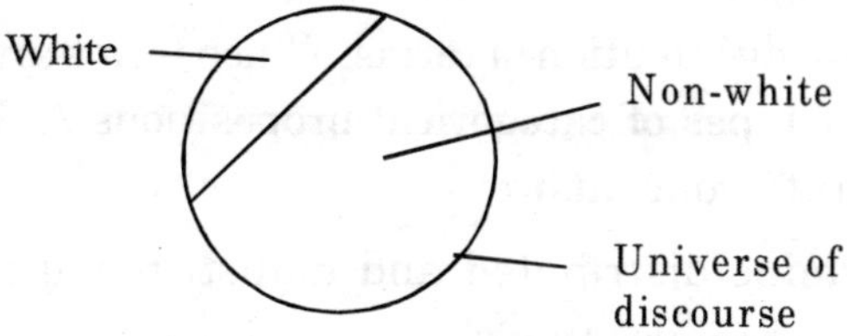

Contrary Terms
(White is contrary to black colour)

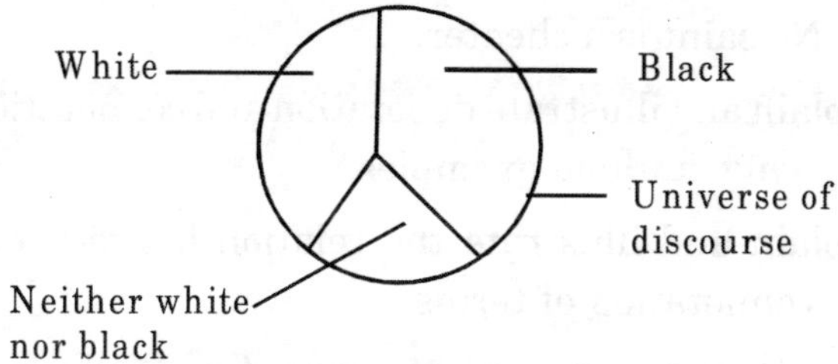

COLLECTIVE AND DISTRIBUTIVE TERMS

Collective terms apply to group of persons, things or objects but not to the individuals composing the group. For instance, terms like club, parliament, society, library, army, etc. are collective terms. The use of collective terms means the entire class is taken into consideration. On the other hand, distributive term refers to all the members of the class separately. In the following propositions there is a use of distributive terms, "All plays of Shakespeare are outstanding pieces of literature", "All members of Indian army are Indian citizens", "All members of the club are Citibank card holders". However, no term by itself is collective or distributive. The use of the term in a proposition decides whether a term is collective or distributive. The collective use of the term takes term as a whole whereas use of distributive term takes into consideration all the members of the class individually.

Exercises

1. What do you understand by a term? Is it a sub-set of word or a phrase? Explain with the help of examples.
2. Explain distribution of terms. Which terms are distributed in four types of categorical propositions A, E, I, and O? Illustrate your answer.
3. Determine distributed and undistributed terms of the following propositions:
    1. All soldiers are brave people.
    2. Some schemes of social reform are not feasible.
    3. Some ambitious people are successful people.
    4. No saint is a cheater.
4. Explain and illustrate denotation and connotation of term by giving suitable examples.
5. Explain and illustrate the relation between denotation and connotation of terms.
6. Explain 'non-connotative' terms. Are proper nouns 'non-connotative' terms? Discuss.
7. Does the connotation of a term include all the qualities possessed by the object to which it applies, or only some of them? Justify your answer with examples.
8. What are the characteristics of a singular term? Differentiate it from a general term giving suitable examples.
9. Differentiate between contrary and contradictory terms. Illustrate your answer.
10. Write a short note on 'types of terms'.

Chapter 5

Square of Opposition
(Relation among the Categorical Propositions)

FOUR categorical propositions A, E, I and O are related to each other by various 'truth relations'. The relations among them are of 'opposition'. The traditional logicians have explained these relationships by a diagram of square to which they call "Square of Opposition".

Each side of the square and also the diagonals represent different kinds of relations.

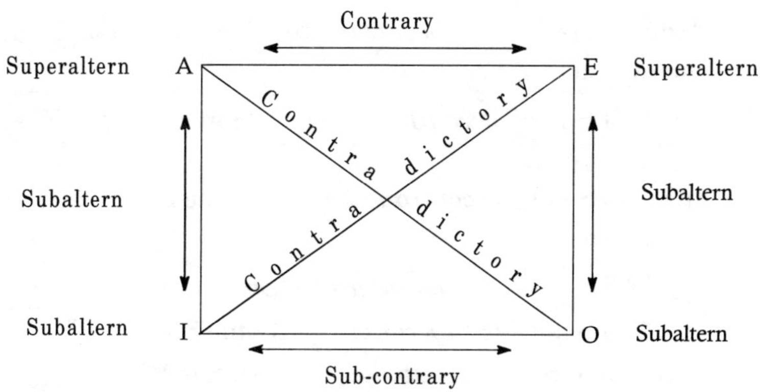

Universal affirmative 'A' proposition, "All S is P" and Universal negative 'E' proposition, "No S is P" are related to each other by the Contrary relation. The proposition "All scientists are philosophers" is contrary to "No scientists are philosophers". Similarly, "No fish is mammal" is contrary to "All fish are mammals".

Particular affirmative 'I' proposition, "Some students are scholarship holders" is related to 'O' proposition "Some students are not scholarship holders" by subcontrary relation. Similarly, 'O' proposition, "Some animals are not carnivorous" is related to 'I' proposition, "Some animals are carnivorous" by subcontrary relation.

The Universal affirmative 'A' proposition, "All S is P" is related to particular negative 'O' proposition, "Some S is not P" by contradictory relation. The contradictory of "All men are mortal" is "Some men are not mortal" and vice versa. The contradictory of 'E' proposition, "No crows are mammals" is 'I' proposition, "Some crows are mammals".

Universal affirmative 'A' proposition, "All men are mortal" is superaltern to 'I' proposition, "Some men are mortal". Similarly, 'E' proposition, "No crow is mammal" is superaltern to 'O' proposition, "Some crows are not mammals".

1. "All S is P" is *contrary* to "No S is P" and vice versa.
2. "Some S is P" is *subcontrary* to "Some S is not P" and vice versa.
3. (i) "All S is P" is *contradictory* to "Some S is not P" and vice versa.
   (ii) "No S is P" is *contradictory* to "Some S is P" and vice versa.
4. (i) "All S is P" is *superaltern* to "Some S is P".
   (ii) "No S is P" is *superaltern* to "Some S is not P".
   (iii) "Some S is P" is *subaltern* to "All S is P".
   (iv) "Some S is not P" is *subaltern* to "No S is P".

The relationship among the categorical propositions is of opposites. Two categorical propositions are said to be opposite if they differ either in:

i. quantity, or
ii. quality, or
iii. both quantity and quality.

Contrary propositions 'A' and 'E' have same quantity (universal) but they differ in qualities. Similarly, subcontrary propositions 'I' and 'O' have same quantity (particular) but they differ in qualities. Propositions related by subaltern relationship such as 'A' and 'I', and also 'E' and 'O' have the same quality but they differ in quantities. Contradictory propositions 'A' and 'O' and also 'E' and 'I', however, differ both in quantities and qualities.

Each opposite relation has certain characteristics. Contrary proposition 'A' and 'E' *cannot be both true together* though they both can be false at the same time. If one of the contrary propositions is true then the other contrary proposition is necessarily false, whereas if one contrary proposition is false, the other contrary proposition is undetermined (it can be true or false).

Subcontrary propositions 'I' and 'O' *cannot both be false together* though they both can be true together. If 'I' is true, 'O' is undetermined; whereas if 'I' proposition is false, 'O' is necessarily true. Similarly, if 'O' is true, 'I' is undetermined but if 'O' is false, 'I' is definitely true.

Subaltern relationship shows if 'A' is true, then 'I' is necessarily true, but if 'I' is true, 'A' remains undetermined. Same is the case with 'E' and 'O'. If 'E' is true, 'O' is true but not the other way round.

Contradictory relation between 'A' and 'O', and also between 'E' and 'I' is of strict opposition. If 'A' is true, 'O' is false; if 'O' is true, 'A' is false. Similarly, if 'E' is true, 'I' is false and if 'I' is true, 'E' is false.

These various relations lay down the foundation for testing the validity of some elementary arguments in logic as Irving M. Copi says, "The relationships diagrammed by this Square of Opposition were believed to provide a logical basis for validating certain elementary forms of arguments".[1]

---

1. Irving M. Copi, and Cohen Carl, *Introduction to Logic* (ninth edition), p. 217.

If 'A' proposition is given as true, then it implies:

E proposition is false

I proposition is true

O proposition is false

If 'A' proposition is given as false, then it implies :

E proposition is undetermined

I proposition is undetermined

O proposition is true

If 'E' proposition is given as true, then it implies :

A proposition is false

I proposition is false

O proposition is true

If 'E' proposition is given as false, then it implies :

A proposition is undetermined

O proposition is undetermined

I proposition is true

If 'I' proposition is given as true, then it implies:

A proposition is undetermined

O proposition is undetermined

E proposition is false

If 'I' proposition is given as false, then it implies:

A proposition is false

O proposition is true

E proposition is true

If 'O' proposition is given as true, then it implies:

A proposition is false

E proposition is undetermined

I proposition is undetermined

If 'O' proposition is given as false, then it implies:

E proposition is false

A proposition is true

I proposition is true.

In 'Square of Opposition', one important point should be noticed, that is in order to find out the other opposite propositions from a given proposition, **the subject and predicate of the implied proposition is same as that of the implying one.**

Here are some solved examples :

Example 1 : The contrary, contradictory and subaltern of the proposition "All men are mortal" are as follows :

Contrary "No men are mortal" (E)

Contradictory "Some men are not mortal" (O)

Subaltern "Some men are mortal"(I)

Example 2 : The subcontrary, contradictory and superaltern of the proposition "Some scientists are mathematicians" are as follows :

Subcontrary "Some scientists are not mathematicians" (O)

Contradictory"No scientists are mathematicians" (E)

Superaltern "All scientists are mathematicians" (A)

Modern Logicians "Square of Opposition"[2]

The traditional "Square of Opposition" was criticized by the modern thinkers in the context of the existential import. You have already read in chapter 3B that universal propositions, "A" and 'E' do not have existential import whereas the particular propositions 'I' and 'O' do have it. This standpoint had a tremendous impact on the traditional "Square of Opposition". Consequently, only one relation of contradictory among the categerical propositions has been accepted as valid. Other relations like contrary, sub-contrary, subaltern have become invalid.

2. Here I am taking mainly Boolean interpretation of categorical propositions.

Let us begin with contrary relation. The traditional account of the contrary relation states that propositions "All S is P" and "No S is P" (which are related by contrary relations) cannot be both true together though they both can be false together. But the propositions, "All houses made of cheese are green houses" and "No houses made of cheese are green houses" are true together because the subject term of these propositions 'houses made of cheese' being empty class is false.

The analysis of "All houses made of cheese are green houses" in modern logic is "If there is a house made of cheese then it is a green house". Since "houses made of cheese" is false (being an empty class), the conditional proposition will be true, because in conditional proposition if antecedent is false then irrespective of its consequent the proposition is true. Symbolically it can be expressed as:

$$\text{False} \supset (\text{True or False})$$
$$\Rightarrow \text{True}$$

Similarly the analysis of "No houses made of cheese are green houses" is analysed as "If there is a house made of cheese then it is not a green house" Since "houses made of cheese" is false (being an empty class) the conditional proposition will be true, because if an antecedent is false, then irrespective of its consequent, the conditional proposition is true. Symbolically it can be expressed as:

$$\text{False} \supset (\text{True or False})$$
$$\Rightarrow \text{True}$$

Now if both 'A' and 'E' propositions are true together, then how can they be contraries?

The subcontrary relation between 'I' and 'O' propositions also becomes invalid. The existential import maintains 'I', "Some S is P" and 'O', "Some S is not P", are true when the subject term 'S' has members; and the propositions 'I' and 'O' are false when the subject term 'S' has no members. The traditional account of the subcontrary relation is that though both 'I' and 'O' propositions can be true together, they cannot be false together. But if there are no member in the subject term of 'I' and 'O' propositions, then both these propositions are false together. For instance, "Some high golden mountains are found in India" and "Some high golden mountains are not found in India" are false together since the subject term 'high golden mountains' is an empty class. The analysis of "Some high gold mountains are found in India" is "There exists at least one gold mountain and that mountain is found in India". This is conjunctive proposition and a conjunctive proposition is false if one of the conjuncts is false. Since there is no 'gold mountain' and the class of 'gold mountain' is an empty class, the conjunctive proposition "There exists at least one gold mountain and that mountain is found in India" will be false. Symbolically it can be expressed as:

False • (True or False)
⇒ False

Similarly the analysis of "Some high gold mountains are not found in India" is "There exists at least one gold mountain and that mountain is not found in India". Since the subject term 'gold mountain' is an empty class, the conjunctive proposition "There exists at least one gold mountain and that mountain is not found in India" is also false. Symbolically it can be expressed:

False • (True or False)
⇒ False.

Now if both 'I' and 'O' are false together, then they are no more subcontraries.

Not only that, the subaltern relation between 'A' and 'I' propositions, and between 'E' and 'O' also becomes invalid. According to the traditional account of subaltern relation, the truth of 'A' proposition implies the truth of 'I' proposition and similarly, the truth of 'E' proposition implies the truth of 'O' proposition. But if one accepts the existential import, then from the truth of 'A' proposition, the truth of 'I' cannot be validly inferred. Similarly, the truth of 'E' proposition does not imply the truth of 'O' proposition. The reason is, 'A' and 'E' propositions being existentially negative propositions cannot imply the truth of 'I' and 'O' propositions respectively because they are existentially loaded. In the deductive reasoning, the conclusion cannot possess anything new or extra which the premisses do not have. The premisses 'A' and 'E' do not have existential import and thus cannot imply the truth of 'I' and 'O' propositions respectively which have existential import.

Modern "Square of Opposition"

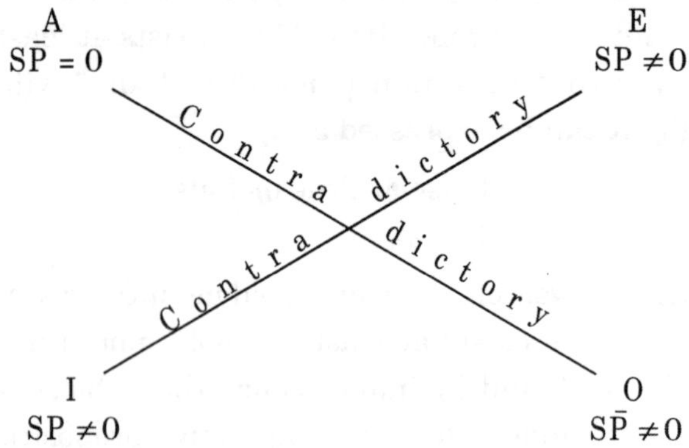

Now you can imagine the big blow the traditional "Square of Opposition" had to suffer because of existential import. The new and modern "Square of Opposition" accepts only one relation of contradiction.

Exercises

1. Find contrary/subcontrary, contradictory and subaltern/superaltern of the following propositions:
   1. All voters are citizens.
   2. No philosophers are traders.
   3. Some leaves are fragrant.
   4. Some good speakers are not good writers.

5. All cats are mammals.
6. No dishonest person is brave.
7. Some politicians are non-statesmen.
8. All non-mortals are non-men.
9. Some non-graduates are not non-citizens.
10. No artists are wealthy persons.

2. If "All butterflies are beautiful creatures" is given as true, then what can be inferred about the following:
   1. No butterflies are beautiful creatures.
   2. Some butterflies are beautiful creatures.
   3. Some butterflies are not beautiful creatures.
3. If "Some lions are black" is given as false, then what can be inferred about the following :
   1. All lions are black
   2. No lions are black
   3. Some lions are not black.
4. Explain the traditional 'Square of Opposition' with appropriate examples.
5. Explain how and why contrary relationship between 'A' and 'E' propositions and sub-contrary relationship between 'I' and 'O' have become invalid in modern logicians' 'Square of Opposition'.
6. Is it true that the modern logicians accept only contradictory relation in the 'Square of Opposition? Do you agree with this? Give reasons.

Chapter 6

Immediate Inference
(Eduction)

Argument is a conceptual term for the arrangement of premiss (or premisses) and the conclusion. Inference, on the other hand, is an actual process of drawing a conclusion from certain premiss or premisses. Inference, however, is of different types. Traditionally it is classified as follows:

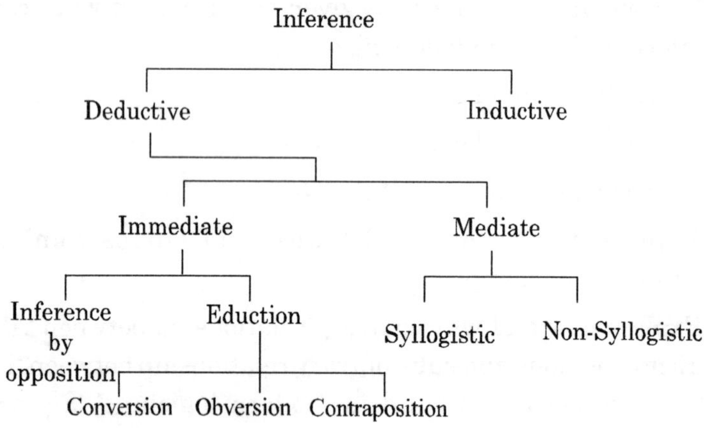

The basis of classification of immediate and mediate inference is the number of premisses in the reasoning. In immediate inference there is one and only one premiss whereas in mediate inference there are at least two premisses, and jointly they imply the conclusion. An argument having two and only two premisses is called syllogistic mediate inference. Aristotle is known for his invention of the theory of syllogism. If the number of premisses is more than two, then the mediate reasoning becomes non-syllogistic.

But every deductive reasoning (immediate or mediate) follows the rule of distribution of terms. The rule states that **if a term is distributed in the conclusion, then it must necessarily be distributed in the premiss.** A piece of deductive reasoning that does not obey this rule becomes invalid. In no valid deductive reasoning conclusion is wider than the premisses.

Immediate inference : In immediate inference there is one and only one premiss and from this sole premiss conclusion is drawn. From "a single proposition expressed in one or other of the four standard forms, it is possible to infer, directly from the given proposition , other propositions implied by it".[1] Immediate inference is of two types:

(i) Inference by Opposition

(ii) Eduction

You have already studied inference by opposition in the previous chapter. In the present chapter, you will study various forms of eduction. In eduction the meaning of the premiss and the conclusion is same. The difference between them is only of forms. But in inference by opposition ("Square of Opposition") the premiss and the conclusion differ both in form and meaning.

Eduction

Eduction is of three types:

(i) Conversion

(ii) Obversion

(iii) Contraposition

Conversion and obversion are independent forms of immediate inference, whereas contraposition is dependent on them.

CONVERSION

In conversion the following rules are observed:

---

1. Mellone, S.H., op. cit. p. 84.

1. The subject of the premiss becomes predicate of the conclusion and predicate of the premiss becomes subject of the conclusion.
2. Quality of the premiss and that of the conclusion remains the same. If the premiss is affirmative, then the conclusion is also affirmative and if the premiss is negative, the conclusion is also negative.
3. Quantity of the premiss and the conclusion should be same as far as possible. If the premiss is universal, then the conclusion should also be universal. Similarly, if the premiss is particular, then the conclusion should also be particular. However, in the conversion of A proposition this rule is not observed.
4. The rule governing distribution of terms must be observed.

Conversion of the four categorical propositions A, E, I and O is as follows:

Conversion of A Proposition

Keeping first three rules in mind, the proposition "All S is P" is converted as:

All S is P.
___
Therefore, all P is S.

But it is invalid reasoning; for the term P which is distributed in the conclusion fails to be distributed in the premiss. We can try an alternative conclusion.

All S is P.
___
Therefore, some P is S.

This is valid. While proposition A could not be converted into A, it can be converted into I proposition. This conversion of A into I, however, is called *conversion by limitation* because here we go from universal premiss to particular conclusion.

"All men are mortal" is converted as "Some mortals are men".

Conversion of E Proposition

No S is P.

Therefore, no P is S.

is valid reasoning, and hence the conversion of E is into E.

"No applicants are graduates" is converted into
"No graduates are applicants".

Conversion of I Proposition

Some S is P.

Therefore, some P is S

is valid.

"Some graduates are employed" is converted as

"Some employed persons are graduates."

Conversion of O Proposition

The conversion of O proposition is not valid. Let us see why.

Some S is not P.

Therefore, some P is not S

is invalid, for the term S which is distributed in conclusion fails to be distributed in the premiss. So, no conversion is possible for O proposition.

Summary

A is converted into I.
E is converted into E.
I is converted into I.
Conversion of O proposition is not valid.

OBVERSION

Obversion is another independent form of immediate inference. The rules for obversion are as follows:

1. Subject of the premiss is the subject of the conclusion.
2. Predicate of the conclusion is contradictory of the predicate of the premiss. One must notice that a negative

proposition is different from the proposition having a contradictory predicate. For instance, "Some S is not P" is a negative proposition whereas "Some S is non-P" is affirmative proposition with contradictory predicate.

3. Quantities of the premiss and the conclusion must be same. If the premiss is universal, conclusion is also universal and if the premiss is particular, conclusion is also particular.
4. Qualities of the premiss and the conclusion, however, are different. If the premiss is affirmative, then the conclusion is negative; and if the premiss is negative, the conclusion is affirmative.
5. The rule of distribution of the terms is to be observed.

Obversion of A Proposition

All S is P.

Therefore, no S is non-P

is valid for it satisfies all the rules of obversion.

"All men are mortal" is obverted as
"No men are immortal".

Obversion of E Proposition

No S is P.

Therefore, all S is non-P

is valid inference

"No politicians are idealists" is obverted as

"All politicians are non-idealists".

Obversion of I Proposition

Some S is P.

Therefore, some S is not non-P

is valid inference.

"Some men are wise" is obverted as

"Some men are not unwise".

Obversion of O Proposition

Some S is not P.
___
Therefore, some S is non-P

is valid inference.

"Some applicants are not Indian citizens" is obverted as "Some applicants are non-Indian citizens".

Summary

A is obverted into E.
E is obverted into A.
I is obverted into O.
O is obverted into I.

CONTRAPOSITION

Contraposition is not an independent form of immediate inference. It is a combination of both conversion and obversion. In contraposition, the subject of the conclusion is contradictory of the predicate of the premiss, and predicate of the conclusion is contradictory of the subject of the premiss. We keep applying obversion and conversion by turns till the required subject and predicate is found.

Contraposition of A Proposition

	All S is P	
=	No S is non-P	by obversion
=	No non-P is S	by conversion
=	All non-P is non-S	by obversion

The required subject and the required predicate are found. Therefore, the contraposition of A proposition is A itself.

"All cats are mammals" is contraposited as "All non-mammals are non-cats".

Contraposition of E Proposition

	No S is P	
=	All S is non-P	by obversion
=	Some non-P is S	by conversion
=	Some non-P is not non-S	by obversion

The required subject and the required predicate are found, therefore, contraposition of E proposition is O.

"No businessmen are philosophers" is contraposited as "Some non-philosophers are not non-businessmen".

Since E is contraposited into O, it is called *contraposition by limitation* because the premiss is universal whereas the conclusion is particular.

Contraposition of I Proposition

	Some S is P	
=	Some S is not non-P	by obversion

Now is turn for conversion but since it is O proposition, its conversion is not possible.

Therefore, there is no valid contraposition of I proposition.

Contraposition of O Proposition

	Some S is not P	
=	Some S is non-P	by obversion
=	Some non-P is S	by conversion
=	Some non-P is not non-S	by obversion

The required subject and the required predicate are found, therefore, contraposition of O proposition is O itself.

"Some philosophers are not radicals" is contraposited as "Some non-radicals are not non-philosophers."

Summary

A "All citizens are voters" is contraposited into
"All non-voters are non-citizens".

E "No politicians are honest" is contraposited into

"Some non-honest beings are not non-politicians".

I "Some applicants are graduates" cannot be contraposited.

O "Some students are not voters" is contraposited as "Some non-voters are not non-students".

Various forms of eduction of the categorical propositions are tabled as follows:

Proposition	Conversion	Obversion	Contraposition
All S is P	Some P is S (conversion by limitation)	No S is non-P	All non-P is non-S
No S is P	No P is S	All S is non-P	Some non-P is not non-S (contraposition by limitation)
Some S is P	Some P is S	Some S is not non-P	Not Valid
Some S is not P	Not Valid	Some S is non-P	Some non-P is not non-S

It should be noticed that in all the forms of eduction, the premiss and the conclusion are equivalent in meanings though the forms of the premiss and of the conclusion are different. Hence, conversion obversion, and contraposition are called equivalent propositions also. Each categorical proposition has at least two equivalent propositions.

The proposition "All S is P" is equivalent to:

(i) All S is P = No S is non-P — Obversion

(ii) All S is P = All non-P is non-S — Contraposition

Conversion of A into I is not equivalent proposition. For, premiss is universal but the conclusion is particular.

The proposition "No S is P" is equivalent to:

(i) No S is P = No P is S — Conversion

(ii) No S is P = All S is non-P Obversion

Contraposition of E proposition into O is not equivalent for premiss is universal and the conclusion is particular.

The I proposition "Some S is P" has again two equivalents :

(i) Some S is P = Some P is S Conversion
(ii) Some S is P = Some S is not non-P Obversion

Contraposition of I proposition is not valid.

Equivalents of O proposition are:

(i) Some S is not P = Some S is non-P Obversion
(ii) Some S is not P = Some non-P is not non-S Contraposition

Conversion of O proposition is not valid.

Note: In order to find out conversion, obversion and contraposition of a categorical proposition, one must make sure that the proposition is in standard logical form. There must be one subject term (noun), one predicate term (noun) and they must be joined by 'is', 'is not', 'was', 'was not', 'are', 'are not', etc. If predicate term of a proposition is not a noun, then it should first be changed into substantive noun and then the forms of eduction are to be applied.

Here are some solved examples:

(1) Find conversion, obversion and contraposition of the following propositions:

(i) All cats eat meat.

The proposition is not in the standard logical form. After changing it into standard form it becomes

All cats are meat eaters.

Conversion Some meat eaters are cats.
Obversion No cats are non-meat eaters.
Contraposition All non-meat eaters are non-cats.

(ii) All boys play football.

Logical form of the proposition is:

All boys are football players.

Conversion	Some football players are boys.
Obversion	No boys are non-football players.
Contraposition	All non-football players are non-boys.

(iii) No politicians are honest.

Logical Form	No politicians are honest beings.
Conversion	No honest beings are politicians.
Obversion	All politicians are dishonest beings.
Contraposition	Some dishonest beings are not non-politicians.

(2) Find conversion, obversion, contraposition, contrary/ subcontrary and contradictory of the following propositions:

(i) Some students are non-radicals.

Conversion	Some non-radicals are students.
Obversion	Some students are not radicals.
Contraposition	Since it is I proposition, its contraposition is not valid.
Subcontrary	Some students are not non-radicals.
Contradictory	No students are non-radicals.

(ii) Some artists are not non-professionals.

Conversion	Since it is O proposition, its conversion is not valid.
Obversion	Some artists are professionals.
Contraposition	Some professionals are not non-artists.
Subcontrary	Some artists are non-professionals.
Contradictory	All artists are non-professionals.

(3) A few more examples:

(i) If "Some students are scholarship holders" is true, what can be said about "All students are non-scholarship holders".

Note : In such types of problems, first change the subject and the predicate of the *given proposition* so that they match the subject and the predicate of the *required proposition* (the proposition whose value you want to find). This can be done by applying either conversion or obversion or contraposition as the situation demands. The forms of eduction can be applied repeatedly also. After that if need arises, apply "Square of Opposition".

Solution:

	Some students are scholarship holders	Given True
=	Some students are not non-scholarship holders	True by obversion

Since we have got the required subject (student) and the required predicate (non-scholarship holders), we will not use any more eduction. Instead, we will apply "Square of Opposition". If "Some students are not non-scholarship holders" is true, then "All students are non-scholarship holders" is *False* by contradictory relation.

(ii) If "All logicians are mathematicians" is true what can be said about "Some non-mathematicians are not non-logicians"?

Solution:

	All logicians are mathematicians	Given True
=	All non-mathematicians are non-logicians	True by contraposition
	Therefore, some non-mathematicians are not non-logicians	False by contradictory relation

(iii) If "No philosophers are businessmen" is true, what can be said about "No businessmen are non-philosophers"?

Solution:

	No philosophers are businessmen	Given True
=	No businessmen are philosophers	True by conversion
=	All businessmen are non-philosophers	True by obversion
	Therefore, no businessmen are non-philosophers	False by contrary relation

(iv) If "All cats are black" is false, what can be said about "Some non-black creatures are not non-cats"?

Solution :

A different method is adopted when the given proposition is false. The contradictory of the given proposition (which will obviously be true), is to be assumed as given proposition. Here given proposition "All cats are black"is false.The contradictory of this is 'O' proposition "Some cats are not black" and it is true. Now proceed as we have done in other cases.

Solution:

Some cats are not black	Given True.
⇒ Some non-black creatures are not non-cats	True by Contraposition.

Therefore, the required proposition "Some non-black creatures are not non-cats" is True.

Why a different strategy is taken here? This is because in deductive logic there is a possibillity of inferring a true as well as false conclusion from the given false premiss. But if the given proposition is true and the reasoning is valid, then it cannot imply a false conclusion. This you have already studied in Truth and Validity Section of chapter 1.

(v) If "Some men are happy beings" is true what can be said about "No happy beings are men"?

Solution:

Some men are happy beings	Given True
Some happy beings are men	True by conversion

Therefore, "No happy beings are men" is False by contradictory relation.

There is yet another method to solve problems of this kind. Consider the following example: If "All men are mortal" is true what may be inferred about the truth and falsehood of the following propositions:

1. No men are non-mortal.
2. Some non-mortals are not non-men.
3. All mortals are men.
4. No non-men are non-mortals
5. Some non-mortals are men.
6. No mortals are non-men.
7. No non-mortals are men.
8. All non-men are non-mortals.
9. All non-mortals are non-men.
10. Some men are not mortals.

To infer values of the above ten propositions, first make a list of all possible immediate inferences of the given proposition "All men are mortal". This can be done by converse, obverse and contraposition. All inferred propositions will be true, for all immediate inferences are equivalent propositions.

List of possible immediate inferences of the given proposition "All men are mortal" are as :

(i) Some mortals are men (converse of the given proposition and it is true)

(ii) Some mortals are not non-men (obverse of (i) and is true)

(iii) No men are non-mortals (obverse of the given proposition and is true)

(iv) No non-mortals are men (converse of (iii) and is true)

(v) Some non-men are not mortals (contraposition of (iv) and is true)

(vi) All non-mortals are non-men (contraposition of the given proposition and is true)

(vii) Some non-men are non-mortals (converse of (vi) and is true).

Now, infer the values of the required propositions one by one.

Solutions:

1. The value of "No men are non-mortal" is *true* by (iii) (obverse of the given proposition).
2. The value of "Some non-mortals are not non-men" is as follows:
   All non-mortals are non-men is true by (vi).
   ∴ Some non-mortals are not non-men is *false* by Contradictory relation.
3. The value of "All mortals are men" is as follows:
   Some mortals are men is true by (i).
   ∴ All mortals are men is *Undetermined* by Superaltern.
4. The value of "No non-men are non-mortals" is as follows:
   Some non-men are non-mortals is true by (vii).
   ∴ No non-men are non-mortal is *false* by Contradictory relation.
5. The value of "Some non-mortals are men" is as follows :
   No non-mortals are men is true by (iv).
   ∴ Some non-mortals are men is *false* by Contradictory relation.
6. The value of "No mortals are non-men" is as follows:
   Some mortals are not non-men is true by (ii)

∴ No mortals are non-men is *Undetermined* by Superaltern.

7. The value of "No non-mortals are men" is *true* by (iv)
8. The value of "All non-men are non-mortals" is as follows: Some non-men are non-mortals is true by (vii)

   ∴ All non-men are non-mortals is *Undetermined* by Superaltern.
9. "All non-mortals are non-men" is *true* by (vi).
10. The value of "Some men are not mortals" is *false* because it is Contradictory of the given proposition "All men are mortals".

Immediate Inference (Eduction) in Modern Logic

The traditional "Square of Opposition" and other forms of immediate inference, say conversion, obversion and contraposition have been criticized by the modern logicians in the context of existential import. In the chapter 3B of this book you have already read that 'A' and 'E' propositions are existentially negative whereas particular propositions 'I' and 'O' are existentially affirmative. If this standpoint is accepted, then conversion of 'A' into 'I' and contraposition of 'E' into 'O' will become invalid. The conclusion of 'I' from 'A' premiss and 'O' from 'E' premiss is against the basic tenets of deductive logic. In deductive reasoning, the conclusion cannot have anything extra which the premiss or premisses do not have. It will be to "go beyond the evidence". An existentially empty proposition cannot imply existentially loaded proposition. 'I' or 'O' proposition (conclusion) has existential import, whereas 'A' or 'E' (premiss) does not have existential import. Therefore, from 'A' premiss, 'I' conclusion cannot be validly inferred. Similarly, from 'E' premiss, 'O' conclusion cannot be validly inferred. Eduction thus in the Modern Logic takes the following form:

Conversion:	E into E
	I into I

Obversion	A into E
	E into A
	I into O
	O into I
Contraposition	A into A
	O into O

A question may arise : Is there any way to save traditional logic and all the forms of immediate inferences (Eduction as well as "Square of Opposition")? This is possible provided we allow all the propositions universals as well as particulars to have existential import. But if all the categorical propositions, universal and particular, have existential import, then the relationship of contradiction will become invalid and if that happens, then the entire logic will collapse. The contradictory relation states that two contradictory propositions, theorems, viewpoints, or standpoints cannot be accepted true at the same time. Similarly they cannot be false together at the same time. But if all the categorical propositions have existential import, then A and O propositions (which are contradictory) can both be false at the same time. For instance, the proposition "All golden mountains of the world are situated in India" and "Some golden mountains are not situated in India" are both false propositions because the class of 'golden mountain' is empty. Thus, if all the categorical propositions have existential import, then we will have to pay heavier price in logic. In order to avoid all that, the modern logicians have assigned existential import only to the particular propositions, and not to universals.

Exercises

1. Give converse, obverse and contrapositive of the following propositions (wherever possible):
   1. All scientists are philosophers.
   2. Some cats are black.
   3. Some socialists are not democrats.

4. All fish are vertebrate.
5. No man is angel.
6. Some teachers are good writers.
7. Some traders are not cheaters.
8. No sinners are saints.
9. Some good football players are Europeans.
10. All businessmen are wealthy persons.
11. Some poets are not idealists.
12. Some leaders are good statesmen.
13. All trees are useful things.
14. No mathematicians are dishonest beings.
15. All triangles are three-sided polygons.
16. No giraffes are short-necked.
17. All giraffes are long-necked animals.
18. Some non-artists are non-honest beings.
19. No non-citizens are voters
20. Some non-mammals are not birds.
21. All non-honest persons are non-artists.
22. No non-artists are honest.
23. No circle is polygon.
24. Some non-honest persons are artists.
25. Some non-graduates are non-girls.

2. If "Some students are radicals" is true, what can be inferred about the truth or falsity of the following:
    1. Some students are not non-radicals.
    2. All non-radicals are non-students.
    3. No radicals are students.
    4. No students are radicals.

3. If "No politicians are honest" is true, what can be inferred about the truth or falsity of the following:
   1. Some non-honests are not non-politicians.
   2. Some honest persons are not non-politicians.
   3. No non-politicians are honest.
   4. Some non-politicians are not non-honest.
4. If the proposition "No soldiers are officers" is true, what can be inferred about each of the following? Give reasons:
   1. Some soldiers are non-officers.
   2. Some officers are soldiers.
   3. Some non-soldiers are non-officers.
   4. All non-officers are non-soldiers.
5. Assuming that "All journalists are pessimists" is true, what can be inferred about the truth or falsity of the following:
   1. All journalists are non-pessimists.
   2. No non-jounalists are non-pessimists.
   3. Some non-pessimists are non-journalists.
   4. Some journalists are not non-pessimists.
6. If "Some students are not scholarship holders" is true, what can be inferred about the truth or falsity of the following propositions:
   1. No scholarship holders are students.
   2. Some students are scholarship holders.
   3. Some non-scholarship holders are not non-students.
   4. No non-students are non-scholarship holders.
7. If "All students are brave" is false, then what can be inferred about the truth or falsity of the following:
   1. All non-students are non brave.
   2. Some brave persons are not students.
   3. No non-brave persons are non-students.

4. Some students are not non-brave.

8. If "All roses are red" is false, then what can be inferred about the truth and falsity of the following propositions?

   1. Some non-red things are not non-roses.
   2. No roses are non-red things.
   3. All red things are roses.
   4. All non-roses are non-red things.

9. What do you understand by 'inference'? Explain with examples the various kinds of immediate inferences.

10. Is conversion of A into I and contraposition of E into O valid forms of immediate inference? Discuss with reference to existential import.

Chapter 7 – Section A

Categorical Syllogism

SYLLOGISM is mediate inference having two and only two premisses. The premisses jointly imply the conclusion. Aristole, founder of syllogistic reasoning, recognized that all two-premissed reasoning is syllogistic. Syllogisms are classified as categorical or non-categorical (compound). In a categorical syllogism all propositions (two premisses and conclusion) are categorical propositions, that is, A, E, I and O.

All men are mortal.
All professors are men.
Therefore, all professors are mortal.

is an example of categorical syllogism.

In a compound syllogism one premiss or both the premisses are conditional propositions. Here is an example of compound syllogism:

If it rains in time, then harvest will be good.
It harvest is good, then inflation will be reduced.
Therefore, if it rains in time, then inflation will be reduced.

In a categorical syllogism there are three and only three propositions (two premisses and a conclusion) and there are three and only three terms. For example, in the syllogism.

All M is P
All S is M
Therefore, all S is P.

S, P, M are terms. **The term common between the premisses is called middle term; subject of the conclusion is minor**

term; predicate of the conclusion is major term. Each term in a categorical syllogism occurs twice. In the above example,

S - Minor term
P - Major term
M- Middle term

There are two premisses in a categorical syllogism, major premiss and minor premiss. **The premiss which contains major term is called major premiss and the premiss which contains minor term is called minor premiss.** See the following example:

All M is P	Major premiss
All S is M	Minor premiss
Therefore, all S is P Conclusion	

In a standard form categorical syllogism, major premiss occurs first, then the minor premiss comes and the conclusion occurs in the end. A syllogism may not be always in a standard form always. The premisses and the conclusion may not be in the right order. The conclusion may sometimes be stated first and premisses later on. In such cases the syllogism is to be rearranged in the proper order and then the validity of the syllogism is determined.

The main characteristic of a categorical syllogism is that all the three propositions (two premisses and conclusion) are categorical propositions 'A', 'E', 'I' or 'O'. Singular propositions like "Socrates is mortal". "Socrates is a man" in a syllogism like,

All men are mortal
Socrates is a man.
____
Therefore, Socrates is mortal.

are treated as universal affirmative A proposition.

Figures of Syllogism

Position of the middle term in the premisses decides the figure of a syllogism. The middle term can occur in four different ways in a standard form categorical syllogism.

First Figure, M P
S M

Therefore, S P

In the first figure, middle term is subject in the major premiss and predicate in the minor premiss.

Second Figure, P M
S M

Therefore, S P

Middle term is predicate in both the premisses in the second figure.

Third Figure, M P
M S

Therefore, S P

Middle term is subject in both the premisses in the third figure.

Fourth Figure, P M
M S

Therefore, S P

Middle term is predicate in the major premiss and subject in the minor premiss in the fourth figure.

Moods of Syllogism

Mood of a syllogism means arrangement of premisses and conclusion. For instance AAA mood in the first figure is expressed as:

All M is P.
All S is M.

Therefore, all S is P.

In AAA mood, the first letter '(A)' stands for the major premiss, second letter '(A)' stands for the minor premiss and the last letter (A) stands for the conclusion.

AEE mood in the second figure is expressed as:

All P is M.
No S is M.

Therefore, no S is P.

The first letter (A) is for the major premiss, second letter (E) is for the minor premiss and the last letter (E) is for the conclusion.

Standard Form Categorical Syllogism

The validity of a syllogism can be determined only when the syllogism is in the standard form because rules of validity of a syllogism are applicable only to the standard form syllogism. In the standard form categorical syllogism major premiss must occur first and the minor premiss comes after that, and the conclusion is in the end. But sometimes conclusion may not be in the right place; it may come either in the beginning or between the premisses. In that case the syllogism has to be rearranged in the proper form. **In order to rearrange the non-standard form categorical syllogism into standard form first the conclusion should be located.** Afterwards determine the minor and the major terms. The subject of the conclusion is minor term and the predicate of the conclusion is major term. Thereafter major premiss and minor premiss can be located easily, for the major premiss contains major term and the minor premiss contains minor term.

There are conclusion indicator words and there are premiss indicator words. Some of the conclusion indicator words are:

'so', 'hence', 'it follows', 'subsequently', 'it is implied', 'therefore', 'thus', etc. Some of the premiss indicator words are:

'since', 'for', 'because', 'reason' 'being', 'on account of', etc.

Let us examine a few more syllogisms which are not in standard form and then see how they are reduced into the standard form categorical syllogism.

(i) Some dinosaurs were carnivorous but all dinosaurs are extinct, hence some carnivorous animals are extinct.

The standard form categorical syllogism is:

All dinosaurs are extinct.

Some dinosaurs were carnivorous animals.

Therefore, some carnivorous animals are extinct.

This is All mood in the third figure.

(ii) No one whoever dies are phoenix and all phoenix are immortals, so no one whoever dies is immortal.

The standard form categorical syllogism is:

All phoenix are immortals.

No one who ever dies are phoenix.

Therefore, no one whoever dies is immortal.

This is AEE mood in the first figure.

After rearranging the premisses and the conclusion in a proper order, examine all the propositions (premisses as well as conclusion), whether each one of them is in the standard logical form or not. All the propositions should be in one of the following forms:

All S is P.

No S is P.

Some S is P.

Some S is not P.

If either of the premisses or the conclusion is not in the logical form, then it should be reduced into standard logical form proposition. The devices and techniques for doing this is already worked out in the third chapter.

For example the following argument is rewritten in the proper syllogistic order.

Most of the professors are knowledge seekers and every knowledge seeker is not worldly wise hence some worldly wise persons are not professors.

In this argument first two propositions are not in standard form. First those propositions will be reduced in standard form.

Most of the professors are knowledge seekers $\Rightarrow$ Some professors are knowledge seekers.

Every knowledge seeker is not worldly wise ⇒ Some knowledge seekers are not worldly wise.

Conclusion is already in standard form.

The standard form syllogism will be.

Some professors are knowledge seekers.
Some knowledge seekers are not worldly wise.

Therefore, some worldly wise persons are not professors.

This is IOO mood in 4th figure.

Exercises

1. Define syllogism. Explain its nature and structure with suitable examples.
2. What is meant by the figure of a syllogism? Explain different figures of syllogism. Illustrate your answer.
3. Identify major term, minor term and middle term of the following syllogisms. Give their figures and moods also.
    1. All logicians are mathematicians.

       Some mathematicians are musicians.

       Therefore, some musicians are logicians.
    2. Some successful people are rich.

       Some businessmen are rich.

       Therefore, some businessmen are successful people.
    3. All philosophers are scientists.

       Some philosophers are mathematicians.

       Therefore, some mathematicians are scientists.
    4. All sharks bite.

       Some fish are sharks.

       Therefore, some fish bite.
    5. All parrots are birds.

       All crows are birds.

       Therefore, all crows are parrots.

6. Some employees are voters.

   No child is a voter.

   Therefore, no child is employee.

7. Some dinosaurs were carnivorous.

   All dinosaurs are extinct.

   Therefore, some extinct animals were carnivorous.

8. All cowards are unsuccessful people.

   No patriot is coward.

   Therefore, no patriot is unsuccessful people.

9. All naturalists are observant people.

   Some observant people are interested in animals.

   Therefore, some people who are interested in animals are naturalists.

10. Some scientists are not credulous.

    All psychiatrists are credulous.

    Therefore, some psychiatrists are not scientists.

4. Point out the conclusion, the premisses, and the middle term in each of the following arguments:

   Note: If a syllogism is not in the standard form, then first change it into standard form categorical syllogism, and then proceed further.

   1. All saints are polite. No sinners are saints. Therefore, no sinners are polite.

   2. Some professors are not good orators. All good orators are successful persons. Thus, some professors are not successful persons.

   3. No one who believes in human equality are fascist, and all those who believe in human equality are strong defenders of democracy. Subsequently no strong defenders of democracy are fascists.

4. Some trade unions are politically motivated organizations. But some trade unions are for the welfare of the workers. From this, one concludes that some politically motivated organizations are for the welfare of workers.
5. No coward is self-confident person because all self-confident persons are mentally strong whereas no coward is mentally strong person.
6. Since no insects are eight-legged animals and all wasps are insects, so no wasp is eight-legged animal.
7. No Indian woman is a soldier. All soliders serve the country. From them it follows that some who serve their country are not Indian women.
8. All enterprising people have dynamic personality because all those who have dynamic personality look forward and all those who look forward are enterprising people.
9. No civilized person is rude in his behaviour, for all civilized persons are considerate of others and no one who is considerate of others is rude in his behaviour.
10. All bats can fly because all bats have feathers and all those who have feathers can fly.

5. Reduce the following syllogisms into standard term and give their figures and moods:
   1. Only virtuous are happy persons and every happy person is optimist. Thus only those who are optimists are virtuous persons.
   2. Almost all scientists are honest beings and also every scientist is an inquisitive person, from this it is implied that all inquisitive persons are honest beings.
   3. All dogs are intelligent beings but every intelligent being is not faithful, hence every dog is not faithful being.

4. A few old persons are healthy whereas every old person is conservative in attitude. Therefore some those who are conservative in attitude are not healthy.
5. None but brave deserve medals and some students are brave. Therefore some students deserve medals.
6. Many successful businessmen are not really happy because they (successful businessmen) are not virtuous and it is only virtuous who is really happy.
7. Some ambitious persons are not honest beings, for all politicians are ambitious persons and majority of politicians are not honest beings.
8. Many dinosaurs were carnivorous but even a single dinosaur is not alive today which only implies that some of those who are alive today are not carnivorous.
9. All cats are mammals but all cats are not black creatures, therefore some mammals are not black creatures.
10. All philosophers die unsatisfied and Karl Marx was a philosopher therefore Karl Mark died unsatisfied.

Chapter 7 – Section B

Validity of Categorical Syllogism
Traditional Method

ARISTOTLE and other traditional logicians devised certain rules which determine the validity of a syllogism. These rules are mainly based on the distribution of terms. A valid syllogism has to obey all the given rules, and if any of the rules is violated, then the syllogism becomes invalid. There is no uniformity of order regarding these rules in the books of logic.

Rule No. 1

A syllogistic reasoning must have three and only three terms. Since each term occurs twice, the term should be used in the same sense in both of its occurrences. The meaning and context of a term at both places of its occurrences should be same. Sometimes a term carries particular meaning at one place and is used in different sense at another place. In that case the syllogism is invalid and has the **fallacy of four terms.** For example:

e. Right things should be enforced by law.

Charity is right thing.

Therefore charity should be enforced by law.[1]

In this syllogism the term 'right thing' is ambiguous. It refers to legally right thing in the major premiss and in minor premiss it means morally right thing. This syllogism has four terms instead of three, and hence is invalid having fallacy of four terms.

Sometimes more than three terms are used but two of them are either synonymous or contradictory. In that case, terms of

1. Mellone, S.H. op. cit., p 126.

the syllogism can be reduced to three with the help of conversion, obversion or contraposition. For example:

All librarians are faculty members.
Some staff members are non-faculty members.

Therefore, some staff members are not librarians.

In this syllogism, there are initially four terms, namely:

1. librarians
2. faculty members
3. non-faculty members
4. staff members

But the term "non-faculty member" can be replaced by "faculty member" after obverting minor premiss. The minor premiss then becomes

Some staff members are not faculty members.

The syllogism now has only three terms and it is stated as:

All librarians are faculty members.
Some staff members are not faculty members.

Therefore, some staff members are not librarians.

In case of synonymous terms, one synonymous term is replaced by another synonymous term because meaning of the synonymous terms is same. However, if the terms are more than three and none of them is synonymous or contradictory, then there is fallacy of four terms.

Rules Related to Distribution of Terms

Rule No. 2

Middle term must be distributed at least at one of the places of its occurrences. If the middle term is not distributed in any of the premisses, then the syllogism becomes invalid and has the **fallacy of undistributed middle.** For instance, in the following syllogisms, the middle term is not distributed in any of the premisses and hence, they are invalid syllogisms.

(i) All P is M.
All S is M.
Therefore, all S is P.

(ii) All cows (D)* are mammals.(UD)**
All cats (D) are mammals.(UD)
Therefore, all cats are cows.

Rule No. 3

A term which is distributed in the conclusion must necessarily be distributed in the premiss. We had discussed it earlier also in the immediate inference. A syllogism becomes invalid if a term is distributed in the conclusion but undistributed in the premiss. A categorical syllogism having minor term distributed in the conclusion but undistributed in the minor premiss, is invalid having the **fallacy of illicit minor.** For example:

(i) All M is P.
All M is S.
Therefore, all S is P.

The term 'S' is distributed in the conclusion but not in the premiss. So it is invalid syllogism having fallacy of illicit minor.

(ii) No mathematicians (D) are musicians.(D)
All mathematicians (D) are scientists (UD).
Therefore, no scientists (D) are musicians.

In this syllogism there is fallacy of illicit minor and hence it is invalid syllogism.

Similarly, the categorical syllogism having major term distributed in the conclusion but undistributed in the major premiss is invalid, having the **fallacy of illicit major**. For example :

(i) All M is P.
Some S is not M.
Therefore, some S is not P.

* D = distributed ** UD = undistributed

(ii) All mathematicians (D) are logicians (UD).
Some businessmen (UD) are not mathematicians (D).
Therefore, some businessmen (UD) are not logicians (D)

are invalid syllogisms having fallacy of illicit major.

To commit either the fallacy of illicit major or illicit minor means the syllogism violates the very basic tenet of the deductive logic. In the deductive logic the conclusion is already contained in the premisses, that is why, the conclusion cannot be more comprehensive than the premisses. If a term is distributed in the conclusion but not in the premiss, then it means the conclusion goes beyond the premiss, which is not permitted in the deductive reasoning.

Rules of Quality

There are two rules governing the qualities of premisses and conclusion. They are as follows :

Rule No. 4

A valid syllogism must not have two negative premisses. A syllogism having both the negative premisses is invalid and has the **Fallacy of Exclusive Premisses.**

The reasoning behind this rule is that two negative propositions have nothing common. There is no connective thread between the premisses.

The function of middle term 'M' is to relate 'S' and 'P', but here 'M' does not connect them.

(i) No P is M.
No S is M.
Therefore, no S is P.

is invalid syllogism having the fallacy of exclusive premisses.

Similarly, the following syllogism is invalid having the same fallacy.

(ii) No cats are flying creatures.
Some domestic animals are not cats.
Therefore, some domestic animals are not flying creatures.

Rule No. 5

If one of the premisses is negative, then the conclusion should be negative. But if one premiss is negative and conclusion is affirmative, then it has the **Fallacy of drawing affirmative conclusion from a negative premiss**[2]. For example:

(i) All P is M.
No S is M.
Therefore, all S is P

is invalid having the fallacy of drawing affirmative conclusion from a negative premiss. The following syllogism also has the same fallacy.

All athletes are strong-built persons.
No strong-built person is lazy man.
Therefore, all lazy men are athletes.

Rule of Quantity

Rule No. 6

A syllogism having both the universal premisses must have universal conclusion. A syllogism having both universal premisses but a particular conclusion is invalid having the fallacy called **Existential Fallacy.** For example.

All M is P.
No S is M.
Therefore, some S is not P.

is invalid syllogism because of existential fallacy. However, this rule was not there in the traditional logic. For the traditional logicians syllogisms like:

2. The name of fallacy is from Irving M. Copi., and Carl Cohen, *Introduction to Logic* (ninth edition), p. 265.

(i) All M is P.
All S is M.
Therefore, some S is P.

(ii) No M is P.
All M is S.
Therefore, some S is not P.

(iii) All P is M.
All M is S.
Therefore, some S is P.

(iv) No P is M.
All M is S.
Therefore, some S is not P.

are valid, though they were called weak moods. But for the modern logicians, however, all these syllogistic moods are invalid, because they commit existential fallacy.

We have already discussed existential import in the third chapter, and stated that 'A' and 'E' do not have existential import whereas 'I' and 'O' propositions have it. In deductive logic conclusion cannot possess anything which the premisses do not have. The conclusion cannot be particular if all the premisses are universal.

In addition to the six rules which are treated as self-evident and self-explanatory, there are certain corollaries (or hypotheses) which are also applicable to all the moods of syllogism. They are called corollaries or hypotheses because they are not self-evident, and can be proved with the help of the above given six rules.

Corollary 1: From two particular premisses no valid mood follows in a standard form categorical syllogism.

Proof : If both the premisses are particular, the combinations of premisses are : II, IO, OI and OO.

II combination of premisses do not distribute any term and hence the syllogism having II as premisses is always invalid having the fallacy of undistributed middle. The combination of

OO premisses always makes invalid syllogism because of the fallacy of exclusive premisses.

We are left with IO and OI combinations of premisses. From IO combination of the premisses four possible moods can be constructed which are as: IOA, IOE, IOI and IOO.

Out of these moods IOE and IOO are invalid because of illicit major (though there is one more fallacy also in them depending on the figure to which the syllogism belongs).

IOA and IOI are invalid moods having the fallacy of drawing affirmative conclusion from a negative premiss.

Similarly, from OI combinations of premisses we get four syllogistic moods. OIA, OIE, OII and OIO. OIA and OII are invalid, for they have the fallacy of drawing an affirmative conclusion from a negative premiss. OIE definitely has the fallacy of illicit minor though it has one more fallacy also OIO has either fallacy of illicit major or undistributed middle.

Hence, from two particular premisses no valid categorical syllogism can be constructed.

Corollary 2 : If one of the premisses is particular, then the conclusion has to be particular in a valid standard form categorical syllogism.

or

From one particular premiss, universal conclusion cannot be drawn in a valid standard form categorical syllogism.

Proof : The possible combinations of the premisses with one particular premiss are: AI, IA, AO, OA, EI, IE, EO and OE.

Out of these EO and OE combinations of premisses will always make invalid syllogism because of the fallacy of exclusive premisses.

Let us consider all other combinations of premisses one by one. The moods with AI combination of premisses and universal conclusion are: AIA and AIE.

Both of them are invalid syllogisms because of illicit minor, although they have one more fallacy also depending on the figure to which the mood belongs.

From IA again we get two moods: IAA and IAE.

Whereas, IAE definitely has the fallacy of illicit major, IAA has either the fallacy of illicit minor or the fallacy of undistributed middle.

From AO premisses, the two required moods are: AOA and AOE.

AOA is invalid, for it has the fallacy of drawing an affirmative conclusion from a negative premiss. AOE has either the fallacy of illicit major or illicit minor depending on the figure to which the mood belongs.

Similarly, from OA we get two moods: OAA and OAE.

OAA has the fallacy of drawing an affirmative conclusion from a negative premiss, though it has one more fallacy also. OAE has either the fallacy of illicit major or illicit minor depending on the figure to which the mood belongs.

From EI premisses we get EIA and EIE moods. They both have the fallacy of illicit minor.

IE combination of premisses give us IEA and IEE moods.

IEA is invalid mood, for it has fallacy of drawing an affirmative conclusion from a negative premiss. IEE has the fallacy of illicit major.

Thus, from a particular premiss, universal conclusion cannot be drawn in a valid standard form categorical syllogism.

Corollary 3 : In a valid standard form of categorical syllogism no negative conclusion follows from two affirmative premisses.

Proof: Combinations of both affirmative premisses are AA, AI, IA and II.

The combination of II premisses always make invalid syllogism because it does not distribute any term in the premiss and, hence, has the fallacy of undistributed middle.

AA premisses with a negative conclusion form AAO and AAE, moods.

AAO suffers from the existential fallacy and AAE has either the fallacy of illicit major or undistributed middle depending on the figure of the mood.

AI and IA combinations of premisses and a negative conclusion gives us AIO, AIE, IAO and IAE, moods.

Whereas, IAO and IAE definitely have the fallacy of illicit major, AIE has the fallacy of illicit minor. AIO has either the fallacy of illicit major or undistributed middle depending on the figure.

Thus, with two affirmative premisses and a negative conclusion no valid standard form categorical syllogism is possible.

Corollary 4 : If major premiss is particular, then minor premiss cannot be negative in a valid standard form categorical syllogism.

Proof: If minor premiss is negative, then the conclusion is also negative. Otherwise it has the fallacy of drawing an affirmative conclusion from a negative premiss. If minor premiss is negative, then the major premiss has to be affirmative (otherwise there is fallacy of exclusive premisses).

Now since the conclusion is negative, its predicate term (major term) is distributed. The major term then must be distributed in the major premiss also. But since major premiss in this case is particular and also affirmative (I proposition) no term is distributed. The syllogism then has the fallacy of illicit major. Thus, if major premiss is particular, the minor premiss must not be negative.

The six general rules and four corollaries are applicable to every mood of categorical syllogism irrespective of its figure.

However, besides these rules and corollaries there are other special rules also for each figure. Special rules of each figure can be proved with the help of six rules just as the corollaries are proved. Let us study the special rules of each figure and see how they are proved.

Special Rules of 1st Figure

1. The major premiss must be universal in the 1st figure (violation of the rule leads to the fallacy of illicit major).
2. The minor premiss must be affirmative in the 1st figure (otherwise there is fallacy of illicit major).

Proof of the 1st rule: The format of first figure is

MP
SM

Therefore, S P.

In the first figure the major premiss must be universal. If major premiss is not universal but instead is particular then the middle term (M) is not distributed in the major premiss because in the particular proposition subject term is always undistributed. The middle term then must be distributed in the minor premiss. In that case minor premiss should be negative, for only in a negative proposition predicate term is distributed.

Negative minor premiss means:

(i) the conclusion is negative,

(ii) and major premiss is affirmative

Two negative premisses do not make syllogism valid. The negative conclusion means the predicate term (major term P) is distributed. Now in a valid syllogism major term which is distributed in the conclusion must also be distributed in the major premiss. But here major term is not distributed in the major premiss because major premiss is affirmative and in affirmative propositions (A or I) predicate term is always undistributed. Hence, there is fallacy of illicit major. So the major premiss in the 1st figure of categorical syllogism cannot be particular. It has to be universal.

Proof of the 2nd rule: The minor premiss must be affirmative in the 1st figure.

If minor premiss is not affirmative but is a negative proposition, then the conclusion is also negative. In that case, major premiss is necessarily affirmative. The negative conclusion means the predicate term (major term P) is distributed in conclusion, for in a negative proposition predicate term is always distributed. In a valid categorical syllogism a term which is distributed in the conclusion must necessarily be distributed in the premiss. But in this case major premiss being affirmative proposition, cannot distribute its predicate and hence has the fallacy of illicit major. Therefore, if the minor premiss is not affirmative in the 1st figure, then the syllogism is invalid and has the fallacy of illicit major. The minor premiss thus must be affirmative in the first figure.

The application of these two rules gives the following valid moods in the first figure.

AAA	Barbara
EAE	Celarent
AII	Darii
EIO	Ferio

The names of these valid moods were given by the medieval thinkers. The names contain the vowel symbols. The order in which the vowels occur in the name is the same as that of the mood. The 1st vowel stands for the major premiss, 2nd for the minor premiss and the last for the conclusion. For instance, Barbara represents AAA, Celarent is EAE and so on. The logicians provided the names of valid moods in order to memorize them easily.

Special Rules of 2nd Figure

1. One of the premisses must be negative. (The violation of the rule leads to the fallacy of undistributed middle.)
2. The major premiss must be universal (otherwise there is fallacy of illicit major).

Proof of the 1st rule: Format of 2nd figure is:

PM
SM

Therefore, S P

One of the premisses must be negative. If both the premisses are affirmative, then the middle term is not distributed in any of the premisses. In both the premisses the middle term is predicate, and predicate term is not distributed in affirmative propositions. So if both the premisses are affirmative in second figure, then there is fallacy of undistributed middle. Hence one of the premisses must be negative in the second figure.

Proof of the 2nd rule: The major premiss must be universal in the 2nd figure. Since middle term is predicate in both the premisses, one of the premisses has to be negative in order to make middle term distributed. One negative premiss means the conclusion is negative. The negative conclusion distributes its predicate term which is a major term. In a valid categorical syllogism, the major term if distributed in the conclusion then it must necessarily be distributed in the major premiss. But this is possible only if major premiss is universal, for only in a universal proposition A or E, subject term is distributed. If major premiss is not universal in second figure then the syllogism becomes invalid having the fallacy of illicit major. Hence, major premiss must be universal in the second figure.

Valid moods of the second figure are:

AEE	Camestres
EAE	Cesare
AOO	Baroco
EIO	Festino

Special Rules of 3rd Figure

1. The conclusion must be particular (otherwise there is fallacy of illicit minor).
2. The minor premiss must be affirmative (otherwise there is fallacy of illicit major).

Proof of the 1st rule: Format of 3rd figure is:

MP
MS

Therefore, S P

The conclusion must be particular in the third figure. If the conclusion in the third figure is universal, then minor term S is distributed in the conclusion. In a valid syllogism, if a term is distributed in the conclusion, it must be distributed in the premiss also. In order that the minor term is distributed in the minor premiss, the premiss must be negative, for only in a negative proposition the predicate term is distributed. The negative minor premiss implies a negative conclusion. In turn negative conclusion makes its predicate, which is major term, distributed. Now major term must be distributed in the major premiss also. Since major term in the major premiss is predicate it can be distributed there only if major premiss is negative. But two negative premisses do not make a syllogism valid. Thus, if conclusion is not particular in the third figure, the syllogism is invalid having the fallacy of illicit minor.

Proof of the 2nd rule: The minor premiss must be affirmative in the third figure. If the minor premiss is not affirmative but instead a negative proposition, then in a valid categorical syllogism it implies two things:

(i) a negative conclusion, and

(ii) affirmative major premiss.

The negative conclusion means its predicate term (major term) is distributed in the conclusion. In a valid syllogism the major term then must necessarily be distributed in the major premiss also. But major premiss being affirmative does not distribute its predicate, for in the third figure major term is predicate. So major term is distributed in the conclusion but undistributed in the premiss which leads to the fallacy of illicit major. Thus, if the minor premiss is not affirmative in the third figure, then the syllogism will become invalid having the fallacy of illicit major.

Valid moods in the third figure are:

AII	Datisi
IAI	Disamis
OAO	Bocardo
EIO	Ferison

Special Rules of 4th Figure

1. If either premiss is negative, the major premiss cannot be particular (otherwise there is fallacy of illicit major).
2. If the major premiss is affirmative, the minor premiss cannot be particular (otherwise there is fallacy of undistributed middle).
3. If the minor premiss is affirmative, then the conclusion cannot be universal (otherwise there is fallacy of illicit minor).

Proof of 1st rule: Format of fourth figure is:

PM
MS

Therefore, S P

If either of the premisses is negative, then the conclusion is also negative. The negative conclusion distributes its predicate term which is major term. The major term then must necessarily be distributed in the major premiss. But if the major premiss is not universal, then its subject term is not distributed. The syllogism then becomes invalid having the fallacy of illicit major. Thus, if one of the premisses is negative in the fourth figure, then the major premiss must necessarily be universal.

Proof of 2nd rule: If the major premiss is affirmative, then the middle term is not distributed there because in an affirmative proposition, predicate term is undistributed. The middle term then has to be distributed in the minor premiss. This is possible only if the minor premiss is a universal proposition. For the middle term is subject in the minor premiss in the fourth figure, and subject term is distributed only in the universal proposition. Therefore, if the major premiss is affirmative, then the minor premiss cannot be particular otherwise the syllogism becomes invalid having the fallacy of undistributed middle.

Proof of 3rd rule: If the minor premiss is affirmative, the conclusion cannot be universal. The affirmative minor premiss and the universal conclusion make the syllogism invalid in the fourth figure having the fallacy of illicit minor. The universal conclusion distributes its subject term, because universal proposition (A or E) always distributes its subject term. Now if minor term is distributed in the conclusion, then it must also be distributed in the minor premiss. But the minor premiss being affirmative does not distribute its predicate term because in the fourth figure minor term is predicate term. Hence, there is fallacy of illicit minor. So in the fourth figure if minor premiss is affirmative, the conclusion must be particular.

Valid moods in the fourth figure are:

AEE Cameres
IAI Dimaris
EIO Fresison

Its amazing EIO mood is valid in all the four figures, whereas IEO is invalid in all the figures.

Maximum 256 possible moods can be constructed with different combinations of categorical propositions in all the four figures of syllogism. Out of them only 15 moods are valid for the modern logicians. In the first figure 4 moods, in the second figure 4 moods, in the third figure 4 moods and in the fourth figure only 3 moods are valid, which shows validity is so rare and precious.

Let us see how different combinations of 'A', 'E', 'I' and 'O' propositions yield 256 moods.

Taking 'A' as major premiss, we get the following moods:

AAA AIA
AAE AIE

AAI	AII
AAO	AIO
AEA	AOA
AEE	AOE
AEI	AOI
AEO	AOO

There are 16 combinations and each one of them further has four moods in four different figures. For instance, AAA combination of premisses and conclusion has four moods, one each in 1st, 2nd, 3rd and 4th figure. So each one of 16 moods has four moods further. Thus if 'A' is major premiss then 64 moods can be framed (how many of them are valid is a separate question).

Similarly, 64 moods can be framed by taking 'E' as major premiss, 64 moods can be construced taking 'I' as a major premiss, and further 64 moods are there with 'O' as a major premiss.

EAA	IAA	OAA
EAE	IAE	OAE
EAI	IAI	OAI
EAO	IAO	OAO
EEA	IEA	OEA
EEE	IEE	OEE
EEI	IEI	OEI
EEO	IEO	OEO
EIA	IIA	OIA
EIE	IIE	OIE
EII	III	OII
EIO	IIO	OIO
EOA	IOA	OOA
EOE	IOE	OOE
EOI	IOI	OOI
EOO	IOO	OOO

Out of 256 moods, only 15 are valid for the modern logicians whereas for the traditional logicians there are 24 moods. A student can apply six rules of valid syllogism to eliminate the invalid ones.

The other nine moods which were accepted by the traditional logicians are:

AAI In 1st, 3rd and 4th figure.

EAO In 1st, 2nd, 3rd and 4th figure.

AEO In 2nd and 4th figure.

But in the context of existential import these moods have become invalid having the existential fallacy.

Exercises

1. Test the validity/invalidity of the following syllogistic forms by the traditional method of rules and fallacies in the figures indicated against them.

1. AAA - 2	7. AOO - 4	13. IOE - 2
2. AEE - 3	8. EIE - 3	14. EIE - 4
3. AEO - 1	9. IAA - 2	15. IAA - 4
4. AII - 4	10. IOO - 1	16. OIO - 1
5. AOE - 1	11. III - 4	17. OAI - 3
6. AOI - 3	12. IEE - 3	18. OAE - 1
19. OOO - 4	30. OAI - 1	41. AAO - 1
20. IAI - 1	31. OAO - 1	42. OAO - 4
21. EAO - 3	32. OEO - 4	43. EOO - 2
22. EAE - 4	33. EAO - 1	44. EIE - 1
23. AEO - 3	34. AAA - 4	45. IEO - 2
24. EAE - 2	35. AAE - 1	46. IAA - 3
25. AAI - 1	36. OAO - 2	47. AAA - 1
26. OAI - 2	37. EAO - 4	48. AEO - 4
27. IEO - 3	38. IEO - 1	49. AAA - 3
28. OAA - 4	39. EIO - 3	50. EIO - 1
29. EAE - 3	40. EOO - 4	

2. Test the validity/invalidity of the following syllogisms by the traditional method of rules and fallacies, after rearranging them into standard form (wherever necessary):

    1. Some extremists are violent persons and no doctors are extremists. It follows no violent persons are doctors.
    2. All applicants are degree holders and some students are not applicant. Hence, some students are not degree holders.
    3. Since all teachers are critical thinkers and all critical thinkers are good analysers, so it is true all good analysers are teachers.
    4. All those who eat spicy foods are ulcer patients because all spicy foods are unhealthy food and all ulcer patients eat unhealthy food.
    5. Since all dictators are ruthless and no ruthless is lover of art, so some lovere of art are not dictators.
    6. Some games are played for entertainment and some games are played for making profit. Thus, some entertainment acts are for making profit.
    7. All citizens are voters whereas some citizens are not government employees. Therefore, some government employees are not voters.
    8. No Indian is Greek but some Indians are Aryans, therefore, some Aryans are Greeks.
    9. Since no slow thinker solves mathematical problems quickly and Sita is not a slow thinker, so Sita solves the mathematical problems quickly.
    10. All soldiers are slaves because all slaves are loyal and all soldiers are loyal.

3. Examine the validity/invalidity of the syllogisms given in the Exercise No. 4 and 5 on pages 114, 115.

Chapter 7 – Section C

Validity of Categorical Syllogism

Modern Method

THE rules and fallacies for the categorical syllogisms provided by the traditional logicians are primarily based on the distribution of terms. The traditional method of checking validity of syllogism was basically non-mathematical. The modern logicians suggested other alternative methods to determine the validity of the categorical syllogisms. Some of these methods are:

(i) Venn diagram

(ii) Anti-logism Theorem by Mrs. Christine Ladd-Franklin

(iii) Method provided in the Predicate Calculus – Quantifiers

The present chapter, however, deals with the first two methods. Chapter 15 deals with Predicate Calculus and Quantifiers. We start with Venn diagram.

The basis of validity of the categorical syllogisms in the Venn diagram is same as that of the traditional logic, that is, **the conclusion must not contain anything which the premisses do not have.** The logicians examine whether premisses are sufficient or efficient enough to support the conclusion or not. If the conclusion is implied by the premisses jointly then the syllogism is valid, and if the premisses do not imply the conclusion, the syllogism is invalid.

In Venn diagram the terms of a categorical proposition are represented by circles. We have already seen how A, E, I, O propositions are expressed in Venn diagrams in the third chapter. The shaded portion on the diagrams represents empty class. Let us again see how the categorical propositions are shown through diagrams:

All S is P

$S\bar{P} = 0$

No S is P

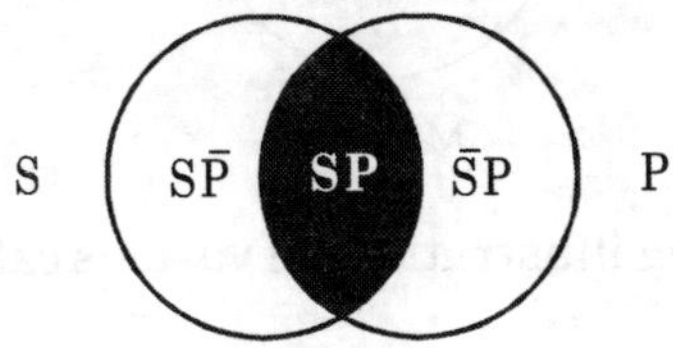

SP = 0

Some S is P

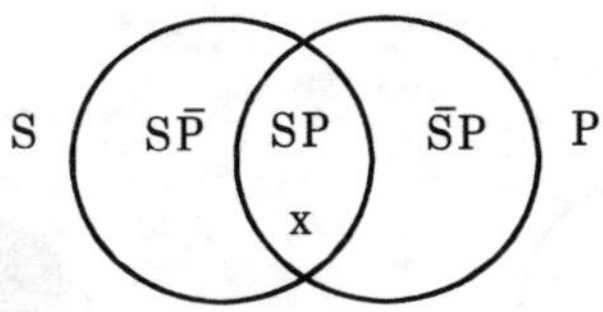

$SP \neq 0$

Some S is not P

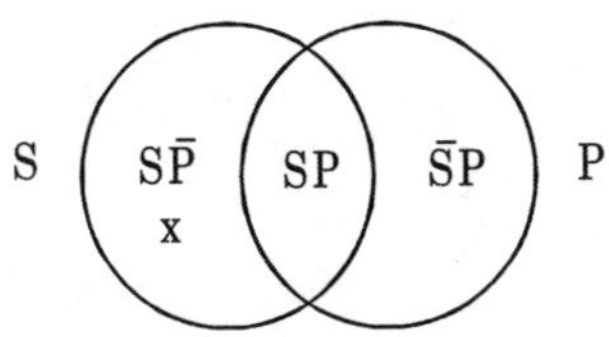

$S\bar{P} \neq 0$

In a categorical syllogism there are three terms. In a diagram representing categorical syllogism there are three circles overlapping each other as has been shown in the following example:

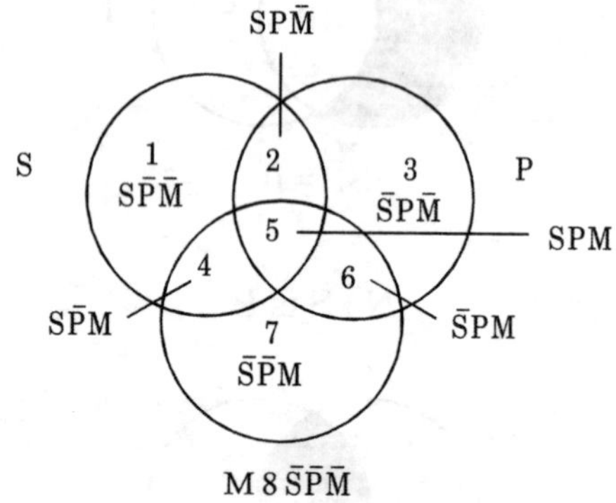

Look at the following illustrations of various categorical syllogistic moods:

1. We begin with AAA mood in 1st figure:

All M is P.
All S is M.
____
Therefore, all S is P

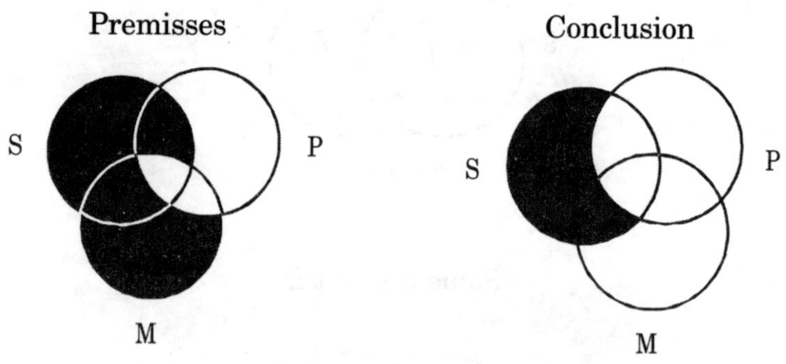

The premisses jointly imply the conclusion. The diagram clearly shows the conclusion is endorsed by both the premisses together. Hence, it is a valid syllogistic form.

2. AEE in 2nd figure:

   All P is M.
   No S is M.
   Therefore, no S is P.

Premisses

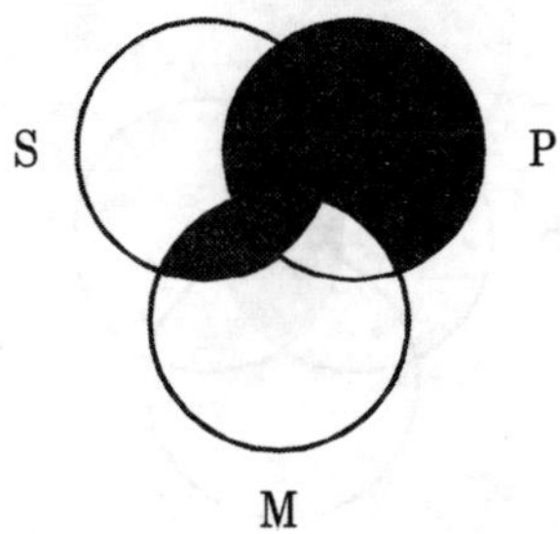

Conclusion

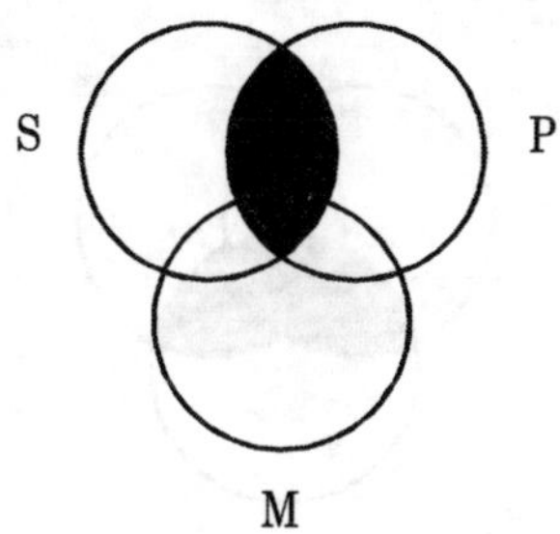

The diagram clearly shows that conclusion is covered by the premisses.

Therefore, the syllogistic mood is valid.

3. AAA in 4th figure:

   All P is M.
   All M is S.
   Therefore, all S is P.

Premisses

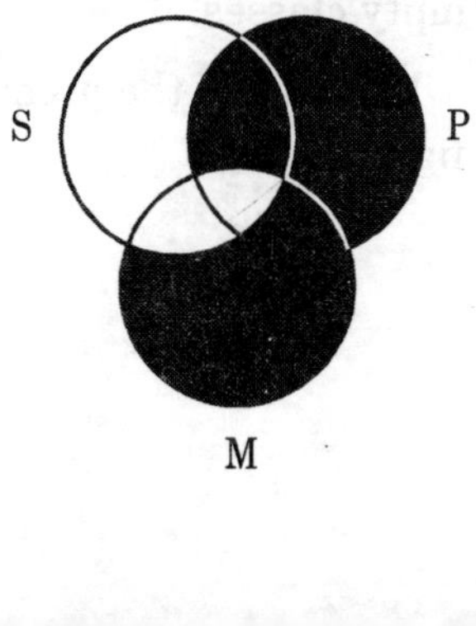

Conclusion

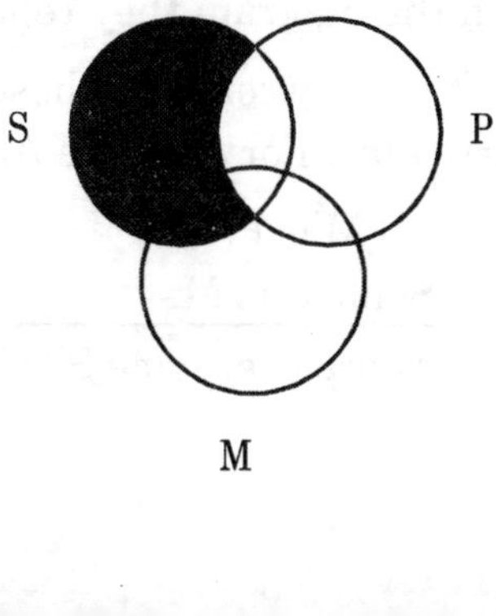

The diagram shows the conclusion is not covered by the premisses. Therefore, the mood is invalid.

Notice, no segment of the conclusion is covered by the premisses. Therefore, the mood is invalid.

4. EEE mood in 1st figure:

   No M is P.
   No S is M.
   Therefore, no S is P.

Premisses

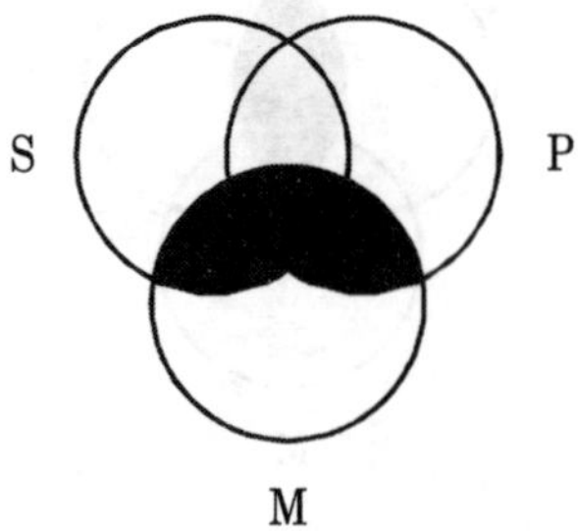

Conclusion

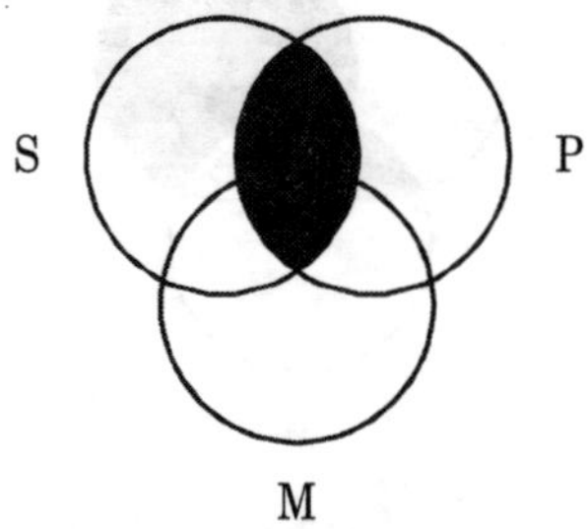

The conclusion is not completely endorsed by the premisses. Therefore, it is invalid syllogistic form

Note SPM segment of the conclusion which states SPM = 0 is covered by the premisses but none of the premisses states anything about $SP\bar{M}$. Since the premisses are silent about $SP\bar{M}$ and do not imply $SP\bar{M} = 0$, therefore it is invalid mood.

So far we were dealing with the universal (propositions) premisses as well as conclusion which are existentially negative, and in the diagram they represent empty classes.

Let us now consider those moods where one of the premisses is particular. For example AII in 1st figure:

5. All M is P.
   Some S is M.

   Therefore, some S is P.

Premisses

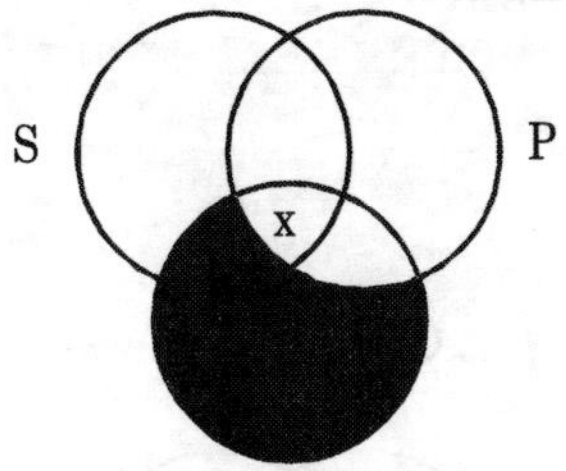

Conclusion

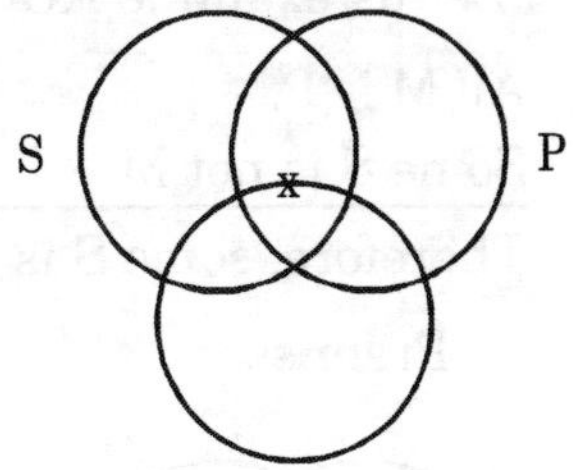

The diagram shows the conclusion is supported by the premisses.

Even if the premisses are silent about SP$\bar{M}$ segment, but they (premisses) jointly and categorically state that SPM has members. Thus the conclusion is upheld and supported by the premisses.

So the mood AII in 1st figure is valid.

6. AOO mood in 2nd figure:

All P is M.
Some S is not M.
___
Therefore, some S is not P .

Premisses

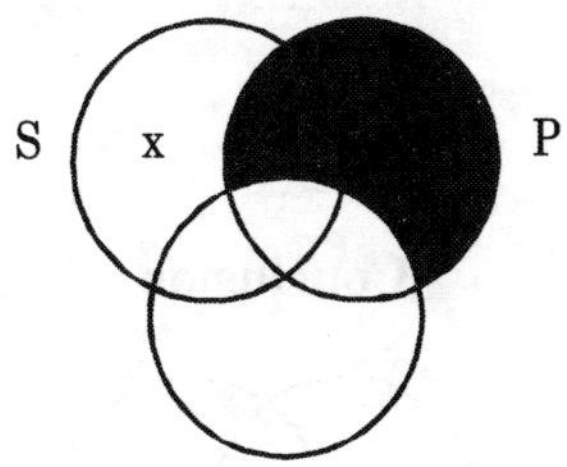

Conclusion

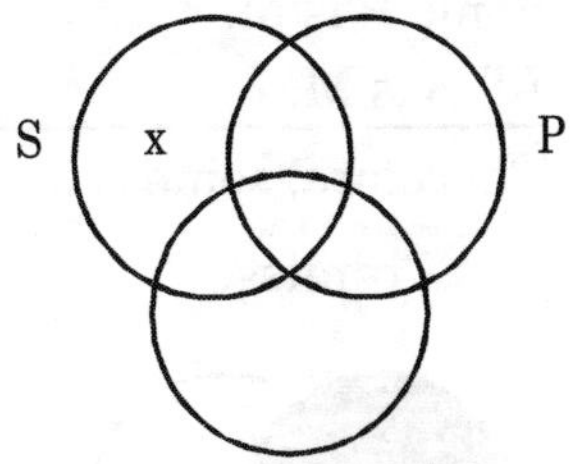

The premisses jointly endorse the conclusion. Even if S $\bar{P}$ M is not covered by any of the premisses yet, they jointly holds conclusions.

$x + ? \neq 0$

Therefore, the mood AOO in 2nd figure is valid.

7. Let us examine AOO in 1st figure:

All M is P.
Some S is not M.

Therefore, some S is not P.

Premisses

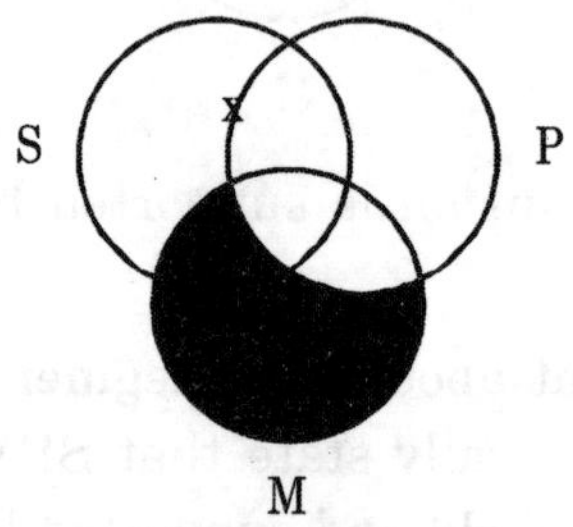

Conclusion

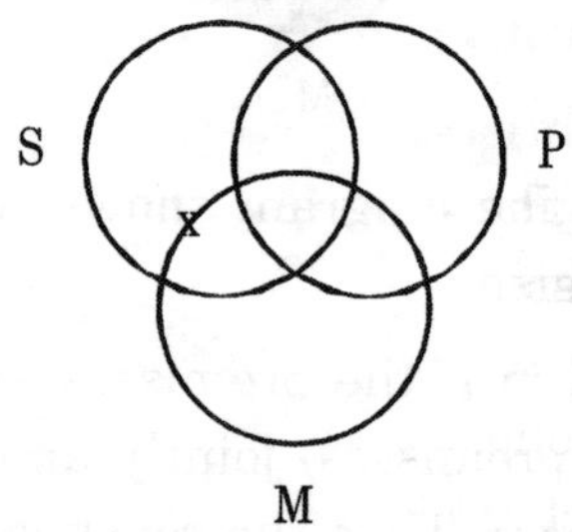

The minor premiss does not very definitely state where exactly the member 'x' lies, that is, whether the members are in $S P \bar{M}$ segment or in $S \bar{P} \bar{M}$ segment or in both $S \bar{P} \bar{M}$ and $SP\bar{M}$. Therefore, the minor premiss must categorically state $S \bar{P} \bar{M} \neq 0$. But it does not do that. The premisses are not clear about $S \bar{P} \bar{M}$. Therefore, AOO in the 1st figure is invalid mood.

8. IAI in 2nd figure:

Some P is M.
All S is M.

Therefore, some S is P.

Premisses

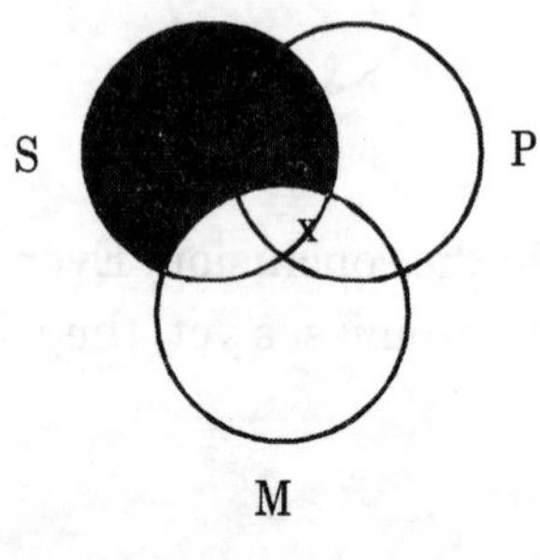

Conclusion

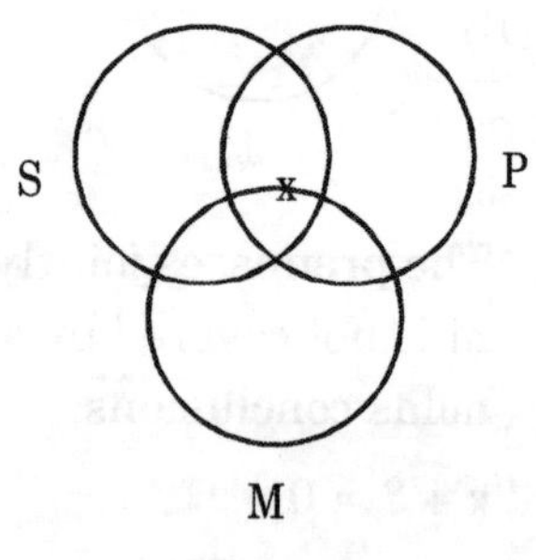

While S P $\bar{M}$ has been shown as zero by the premisses, but they do not categorically state S P M has members. The major premiss does not specify where exactly the members lie. It does not categorically state where the members lie, whether members are in SPM or $\bar{S}$PM or in both.

So the mood IAI in second figure is invalid.

The Antilogism

Mrs Christine Ladd-Franklin[1] had devised yet another method, antilogism, for testing the validity of categorical syllogisms. Antilogism or 'inconsistent triad' (as it is popularly known) is a device to test the validity of syllogisms without using the traditional rules. The antilogism is closely associated with the indirect method.

From the syllogistic mood (whose validity one wants to determine) an antilogism is framed replacing the conclusion (of the given mood) by its contradictory. The premisses of the mood remain the same in the antilogism. For instance, in order to test the validity of AAA mood in first figure, the antilogism derived from the mood AAA is AAO.

Mood	Antilogism
All M is P.	All M is P.
All S is M.	All S is M.
Therefore, all S is P.	Therefore, some S is not P.
	(contradictory of the conclusion)

The contradictory of the conclusion "All S is P" is "Some S is not P" [By Square of Opposition]. The mood AAA is valid if and

1. Christine Ladd-Franklin (1847-1930) like Aristotle believed that one single test would prove all valid syllogisms because every valid categorical syllogism shares a common form and a common denominator. The job of single test is to reduce all syllogisms into that common denominator. Ladd-Franklin's method states that the premisses of all valid syllogisms when taken together with the negation of the conclusion will form an inconsistent set of propositions.

only if the antilogism framed by the mood AAA, satisfies all the following three conditions:

(1) The antilogism must have two universal propositions. They both may be the premisses or one of them may be the premiss and the other is conclusion. The third proposition (it may be a premiss or a conclusion) should be particular. The univeral propositions are equal to zero. They are, therefore, equations. You know from Boolean algebra universal propositions are existentially negative and are equated to zero. The particular proposition is not equal to zero.

(2) The equations (universal propositions) must have one common term which occurs affirmatively at one place and negatively at another place. This means the common term must occur affirmatively in one equation and negatively in another equation.

(3) Now examine the inequation, that is, the particular proposition. This proposition must contain all the remaining terms of the universal propositions identically as they occur there.

Example 1: Let us test the validity of AAA mood in first figure by the antilogism method. The mood is:

Mood

All M is P	$\longrightarrow$	$M\,\bar{P} = 0$
All S is M	$\longrightarrow$	$S\,\bar{M} = 0$
Therefore, all S is P		Therefore, $S\,\bar{P} = 0$

After replacing conclusion by its contradictory, we get the following antilogism:

Antilogism

All M is P	$\longrightarrow$	$M\,\bar{P} = 0$
All S is M	$\longrightarrow$	$S\,\bar{M} = 0$
Therefore, some S is not P		Therefore, $S\,\bar{P} \neq 0$

(contradictory of A proposition is O).

Now we have to see whether this antilogism satisfies *all* the three conditions or not.

(1) There are two universal propositions (equations = 0) and one particular proposition (inequation ≠ 0) in the antilogism. So the first condition is satisfied by the antilogism.

(2) The two equations $(M)\bar{P} = 0$

$$S\,(\bar{M}) = 0$$

contain one common term which occurs once affirmatively and once negatively, M and $\bar{M}$. Thus, the second condition is also satisfied.

(3) The inequation (particular proposition), $S\,\bar{P} \neq O$, contains the remaining terms of equations (universal propositions)

$(M)\bar{P} = 0$

$S(\bar{M}) = 0$

that is, S and $\bar{P}$ as they are in the universal propositions. Since the antilogism satisfies all the three conditions, therefore, the syllogistic mood which imply the antilogism, is valid,

Example 2: AOO mood in second figure.

Mood

All P is M.	⟶	$P\,\bar{M} = 0$
Some S is not M.	⟶	$S\,\bar{M} \neq 0$
Therefore, some S is not P		Therefore, $S\,\bar{P} \neq 0$

After replacing the conclusion by its contradictory, we get the following antilogism:

Antilogism

All P is M.	⟶	$P\,\bar{M} = 0$
Some S is not M.	⟶	$S\,\bar{M} \neq 0$
Therefore, All S is P		Therefore, $S\,\bar{P} = 0$

(contradictory of the conclusion O is A).

Let us examine whether the antilogism satisfies *all* the conditions or not:

(1) There are two equations $P\,\bar{M} = 0$ and $S\,\bar{P} = 0$. There is one inequation $S\,\bar{M} \neq 0$.

(2) The equations $(P)\bar{M} = 0$

$$S\,(\bar{P}) = 0$$

contain one common term, which occurs once affirmatively and once negatively (P and $\bar{P}$).

(3) The inequation $S\,\bar{M} \neq 0$ contains the remaining terms of both the equations,

$$(P)\,\bar{M} = 0$$

$$S\,(\bar{P}) = 0$$

S, $\bar{M}$, exactly as they are there in the equations.

Thus, you notice the antilogism satisfies all the conditions. Therefore, the syllogistic mood from where the antilogism is formed, is valid.

Example 3: AEE mood in third figure.

Mood

All M is P	⟶	$M\,\bar{P} = 0$
No M is S	⟶	$M\,S = 0$
Therefore, no S is P		Therefore, $S\,P = 0$

After replacing the conclusion by its contradictory, we get the following antilogism:

Antilogism

All M is P	⟶	$M\,\bar{P} = 0$
No M is S	⟶	$M\,S = 0$
Therefore, some S is P		Therefore, $S\,P \neq 0$.

(contradictory of E is I)

Let us examine whether the antilogism satisfy *all* the conditions or not:

(1) The antilogism satisfies the first condition. There are two equation.

$M\,\bar{P} = 0$

$M\,S = 0$

and one inequation $SP \neq 0$.

(2) But the second condition is not satisfied. The equations

$(M)\bar{P}$

$(M)S$

do not contain a common term which once occurs affirmatively and at another place occurs negatively. The common term here occurs only affirmatively at both the places (M and M). Since the second condition is not satisfied so the syllogistic mood from where the antilogism is derived, is invalid.

The student should notice that even third condition is *also not* satisfied.

Example 4:

Some politicians (P) are not married ($\bar{M}$) ⟶ $P\,\bar{M} \neq 0$
All scientists (S) are married (M) ⟶ $S\,\bar{M} = 0$

Therefore, some scientists are not politicians ⟶ $S\,\bar{P} \neq 0$

After contradicting the conclusion, we get the following antilogism:

Some politicians are not married ⟶ $P\,\bar{M} \neq 0$
All scientists are married ⟶ $S\,\bar{M} = 0$

Therefore, all scientists are politicians ⟶ $S\,\bar{P} = 0$

(contradictory of the conclusion O is A)

Now, let us examine whether the antilogism satisfies *all* the three conditions.

(1) The antilogism satisfies the first condition. There are two equations $S\,\bar{M} = 0$, $S\bar{P} = 0$ and one inequation $P\bar{M} \neq 0$

(2) But the second and third conditions are not satisfied. The equations

(S) $\bar{M} = 0$

(S) $\bar{P} = 0$

though have a common term but it occurs only affirmatively (S, S) at both the places. That is why the second condition is also not satisfied. Notice even the third condition is also not satisfied. The inequation $P\bar{M} \neq 0$ does not possess the remaining terms of equations

(S) $\bar{M} = 0$

(S) $\bar{P} = 0$

exactly in the same form. Therefore, the syllogistic mood from where the antilogism is derived, is invalid.

Example 5 :

Some fast readers (R) are slow thinkers (T) ⟶ $RT \neq 0$
Some children (C) are fast readers (R) ⟶ $CR \neq 0$

Therefore, some children are slow thinkers ⟶ $CT \neq 0$

Replacing the conclusion by its contradictory, the syllogistic mood implies the following antilogism:

Some fast readers are slow thinkers ⟶ $RT \neq 0$
Some children are fast readers ⟶ $CR \neq 0$

Therefore, no children are slow thinkers ⟶ $CT = 0$

(contradictory of the conclusion I is E)

Let us see whether the antilogism satisfies all the three conditions or not

(1) The antilogism does not contain two equations. There is only one equation $CT = 0$. Since the very first condition is not satisfied, the syllogism from where the antilogism is derived, is *invalid.*

Exercises

1. Test the validity/invalidity of the following syllogistic moods by Venn diagram:

1. EAE 2	9. AII 3
2. AEE 4	10. IAI 4
3. EAE 1	11. IIO 3
4. AAA 2	12. OAO 1
5. EAA 1	13. IEO 2
6. EAE 3	14. OIE 4
7. AAI 4	15. IAI 3
8. EIO 1	

2. Test the validity/invalidity of the followbing syllogistic moods by the antilogism theorem:

1. AAA 3	11. OIO 1
2. EAE 2	12. EAO 4
3. OAO 3	13. AAI 1
4. AEE 4	14. OAO 2
5. AII 1	15. EAE 4
6. AOO 4	16. AAE 1
7. AEE 2	17. AIO 4
8. EIO 3	18. IAO 3
9. IAI 4	19. OAI 3
10. EAE 1	20. IEO 4

Chapter 7 – Section D

Non-Categorical Syllogism
(Compound Syllogism)

NON-CATEGORICAL syllogism or compound syllogism is mediate reasoning having two premisses and a conclusion. But all the propositions (premisses and conclusion) are not categorical propositions. One of the propositions or all of them are compound propositions. Here are some examples of non-categorical syllogisms.

1. Either I go to his house or I will talk to him on the telephone.

   I shall not go to his house.

   Therefore, I will talk to him on the telephone.

2. If wages are high, then prices will rise.

   Wages are high.

   Therefore, prices will rise.

3. If Congress is united, then Congress will win the election.

   If Congress wins the election, then liberal policies will continue.

   Therefore, if Congress is united, then the liberal policies will continue.

The above syllogisms are compound for they have either one or all compound propositions. For the traditional logicians any reasoning having two premisses is syllogistic. But modern logicians[1] differ on this issue. For modern logicians a syllogism means only categorical syllogism. The compound syllogisms for

---

1. G. Boole and those who came after him in the mid-nineteenth century.

them are not syllogisms at all. The examples cited above are not accepted as syllogistic reasoning by the modern logicians. In other words, whereas any reasoning having two-premisses and a conclusion is called syllogistic by the traditional logicians, for the modern logicians all two premissed reasonings are not necessarily syllogistic. For the latter, syllogism means only categorical syllogism, but for the former, any two-premissed reasoning is syllogistic, categorical or non-categorical. I will not enter into this controversy here. In this chapter I am dealing with different types of compound syllogisms.

There are two prominent types of compound syllogisms:

i. Disjunctive Syllogism

ii. Hypothetical Syllogism

Disjunctive Syllogism

Either Ram goes to library, or he will attend the seminar.
Ram does not go to library.
Therefore, he will attend the seminar.

This is an example of disjunctive syllogism. The first premiss of the syllogism, "Either Ram goes to library, or he will attend the seminar", is a disjunctive proposition. It is a compound proposition having categorical propositions "Ram goes to library", "He will attend the seminar", which are joined by 'either-or'. Both of these categorical propositions are called disjuncts. The second premiss is negation of one of the disjuncts and the conclusion is remaining disjunct or disjuncts. Symbolically, the formation of disjunctive syllogism is like:

Either p or q

not p

Therefore, q.

Validity of disjunctive syllogism:

A disjunctive syllogism is valid when:

(i) The first premiss is a disjunctive proposition.

(ii) The second premiss is negation of one of the disjuncts of the first premiss.

(iii) The conclusion is the remaining disjunct or disjuncts.

A disjunctive syllogism is valid when it satisfies all the above conditions. The above given example of disjunctive syllogism, since satisfies all the conditions, is valid.

In symbolic form, a valid disjunctive syllogism can be one of the following types:

(i) Either p or q

not p

Therefore, q.

(ii) Either p or q

not q

Therefore, p.

An *invalid* disjunctive syllogism can be one of the following types:

(i) Either p or q

p

Therefore, not q.

Here the second premiss is not in the right form,

(ii) Either p or q

q

Therefore, not p.

Hypothetical Syllogism

In a hypothetical syllogism one or all the propositions are hypothetical. Hypothetical propositions are compound propositions combined by 'if, then' relationship. For example, "If Ram is qualified, then he will get job" is a hypothetical proposition.

Hypothetical syllogisms are of two types:

(i) Mixed hypothetical syllogism

(ii) Pure hypothetical syllogism

MIXED HYPOTHETICAL SYLLOGISM

In a mixed hypothetical syllogism one of the premisses is conditional proposition having a relation of 'if then' but the other premiss and the conclusion are not conditional propositions. For example,

If it is pleasant, then we shall go for picnic.
It is pleasant.
Therefore, we shall go for picnic,

is a mixed hypothetical syllogism.

"If it is pleasant, then we shall go for picnic" is conditional or hypothetical proposition. In the above syllogism 'it is pleasant' is antecedent and "we shall go for picnic" is consequent.

Since in this syllogism only one premiss is hypothetical proposition, (the other premiss and the conclusion are categorical), it is called mixed hypothetical syllogism. The minor premiss in the mixed hypothetical syllogism is antecedent of the hypothetical proposition.(major premiss)

Validity of mixed hypothetical syllogism

A mixed hypothetical syllogism is valid when it satisfies all the following conditions:

(i) The first premisss should be a hypothetical proposition.

(ii) The second premiss of the mixed hypothetical syllogism is antecedent of the first premiss.

(iii) The conclusion is consequent of the first premiss.

A valid mixed hypothetical syllogism must obey all of the above conditions. Here is an example of valid mixed hypothetical syllogism:

If I get ticket, then I will go to concert.

I get ticket.

Therefore, I will go to concert.

Symbolically, valid mixed hypothetical syllogism can be expressed as:

If p, then q

p

Therefore, q.

The rule of inference involved here is **Modus Ponens.** Ponens means to affirm; the antecedent of the hypothetical proposition, is affirmed in the second premiss; and the consequent is affirmed in the conclusion.

Valid mixed hypothetical syllogism can also be expressed as:

If p, then q.

not q

Therefore, not p.

The rule of inference involved here is **Modus Tollens.** Tollens means to negate. The consequent is negated in the second premiss, and the antecedent is negated in the conclusion.

Invalid mixed hypothetical syllogism

Mixed hypothetical syllogism is invalid if it has any of the following forms:

If p, then q

not p

Therefore, not q.

or

If p, then q

q

Therefore, p.

One is not allowed to negate the antecedent in the second premiss, and also one is not allowed to affirm the consequent in the premiss.

PURE HYPOTHETICAL SYLLOGISM

In a pure hypothetical syllogism, all the propositions (premisses as well as conclusion), are hypothetical propositions. For example,

> If Joy catches the plane, then he will attend the meeting.
>
> If he attends the meeting, then company will launch new product in the market.
>
> ---
>
> Therefore, if Joy catches the plane, then the company will launch new product in the market.

Symbolically pure hypothetical syllogism can be expressed as :

> If p, then q
>
> If q, then r
>
> ---
>
> Therefore, if p, then r.

Validity of pure hypothetical syllogism

A pure hypothetical syllogism is valid when:

(i) Both of the premisses have one common categorical proposition. In the above example, "he will attend the meeting", is common categorical proposition in both the premisses.

(ii) The common proposition should be antecedent in one premiss, and consequent in another premiss. The common proposition neutralizes each other diagonally.

(iii) The conclusion should not have the common term. It should have the antecedent of one premiss (other than common proposition) and consequent (other than the common proposition) of another premiss.

Valid pure hypothetical syllogisms can be expressed as:

(i) If p, then q
If q, then r

Therefore, if p, then r.

(ii) If q, then r
If p, then q
____
Therefore, if p, then r.

Both of the above pure hypothetical syllogisms are valid.

The following are invalid pure hypothetical syllogisms:

(i) If p, then q
If q, then r
____
Therefore, if r, then p.

(ii) If q, then r
If p, then q
____
Therefore, if r, then p.

(iii) If p, then q
If r, then q
____
Therefore, if p, then r.

(iv) If p, then q
If p, then r
____
Therefore, if q, then r.

Dilemma

Dilemma is yet another syllogistic reasoning. It has two premisses and a conclusion. Major premiss has two hypothetical propositions combined with conjunction. The minor premiss is a disjunctive proposition. The conclusion can be categorical proposition or it may be a disjunctive proposition. The logical form of a dilemma is:

If A then B, and if C then D
Either A or C
____
Therefore B or D

See the following examples:

1. If the pilots work longer hours, then they are dissatisfied and if they earn less, then they are dissatistfied.
Pilots either will work longer hours or they will earn less.
____
Therefore the pilots will be dissatisfied.

2. If the university makes strict attendance rules for the students, then many students will be detained; and if university does not make strict attendance rules for the students, then they will be careless about their studies (major premiss). Either university makes strict rules of attendance for students or it does not make strict rules of attendance (minor premiss). Therefore either many students will be detained or they will be careless about their studies (conclusion).
3. If the medium of instruction is regional language, then students will not be able to read advanced books in the subject, and if the medium of instruction is English, then they will not be able to understand the subject (major premiss).

   Either the medium of instruction is regional language or the medium of instruction is English. (minor premiss).

Therefore either students will not be able to read advanced books in the subject or they will not be able to understand the subject (conclusion).

The word 'dilemma' is known to all of us. We sometimes express ourselves by saying "I am in dilemma, I do not know what to do. Whatever I do I cannot avoid unpleasant consequences" In a dilemmatic situation a person is faced with two or more alternatives all of which have unpleasant consequences. Hamlet was in dilemma when he said "to be or not to be." Prince Arjun in *Mahabharata* was in dilemma whether he should be fighting his cousins, the Kauravas, in the battlefield of Kurukshetra.

From the viewpoint of logic, dilemma is not of great importance, though constructive dilemma and destructive dilemma are two valid forms of inference. A constructive dilemma is one in which the minor premiss (which is a disjunctive proposition) affirms the antecedents (of major premiss). A destructive dilemma is one in which the minor premiss denies the consequents (of the major premiss). The logical form of constructive dilemma is as follows:

If p then q and if r then s	major premiss
Either p or r	minor premiss
Therefore either q or s	conclusion

Symbolically one can express this as:

$(p \supset q) \bullet (r \supset s)$

$p \vee r$

$\therefore q \vee s$

The logical form of destructive dilemma is as follows:

If p then q and if r then s	major premiss
Either not q or not s	minor premiss
Therefore, either not p or not r	conclusion

symbolically one can express this as:

$(p \supset q) \bullet (r \supset s)$

$\sim q \vee \sim s$

$\therefore \sim p \vee \sim r$

Dilemma has great value as a rhetorical device because one can formulate dilemma in such a way that either it can be avoided or can be shown to have "fallacy of false dilemma". It is not necessory that a dilemma has an unwelcome conclusion, but because of its use in rhetoric the word 'dilemma' has come to mean a situation in which each of the alternative courses of action leads to some unsatisfactory consequences. Dilemma when used as a rhetoric device offers to an opponent a choice between two equally unfavourable alternatives neither of them is practically acceptable. The two alternative, or choices traditionally are referred as 'two horns'. Some other related phrases used for the alternative possibilities are "lesser of two evils", "between a rock and a hard place" "between devil and the deep blue sea"

The main question regarding dilemma is — How to defuse a dilemma? or How to get out of a dilemmatic situation?

Traditionally there are two ways to handle dilemma. First, in order to make dilemma ineffective one presents a counter-dilemma which is popularly known as "**rebuttal of dilemma**". This is more a rhetoric device than logical. Second, to prove the given dilemma invalid or unsound by either attacking minor premiss (which presents two alternative situation) or attacking major premiss (which is conjunction of two conditional propositons). This is more a logical device rather than rhetoric one. Traditionally this is called "refutation of dilemma".

The famous example of rebuttal dilemma is of an Athenian mother who did not want her son to enter into public life. She said:

"If you say what is just, men will hate you; if you say what is unjust, Gods will hate you. You will say either what is just or what is unjust. Therefore either men will hate you or Gods will hate you".

The son was smart and was looking for the brighter side of situation. In order to defuse mother's dilemma he presented a counter-dilemma with the same premisses but with different conclusion. "If I say what is just, Gods will love me, and if I say what is unjust, men will love me. I will say either what is just or what is unjust. Therefore either Gods will love me or men will love me".

Take another example.

"If I stay in the suburbs, then I will have no company, and if stay in the city, then I will have no peace of mind.

Either I stay in the suburbs or I stay in the city.

Therefore either I will have no good company or I will have no peace of mind.[2]

One can defuse this by framing a counter-dilemma.

---

2. Jhagirdar (K.T.) and Mudgal (S.G.), op. cit., p. 194.

"If stay in the suburbs then I will have peace of mind, and if I stay in the city, then I will have good company. Either I stay in the suburbs or I will stay in the city. Therefore either I will have peace of mind or I will have good company". Rebuttal is an ingenious process and a devastating weapon. This has stunning impact on the audiences and takes the opponents by surprise. To retort the dilemma means to turn the table against one who presents the dilemma. But it requires a lot of practical wisdom and skill. To provide a counter-dilemma means to provide equally powerful and effective dilemma which proves opposite conclusion from that of the given dilemma. Logically rebuttal of a dilemma can be presented as:

The given (original) dilemma	Rebuttal dilemma
If p then q, and if r then s	If p then not s, and if r then not q.
Either p or r	Either p or r.
Therefore either q or s	Therefore either not s or not q

Symbolically this can be expressed as:

The given (original) dilemma	Rebuttal dilemma
$(p \supset q) \bullet (r \supset s)$	$(p \supset \sim s) \bullet (r \supset \sim q)$
$p \vee r$	$p \vee r$
$\therefore q \vee s$	$\therefore 2 \sim s \vee \sim q$

In the rebuttal of dilemma minor premiss remains the same. There is change in the major premiss, hence there in change in the conclusion.

Rebuttal is a rhetorical device which may be logically as incorrect as the given dilemma. But it is an effective device which turns opponent's argument against opponent. In public debates and also in persuading others rebuttal dilemma is a smart weapon.

However, every dilemma is not rhetorical in nature. There are true dilemmas also. When a person is really confronted with two choices which give unpleasant results, then the person is really facing true dilemma. A true dilemma is valid inference and it cannot be shown to be invalid. A false dilemma, on the other hand, has defects in its premisses, major or minor or in both. To prove the defects in either of the premisses of dilemma is known as "refutation of dilemma".

The dilemma is based on the assumption that there are two and only two alternatives. Minor premiss of dilemma being disjunctive offers a person with two choices and both of them lead to unpleasant consequences. One of the ways to refute dilemma is to expose the errors in the minor premiss by showing that the two alternatives are not mutually exhaustive. There can be a third alternative which the person can take. Arguing and showing that there are more alternatives available is called "**escaping between the horns**".

Dilemma is compared with bull and its alternatives with horns. Logically alternatives can be shown as:

Either p or r

Symbolically it can be writen as:

p v r

Now if both 'p' and 'r' are false the disjunctive proposition (which is minor premiss of a dilemma) can be shown false also. It can be worked out like this:

p v r

$\Rightarrow$ False v False

$\Rightarrow$ False.

Now see a concrete example:

"If a student is fond of learning, then he needs no stimulus, and if he dislikes learning, no stimulus will be of any use. (major premiss). A student is either fond of learning or dislike it (minor premiss). Therefore a stimulus is either needless or of no use"[3] (conclusion).

The disjunctive minor premiss assumes improperly that a student is either fond of learning or dislikes it. But these are not

---

3. Mellone, S.H., *Elements of Modern Logic*, pp. 169-70.

the only two alternatives available, for there may be some children who are neither fond of learning nor dislike it and for them a stimulus may be desirable,

See another example:

"If taxes increase, the economy will suffer and if taxes decrease, then essential government services will be curtailed. Taxes will either increase or decrease. Therefore the economy will suffer or the essential government services will be curtailed".[4]

One can show that taxes are neither increased nor decreased. They are kept where they are. In this manner the minor premiss is shown to be false and that makes dilemma false. It is very easy to show the fallacy in dilemma by exposing the "false dichotomy" because it is not possible always to find instances where two alternatives exhaust all the possible cases.

However, if the minor premiss is a tautology (that is p v ~ p) then to refute dilemma by "escaping between the horns" is not possible. In that case one must examine the major premiss which has two conditional statements.

Let us take another example:

"If we encourage competition, we will have no peace, and if we do not encourage competition, we will make no progress (major premiss). We must either encourage competition or not encourage it. (minor premiss). Therefore we will either have no peace or make no progress"[5]

Here the minor premiss is tautology (p v ~ p).

Therefore this piece of dilemma cannot be refuted by showing 'false dichotomy'. Here the dilemma is refuted by showing errors in the major premiss which is a conjunctive proposition having two hypothetical propositions as conjuncts. Major premiss looks like this: If p then q and if r then s.

---

4. Hurley, J. Patrick., *Introduction to Logic*, pp. 296-97.
5. Ibid. pp. 296-97.

'p' and 'r' are antecedents and 'q' and 's' are consequents. The dilemma can be proved unsound by showing that either 'q' does not follow from 'p' or 's' does not follow from 'r'. This device is called "**taking the dilemma by the horns**" or sometimes "grasped by the horns".

Symbolically it can be expressed as:

$(p \supset q) \bullet (r \supset s)$

either (T **F** F) • (Anything true or false)

or $(p \supset q) \bullet (r \supset s)$

(Anything true or false) • (T **F** F)

In the above example "we will have no peace" does not follow from "we encourage competition". Encouraging healthy competion does not make a man peaceless. We may also show the consequent "we will make no progress" does not follow from antecedent "we do not encourage competition".

See another example:

"If men are good, then moral teaching is unnecessary, and if they are not good, then moral teaching is useless (major premiss). Either men are good or they are not good (minor premiss). Therefore either moral teaching is unnecessary or it is useless[6] (conclusion).

This is a complex constructive dilemma and formally valid. But it is not materially sound.

If men are good, then it is all the more necessary to teach them what goodness consists in it. If they are not good, it is useful to teach them to be moral. Thus the consequent does not necessarily follow from the given antecedent. Therefore, the dilemma commits the fallacy of "taking the dilemma by the horns".

There are thus three strategies with which one can encounter a dilemma.

1. By presenting 'Rebuttal' dilemma.

---

6. Jhagirdar K.T. and Mudgal. S.G., op. cit., pp. 188-89.

2. "Escaping between the horns" by showing 'false dichotomy' in minor premiss of the dilemma.
3. "Taking the dilemma by the horns" by showing consequent does not follow from the antecedent in major premiss.

Exercises

1. Identify the form of the following arguments and determine their validity/invalidity:
    1. If it rains in time, then there will be good harvest. It rains in time. Therefore, there will be good harvest.
    2. Either she is innocent or she is pretending to be so. She is not innocent. Therefore, she is pretending to be so.
    3. If the UGC stops funding the existing research projects, then there will be widespread unrest among the scholars. There is widespread unrest among the scholars. Therefore, the UGC stops funding the existing research projects.
    4. Either the coalition government wins the vote of confidence or there will be mid-term election. There will be a mid-term election. Therefore, the government will not win the vote of confidence.
    5. If the weather is pleasant, then we shall go for picnic. If we go for picnic, then we will hire two taxies. Therefore, if the weather is pleasant, then we will hire two taxies.
    6. Either Radha joins regular college or she joins the correspondence course and takes up full-time job. Radha does not join regular college. Therefore, she joins correspondence course and takes up full-time job.

7. Either the dictator leaves the country or he will be prosecuted. He will not be prosecuted. Therefore, the dictator leaves the country.
8. If a person believes that everything makes for the best, then he is an optimist. He is not an optimist. Therefore, he does not believe that everything makes for the best.
9. If Mr X gets assistance from the Bank, then he will start his business. If he starts his business, then his family will prosper. Therefore, if his family prospers, then Mr X gets assistance from the Bank.
10. If Sunny has malaria, then he needs Quinine. He does not need Quinine. Therefore, Sunny does not have malaria.
11. If the patient is late for her appointment, then she has lost confidence in the doctor. If she has lost confidence in the doctor, then there is no chance of her recovery. Therefore if she is late for her appointment, then there is no chance of her recovery.
12. If a man is happy, then he is virtuous. Ram is virtuous. Therefore, he is happy.
13. He is either intelligent or hard-working. He is intelligent. Hence, he is not hard-working.
14. If there is a change in economic policy, then confidence in rupee will not be restored. If the confidence in rupee is not restored, then imports will be restricted. Therefore, if there is change in economic policy, then imports will be restricted.
15. If Sita goes to market, then she will buy sufficient eatables. If she buys sufficient eatables, then the guests will be properly looked after. Therefore, if Sita goes to market, then the guests will be properly looked after.

2. Explain and illustrate disjunctive syllogism.
3. Explain and illustrate mixed hypothetical syllogism.
4. Explain with suitable examples pure hypothetical argument.
5. Explain with suitable examples the fallacies of:
    1. affirming the consequent.
    2. denying the antecedent.
6. Define dilemma. Explain with examples.
7. What is meant by "escaping between the horns" and "taking the dilemma by the horns". Illustrate your answer.
8. What is meant by the "rebuttal of a dilemma" and what is its value? Explain with examples.
9. Distinguish between 'rebuttal' and 'refutation' of dilemma.
10. Give rebuttal of the following dilemma:

    (Arjun's dilemma)

    If I kill them (Kauravas), then I will not go to heaven and if am killed, then I will not get the kingdom. Either I will kill them or I will be killed. Therefore either I will not go to heaven or I will be killed.[7]
11. If I go to a foreign country, then I will lose contacts with my people here and if I stay in my country, then I will not be able to do my advanced studies in Astronomy. Complete above dilemma and test its validity.

7. Jhagirdar K.T. and Mudgal. S.G., op. cit., p. 190.

Chapter 8

Laws of Thought

TRADITIONALLY logic is defined as the study of laws of thought. The customary interpretation of the laws of thought is restricted to three laws, namely Law of Identity, Law of Excluded Middle and Law of Non-Contradiction.

These three laws, however, are related exclusively to propositions. Elementary logic is two-valued logic. A proposition (which is unit of reasoning) is either true or false. A proposition cannot be both true and false at the same time. It cannot be neither true nor false at the same time. The truth values of propositions (truth and falsehood) are **exclusive and exhaustive**. Elementary logic is based on these properties of propositions.

The laws of thought are basis of all our valid and consistent thinking. They (laws of thought) however, by themselves are beyond proof because they are self-evident, self-illuminating and intuitive. They are thus necessary conditions of the valid thinking. The laws of thought are formulated variously but the most accepted form is as follows:

The Law of Identity states if a proposition is true, it is true, and if a proposition is false, it is false. If anything is A, then it is A. If anything is not A, then it is not A.

p	⊃	p
T	T	T
F	T	F

It is a tautology. A thing implies itself. The law of identity is necessary condition of our consistent and valid thinking.

The Law of Excluded Middle states a proposition must be either true or false. It cannot be neither. If a thing is 'A', then it is not non-'A'. The meaning of the law of excluded middle means middle path is not there. There is no third alternative. There are only two alternatives — truth and falsehood; 'A' and non-'A'. One must accept one of the alternatives and reject the other. A proposition cannot be neither 'true' nor 'false'.

p	v	~	p
T	T	F	T
F	T	T	F

It is a tautology. A thing must necessarily possess either of the two contradictory characteristics.

The Law of Non-Contradiction states a proposition cannot be both true and false at the same time. Out of two contradictory values true and false, a proposition can have only one value at one time. It cannot be both true and false at the same time. A thing cannot be 'A' and non-'A' at the same time. If a thing is white, then it cannot be non-white. If, on the other hand, a thing is non-white, then it cannot be white.

Symbolically the law of non-contradiction is stated as:

p	•	~	p
T	F	F	T
F	F	T	F

There cannot be any conjunction of two contradictory qualities.

The principle of non-contradiction (a thing cannot at the same time be and not be; a statement cannot be true and false at the same time) is the most important of the three laws. Aristotle[1]

1. Aristotle (384–322 BC), a Greek philosopher, educator, and scientist, was one of the greatest and the most influential thinkers in Western culture.

puts it at the base of all sciences. The realm of human discourse and the totality of nature all obey this pervasive law. Leibniz[2] considered the law of non-contradiction as the foundation of mathematics. This law according to Leibniz holds good for everything not only for things in this world but for all possible worlds. Thus, the law of non-contradiction is all- pervasive law on which the entire logic, language and nature is based.

But the laws of thought have been criticized since the time of their formation. Some of the criticisms, however, are very trivial while some other criticisms need thorough analysis.

The standard criticism against the law of identity is that a proposition may be true and false also. For example, "It is raining" is true now but it may be false some other time. But this criticism is misleading. The proposition "It is raining" is to be seen in the matrix of space and time. If there is change in the spatio-temporal framework, then the proposition "It is raining" may not be true. But as long as framework of space and time does not change the proposition "It is raining" remains true and will always remain true.

Thus the critics of the law of identity are not right. They have wrongly interpreted the proposition "It is raining". The right formulation of the proposition is "It is raining in Delhi at 2.00 p.m. on 10th July 2003" which is true and will always be true. If the reference of space and time changes then the proposition "It is raining" can be false. Each proposition has a unique reference and a fixed spatio-temporal dimension. The unique reference of space and time makes a proposition (or a fact) identical. All the propositions presuppose unconsciously this framework of space and time. In this lies the validity of the law of identity.

The principle of excluded middle is criticized on the ground that there is a third alternative for the propositions besides being

2. W.G. Leibniz (1646–1716) was a German philosopher, mathematician, and scholar. He and Sir Isaac Newton independently developed the theory of the differential and integral calculus.

true and false. A proposition may neither be true nor false; it may be a meaningless statement. For example "If Ram has killed Ravan, then 2+2=4" is neither true nor false. It is pseudo-proposition. The law of excluded middle, however, is applied only to the propositions which are meaningful. A meaningless expression is not worth considering.

Besides, it is argued there are propositions which are not fully known. It is premature to assign truth values for them. But this point is also not correct. One can wait till the unclear sentences become clear and fully understandable. One must withhold the truth values to such unclear propositions till they are fully known. Only clear and meaningful proposition is either true or false.

At the same time one must be aware of the fact that nowadays the logicians are working on the multi-valued logic which has 'n' values. It means the values of propositions can be one, two, three, four or more. But as long as we are dealing with two-valued logic, there is no third alternative. A proposition has to be either true or false.

Against the law of non-contradiction it is stated since nature changes quickly[3] (nothing is permanent) a proposition may have contradictory values. It may both be true and false. A floor is wet now but it may not be wet after some time. So a proposition has two contradictory values. But again this criticism of the law of non-contradiction is not sound. This criticism falls to ground in the same manner as the law of identity had. A proposition can have two different, rather two contradictory values in different contexts, at different times in different space. But in the same space and at the same time a proposition cannot have two contradictory values.

Besides these individual and specific criticisms against each of the laws of thought, there are general criticisms against these

3. Heraclitus, an ancient Greek philosopher, about 500 BC, says a person cannot step into the same river twice.

laws of thought as well. There are charges that these laws of thought are merely trivial, or they are no more than truisms. A truism may be defined as a proposition which is (1) true, and (2) accepted by everybody on mere inspection as true. But what's the harm if these laws of thought are truism? The laws of thought are supposed to be always true and they are to be accepted by everyone. Hence to charge the fundamental principles of logic with being mere truism is not to condemn them, but to admit that they are fitted to fulfil the function for which they are intended.

Along with these trivial criticisms certain genuine questions are asked regarding the validity and justification of these laws. The two common questions which are raised against these laws are as follows:

1. Are these laws exclusively for logic and language or they are applicable to things and nature also?
2. Are these laws sufficient, and complete logical principles?

The three laws of thought are applied not only to logic and language but to every realm of nature. Our entire thinking is governed by these laws and the subject matter of thinking may be any sphere of reality or nature.

Regarding the second point whether these laws are sufficient for valid thinking one can say that it is true these laws are indispensable for valid thinking, but they are not "exhaustive statement of logical principles". The principle of the syllogism, the principles of tautology, laws of inferences and laws of replacement are equally important and have 'equal claim' to belong to the foundation of logic. These laws of thought are not sufficient basis from which to deduce all other logical principles. The traditional three laws of thought are indispensable but not exhaustive for valid and consistent thinking.

Exercises

1. Explain the law of Identity and Excluded Middle with examples.

2. The law of Non-Contradiction is the basis of all human thinking. Discuss.
3. The "Laws of thought refer to propositions" and not to terms. Explain.
4. Are three laws of thought sufficient and complete to regulate human thinking? Discuss.
5. Are the conventional criticisms against these laws of thought justified? Elaborate.

Part II

Chapter 9

Symbolic Logic
Its Nature and Character

ARISTOTLE, (384BC – 322BC), the Greek thinker, laid the foundation of logic as a science. Since then for nearly two thousand years his work and his style of reasoning dominated the field of logic. Whatever was written by him, was considered as the 'Bible' in logic. The medieval scholastic thinkers developed over 'Aristotelian' logic but they adopted mainly his line of reasoning. The basic structure of logic remained more or less the same. 'Aristotle's' contemporaries and the medieval thinkers added nothing significant to his works and they were under the impression that the last word in logic is already written by him. Some cosmetic changes were made here and there by his followers but nothing significant was added in the field of logic.

In the seventeenth century G.W. Von Leibniz, a mathematician turned philosopher, however, could see that Aristotelian and his contemporaries' style of reasoning needs modification. But he merely suggested, and never worked or showed the direction which logic possibly could take. Logical calculus was discussed by Leibniz but no school was formed and the isolated attempts went unnoticed.

It is only in the nineteenth century that the thinkers started actualizing the ideas conceived by Leibniz. It is for the first time the traditional logic was seen with sharper eyes in equally sharper lights. For nearly two thousand years since its inception, logic did not progress so much as it had done in last one hundred and fifty years. This is mostly because of rapid development in mathematics and its use in logic. Since Leibniz's discovery of Differential Calculus, mathematics developed rapidly. Very soon, it became 'key-science'. The other branches of knowledge started using mathematical techniques in their studies. Mathematical techniques thus started creeping into other sciences. All disciplines of knowledge started reshaping their methods and methodologies in the light of mathematical developments. Logic also joined the race.

Interestingly, all modern logicians were primarily mathematicians, and since they all were aware of mathematical techniques, it became all the more easy for them to make logic look like maths. George Boole (1815-1864) mathematized logic by highlighting the resemblances between disjunction and conjunction of concepts and addition and multiplication operations in mathematics. Class calculus was his contribution to modern logic. While prominent thinkers like De Morgan (1806-1871) and Charles Sanders Peirce (1839-1914) were mathematizing logic, Gottlob Frege (1842-1925), a German mathematician, was doing something totally different. He tried to reduce all mathematics into logic by analysing the concept of number. This is popularly called "thesis of logicism". For this he introduced new language Begriffsschrift (language of thought) which makes use of only logical notations. These notations have capacity to express much more complex sentences than Aristotle's logic could do. This achievement started age of symbolic or mathematical logic for which he is correctly called the father of modern symbolic logic.

In the beginning, it was logic which was borrowing the basic binary operations and use of variables and symbols from maths, but soon the logicians realized mathematics is actually based on logical apparatus. Logic thus became more fundamental and basic than mathematics. It started using logical properties. Modern mathematics, modern algebra, the set theory are just few examples of it. Logicians too became busy in showing logic as the foundation of mathematics. Bertrand Russell and A.N. Whitehead's *'Principia Mathematica'* is leading example of it.

While the traditional logicians were using non-mathematical methods to differentiate correct reasoning from incorrect ones, the modern logicians are using mathematically oriented methods to achieve this aim. But it is not only the methods which are different in these two types of logic, modern logic is a further development of traditional logic. New avenues and fields of investigations are opened by them. The traditional logic is poorer than the modern logic in its formal character. In the classical logic the number of formulae were less and so were the number of valid inference patterns. But at the same time it is not wrong to say that what was implicit in Aristotelian logic has become explicit in modern logic.

The aim of all logicians, traditional as well as modern, is to provide methods and devices to differentiate valid reasoning from invalid ones. Difference between classical logic and symbolic logic may be considered as a difference of degrees rather than of kinds.[1] For example, the difference between a big girl and a small girl is a difference of degrees and not of kind whereas difference between a girl and a boy is of kind and not of degrees. In spirit and essence both logics are still the same and the terminus for all logicians is to determine the validity/invalidity of arguments.

Logical Form and Validity

The rules provided by the logicians to test the validity of arguments are based primarily on the form of argument and not on the content. Each argument is consisted of both form and matter (this was discussed in detail in the first chapter), but it is the form which is fundamental from the viewpoint of validity. Arguments are classified according to the forms they have. Content of an argument is absolutely insignificant as far as the validity of the deductive argument is concerned.

For example any argument having either of the following forms is valid:

---

1. Cf. A.H. Basson and D.T. O'Connor, *Introduction to Symbolic Logic,* pp. 1-2.

(i) All M is P
All S is M
Therefore, all S is P

(ii) If p then q
p
Therefore, q

Whatsoever may be the value of S, P, M or p and q, argument bearing either of the above forms is always valid. On the other hand, the argument having any of the following forms is always invalid:

(i) All P is M
All S is M
Therefore, all S is P

(ii) If p then q
q
Therefore, p

Whatever may be the value of S, P, M or p, q argument having any of the above forms is always invalid.

The symbols like S, P, M or p, q are variables. They are "dummies" in place of which any desired statements may be imagined.[2] They keep changing their values from argument to argument. By giving different values to S, P, M or p, q innumerable arguments can be constructed having similar form but with different content. Rules and formulae to decide the validity of arguments are made according to the form they have, and not according to their content.

For this reason, all the logicians specially deductive logicians, both ancient as well as modern, are interested in the form of an argument. The entire show in the deductive logic is of forms, and because of this deductive logic, like mathematics, is called formal science.

However logic, "seems to differ from mathematics in that in logic we talk about statements and their interrelationships, notably implication, whereas in mathematics we talk about abstract non-linguistic things: numbers, functions, and the like".[3] Yet logic sometimes makes use of the mathematical jargons like

2. W.V. Quine, op.cit., p. 29.
3. Ibid., p. 5.

'law of association', 'law of commutation', 'law of distribution', De Morgan's laws, etc. about which you will study later on.

Advantages of Using Symbols

In sharing the same platform with mathematics, modern logicians made extensive use of symbols. Symbols are ideograms, whereas spoken and written words are phonograms. Ideograms stand directly for ideas whereas phonograms stand for sound that we make while speaking words. All words of all languages are phonograms. For example the written words 'multiplication' is phonogram because they are the written characters of the sounds we make while uttering these words. But 'x' is an ideogram. This does not represent written character of the sound but stands for the idea directly. Symbolic logic makes use of ideograms instead of phonograms.

The classical logic used symbols like S, P, M which denote minor term, major term and middle term in a categorical syllogism, respectively. Also A, E, I, O symbols were used to denote various categorical propositions. The modern logicians extended the use of symbols in logic. The phrase 'symbolic logic' itself suggests their predomination in logic.

Two types of symbols are used — 'variable' and 'constant'. A variable symbol keeps on changing its value from argument to argument. These symbols are "dummies". They do not have fixed values. For example, P in one argument may stand for "You will pass", in another argument P may represent "It is very pleasant today" and yet in third argument it may be assumed for "We will go for picnic". Here symbol P is variable. Many types of variables are used in modern logic such as propositional variables, predicate variables, class variables, free and bound variables and many more. In the traditional logic only three variable symbols were used, that is, S, P and M for minor, major and middle terms of a categorical syllogism respectively. This suggests that the use of variable was known to Aristotle though it was restricted only to a few symbols.

The use of symbols for constants, however, was done for the first time by the modern logicians. Constant symbols do not change their value throughout the domain of logic. Some important constant symbols are as follows:

~ for negation

v for the relation of 'either or'

• for the relation of 'and'

⊃ for 'if then' relationship

A question may arise why the modern logicians make extensive use of symbols? What are the advantages of using symbols in logic? Symbols are of big use to a logician in at least two ways. Firstly, the logical form of an argument becomes explicit by using symbols. The complexity of language may obscure the structure of an argument, and this can conceal its logical form. Not only in logic, language even otherwise is considered a villain in philosophy. The use of language in logic can even be more nasty as slightest variation in the interpretation of terms or propositions can change the form of reasoning. By replacing language by symbols the logical form of an argument becomes explicit. Once right logical form of an argument is captured, its validity can be decided quickly and accurately.

Secondly, the use of symbols in logic is seen as an economical device. The long and big arguments become small and handful expressions after symbolization. They then can be operated quickly and easily. The chances of committing errors in deciding their validity are thus reduced.

Not only in logic but even otherwise there is an increased use of symbols and code language nowadays. 'All sciences', social as well as natural, make use of more and more symbols for being precise and accurate.

Inference and Implication

The chief characteristic of deductive logic is that it is impossible to have all true premisses and a false conclusion. In other words, in a valid deductive argument if all the premisses are true, then the conclusion must necessarily be true. However, this relationship between premisses and conclusion in logic is expressed in two ways, inference and implication. Though sometimes the difference between them is very thin, none the less, the difference is there.

The inference is made *by person,* but it is *propositions* which imply. In inference, the agent, the man believes in the truth value of premisses, and because of this he believes in the truth value of the conclusion. For example, when I say:

All men are mortal.
Socrates is a man.
____
Therefore, Socrates is mortal.

I assert the premisses and thus I assert the conclusion. In order an inference is logically sound or logically justifiable, it must satisfy two conditions:

(i) the inferer believes in the truth value (truth and falsity) of the premisses.

(ii) the conclusion follows from the premisses in accordance with the logical rules. In other words, the premisses and the conclusion are logically related to each other.

But in order an implication is logically valid, it must satisfy just one condition, that is, the relation between antecedent (premisses) and consequent (conclusion) should be logically acceptable. The second condition of true inference is the only condition which applies to valid implication.

An implication is totally formal and the logician may or may not believe in the truth value of the antecedent (premisses) and consequent (conclusion). The logician may also not believe that the meaning of antecedent and consequent are related to each other. For example, "If Ram has killed Ravan, then 2+2 = 4" is logically true implication in spite of the fact that the meaning of the premiss (antecedent) is not related to the conclusion (consequent) at all. Whereas the former is mythical proposition, the latter is a mathematical one. Thus in order that an implication is logically acceptable, it must satisfy only one condition that if antecedent proposition is true, each proposition "implied by it must also to be held as true". The logicians belief or disbelief in the antecedent plays no role in evaluating an implicative relation.

The formats of inference and implication are also different. For example:

All men are mortal.
Socrates is a man.
___
Therefore, Socrates is mortal.

is an inference. The same content can be expressed in implicative form as follows:

If all men are mortal and Socrates is a man, then Socrates is mortal.

An inference is expressed in the form like: Such and such premisses *therefore* the conclusion. Implication is expressed as: if such and such propositions *then* this proposition.

An inference can be expressed in implication and an implication can be expressed in inference after changing their formats. **Whereas in the traditional logic there is extensive use of inferences, the modern symbolic logic makes use of implication only.** This is a big difference. This highlights that the traditional logic is not totally formal whereas the modern logic is completely formal in character. Modern logic is basically a calculus whose rules of operation are determined by form and not by the meaning of the symbols it employs, as in the mathematics.

Exercises

1. What is Leibniz's contribution in symbolic logic? Can we say he is the trendsetter? Discuss.

2. Discuss the relationship of symbolic logic with mathematics. In what way mathematics has influenced logic? Elaborate.
3. What are the advantages of using symbols in logic? Explain with the examples.
4. What do you understand by the notions of 'ideogram' and 'phonogram'. Justify your answer with the help of examples.
5. Give a brief account of George Boole's contribution in modern logic.
6. Which is fundamental science, mathematics or symbolic logic? Support your answer with the help of examples.
7. In what sense Gottlob Frege is considerd father of modern symbolic logic.
8. Explain similarities and dissimilarities between inference and implication.
9. In what way modern symbolic logic is an improvement over traditional Aristotelian logic? Justify your answer.
10. Give a brief history of the development of symbolic logic.

Chapter 10

Symbolization

THERE are twofold tasks in the elementary symbolic logic for the beginners. They are:

(i) Symbolization of propositions and arguments stated in ordinary language.

(ii) Testing the validity of various types of arguments, evaluating, whether statement expressions are tautologous or not, and also construction of demonstration showing whether a statement implies or is equivalent to another statement.

This chapter is concerned with the first of these tasks, that is, with symbolization. For a simple proposition which is a simple sentence also, one letter from alphabet is assigned. For example:

Ram is graduate, is symbolized as G
Sita is good student, is symbolized as S
New Delhi is capital of India, is symbolized as C

Rita is intelligent and she is good student, is symbolized as: I and S.

If it rains, then we shall go for picnic, is symbolized as: If R, then G.

Either I will go to library or attend the seminar is symbolized as: Either G or A.

You will get job if and only if you qualify this test, is symbolized as: G if and only if Q.

Negative proposition: Propositions like "Ram is not a good student", "It is not pleasant today", "We shall not attend the seminar", etc. are negative propositions. They are symbolized as follows:

(i) Ram is not a good student

~ S

S - Ram is a good student

~ - not

(ii) It is not pleasant today

~ P

P - It is pleasant today

~ - not

(iii) We shall not attend the seminar

~ A

A - We shall attend the seminar

~ - not

'~' is sign for "not" and is read as tilde or curl.

There are other words and phrases besides 'not' for which '~' sign is substituted, such as 'it is not the case', 'it is false', 'it is not true', 'it is untrue'.

It is not the case that the indiscipline is tolerated = ~ T

It is false Congress has won the assembly election = ~ W

It is not true that an honest man is a man of millions = ~ M

It is untrue that Indians are indisciplined citizens = ~ I

However, symbolization of propositions like "It is true Indians are religious-minded people" is P.

Symbolization of Compound Propositions

Simple propositions are combined by various relations to form compound propositions.

Compound propositions are of various types: conjunctive, disjunctive, conditional (implicative) and bi-conditional (equivalence).

1. CONJUNCTIVE

In conjunctive proposition, two simple propositions are joined by 'and'. For instance, Ram is intelligent and he is a hard-working student. This is symbolized as follows:

I• H
I Ram is intelligent
H He is hard-working student
'•' is a constant symbol used for 'and' and is read as 'dot'.

There are many other words besides 'and' for which '•' sign is used. These words are: but, yet, both, although, however, moreover, neither nor, as well as, while, etc. For example:

He is poor but he is honest
P•H

It is hot yet tolerable
H•T

He is intelligent although not very careful
I•~C

Both Mohan and Rohit are students of this college
M•R

Not both Sita and Radha attended the convocation
~ (S•R)

But *both not* is symbolized differently.

A and B both were not selected for the job
~A•~B

Conjunctive sign '•' is used for 'neither nor' relationship also. "Neither Radha nor Mohan are graduates" is symbolized as ~ R•~ M. This means Radha is not graduate and Mohan is also not graduate.

2. DISJUNCTIVE

Two simple propositions when combined by 'either or' is called disjunctive proposition. "Either I will telephone him or I will write to him", is symbolized as:

T v W
T - I will telephone him
W - I will write to him

'v' - 'either or'

'v' sign shows the relationship of 'either or'. It is read as 'wedge'. "Either it rains or we shall not go for picnic", is symbolized as:

R v ~ G

R - It rains

~G - We shall not go for picnic

v - sign for 'either or' and is constant.

Either Indians are coward or they are God-fearing.

C v G

C - Indians are coward

G - God fearing

v - 'either or'

Either A is not honest or B is not telling truth.

~H v ~T

If two propositions are joined by 'unless' then also disjunctive sign can be used. For example:

I do not go to market unless it is very necessary, is symbolized as:

~G v N

-G - I don't go to market

N - It is very necessary,

v - disjunctive sign

Take another example: Unless you work hard you will not pass, is symbolized as:

~P v H

H - You work hard

~P - You will not pass

v - disjunctive sign

'Neither nor' relationship to join two simple propositions can also be symbolized by using 'v' sign. For example:

Neither soldiers nor officers are demoralized by this incident.

~(S v O)

S - Soldiers are demoralized

O - Officers are demoralized

Earlier 'neither nor' relation was symbolized by using '•' sign. The above proposition can also be symbolized in terms of '•' like:

~S•~O

Thus,

~(S v O) ≡ (~S• ~O)*

"Neither Ram nor Mohan was elected in the assembly election" can be symbolized in two ways:

(i) ~R• ~M

and

(ii) ~(R v M)

3. IMPLICATION

Simple propositions when combined by 'if, then' relation is called hypothetical, conditional or implicative proposition. When two propositions are joined into an implicative proposition then the first is said to imply the second, or second is implied by the first.

A conditional or implicative proposition is symbolized by '⊃' and is called 'horse shoe' for it looks like shoe of a horse.

If it rains, then we shall go for picnic.

R⊃G

R - It rains

G - We shall go for picnic

⊃ - sign of 'If then'

If it does not rain, then we shall not go for picnic, is symbolized as:

~R ⊃ ~G

In the "p ⊃ q" statement form p is 'antecedent' and q is 'consequent'. While symbolizing an implicative proposition, it is

* More such bi-conditionals are discussed in the next chapter.

important to identify the correct antecedent and correct consequent. For instance in the proposition.

"You will get job only if you qualify the test", is symbolized as:

$G \supset Q$

You will get job	-	G	-	antecedent
You qualify the test	-	Q	-	consequent

You will get job if you qualify the test, is symbolized as:

$Q \supset G$

You qualify the test	-	Q	-	antecedent
You will get job	-	G	-	consequent

All the following statement forms are symbolized as $p \supset q$:

p only if q
q if p
q provided that p
q on condition that p
q in case p
p hence q
p implies q
Since p, then q
"q is a necessary condition for p"
"p is a sufficient condition for q"
"only if q, p".

4. EQUIVALENT OR BICONDITIONAL PROPOSITION

Bi-conditional compound proposition is obtained by combining two simple propositions with equivalent relation. For example "You will catch plane if and only if you reach in time" is equivalent or bi-conditional proposition, and is symbolized as:

$C \equiv R$

C - You will catch plane
R - You will reach in time
$\equiv$ - symbol used for "if and only if" relation

You will get job if and only if you qualify the test.

$G \equiv Q$

In English language "if and only if" phrase stands for equivalent relation between propositions, and is symbolized as "=".

Look at the following compound propositions having similar but logically different forms:

(i) Mr. X will catch bus if he reaches in time
$R \supset C$

(ii) Mr. X will catch bus only if he reaches in time
$C \supset R$

(iii) Mr. X will catch bus if and only if he reaches in time

$C \equiv R$

R - Mr. X reaches in time

C - Mr. X catches the bus

One has to be very careful in symbolizing the propositions. For a slight variation in the symbolization results in wrong evaluation of the truth value of statements and arguments.

Now let us see how arguments are symbolized. Consider the following arguments.

Example 1 : He is either insecure or he is guilty. If he is guilty, he must tell everything to police. He will not tell everything to police. Therefore, he is insecure.

The following symbols are substituted:

He is insecure	-	I
He is guilty	-	G
He must tell everything to police	-	T
1st premiss	-	$I \vee G$
2nd premiss	-	$G \supset T$
3rd premiss	-	$\sim T$
Conclusion	-	I

In an argument one premiss means one complete sentence. Full stop marks the completion of a sentence. The sentence with any of the words, 'therefore', 'thus', 'hence', 'so' is conclusion.

Example 2 : If I watch late night TV, then I will not study for the test. If I do not study for the test, then tomorrow either I will miss my class or I will have to take an off. I will not miss my class. Therefore, I will study for test.

Symbolization:

I watch late night TV	-	W
I will not study for test	-	~S
I will miss my class	-	M
I will have to take an off	-	T
1st premises	-	W ⊃ ~ S
2nd premiss	-	~ S ⊃ (M v T)
3rd premiss	-	~ M
Conclusion	-	S

Example 3 : A car gives good service if and only if it is properly maintained. If this car is properly maintained, then it consumes *less* petrol. This car consumes *'more'* 'petrol'. Therefore, this car is not properly maintained.

Symbolization:

Car gives good service	-	G
Car is properly maintained	-	M
Car consumes less petrol	-	C
1st premiss	-	G ≡ M
2nd premiss	-	M ⊃ C
3rd premiss	-	~ C
Conclusion	-	~ M

One important point which the student should notice is that there is difference between

(i) *argument* and *argument form*

(ii) *statement* and *statement form*

The above given examples are of arguments. They are concrete, individual arguments. The capital letters of the alphabets are used to symbolize them. The argument form, however, is an abstract arrangement of premisses and conclusion in which 'dummies' are used for premisses and conclusion. Countless arguments can be obtained from the same argument form. For instance.

$p \supset q$
$q \supset r$
Therefore, $p \supset r$

is an argument form and p, q and r are propositional variables and are no more than "dummies". The argument forms are symbolized by using small letters of the alphabets whereas arguments are symbolized by using capital letters.

Similarly the statement form is an abstract arrangement of the prepositional variables. A statement form is symbolized by using small letters of the alphabets. For instance $(p \supset q) \vee p$ is statement form and p, q are prepositional variables whereas, "He is poor yet he is honest" is a statement symbolized as (P•H). A statement form can be replaced by statement, and also argument form by argument. In doing so the prepositional variables p, q, r are replaced by prepositional symbols P, Q, R, etc.

Exercises

1. Symbolize the following statements:-
    1. Either a or b.
    2. Both a and b.
    3. Either not a or b.
    4. Neither a nor b.
    5. a only if b.
    6. a if b.
    7. a if and only if b.
    8. If a, then b and c.

9. If a then b, and c.
10. If either a or b then c.
11. If a, then either a or b.
12. a, if b and c.
13. If not a, then b and c.
14. If both a and b then both c and d.
15. a implies b, and c implies d.
16. a provided b.
17. not p unless q.
18. unless p, not q.
19. p in case q.
20. Either both p and q or neither p nor q.
21. Either not both p and q or both not p and not q.
22. p implies q if and only if q implies p.
23. It is not the case that p and q.
24. It is not the case that p, and q.
25. It is not the case that either p or q.
26. It is not the case that either p, or q.
27. It is not the case that if p then q.
28. It is not the case that if p, then q and r.
29. It is not the case that both p and q.
30. It is not the case that either not p or q.

2. Symbolize the following statements using suggested notions:

   1. She attended to her duties and earned promotion. (A, E)
   2. They saw the uselessness of violence yet did not change their policies. (S, C)
   3. I sit on the chair but my cat sits on the floor. (C, F)

4. If he runs at top speed, then he will catch the train (R, C)
5. Either he leaves the country or he is prosecuted. (L, P)
6. Mr. X will be prosecuted unless he co-operates with the investigating team. (P, C)
7. Two triangles are formed if a square is divided diagonally. (T, S)
8. He was annoyed, still he kept quiet. (A, K)
9. He failed though he tried. (F, T)
10. She was waiting for her uncle at the railway station whereas he was waiting for her at bus stop (R, B)
11. Be neither a borrower nor a lender (B, L)
12. I cannot drive a car, if it is dark. (C, D)
13. A child is suspended from the school only if his behaviour is indecent. (S, I)
14. He is both fool and coward. (F, C)
15. We will miss the train unless we run. (M, R)
16. He escaped several times but was finally caught. (E, C)
17. Either the principal did not notice the change or else he approved of it. (N, A)
18. We will go if it does not rain. (G, R)
19. Asha wins only if Bela does not contest. (A, B)
20. He is neither hard-working nor intelligent. (H, I)
21. It is not the case that he is hard-working and he is intelligent. (H, I)
22. Unless it rains in time, harvest will not be good. (R, H)
23. It is not the case that if any metal is heated, then it will not expand. (M, E)
24. It is false that the guard raised his gun yet could not scare away the theives. (G, S)

25. He is a good student therefore he is loved by all. (G, L)
26. It is not true that he reads *Patriot* but not *Reader's Digest*. (P, R)
27. It is not true that either Joyti did not win or that Smita did not win. (J, S)
28. It is not true that neither Jyoti won nor Sheela won. (J,S)
29. A will dance only if both B and C sing. (A, B, C)
30. A will dance if B sings and C also sings. (A,B, C)

3. Symbolize the following statements:-
   1. Sahil will go to college if and only if Karan also goes to college. (S, K)
   2. Either she is too good and innocent or she is pretending to be so. (G, I, P)
   3. If Anu and Babita both do not win, then not both Chetna and Dolly win. (A, B, C, D)
   4. Karan and Belu will go to market if Sita goes to school. (K, B, S)
   5. Aarti and Bindoo go to the market only if Shiva goes to school. (A, B, S)
   6. It is not true that Sheela goes to market but does not buy anything. (S, B)
   7. If mathematics is difficult, then you will pass only if you work hard. (D, P, W)
   8. Rohit will get job only if Mohan does not, but it is not the case that both Rohit and Mohan get job. (R, M)
   9. Either both Aarti and Belu both go to library or neither will. (A, B)
   10. If the wind blows fast, then tents will be uprooted and soldiers will have tough times (B, V, T)

11. If the boats are made of bark, then they are very light and can easily be carried on the shoulders. (B, L, C)
12. Either make haste and get ready soon or you will be late for the meeting (H, R, L)
13. If I do not go to Bombay, then I will meet my dentist and fix an appointment for the operation. (G, M, A)
14. If the police arrives in time and starts firing, then the crowd will disperse (A, S, C)
15. If hydrogen and oxygen are mixed in the required proportion, water is produced. (H, O, W)
16. Manish is a big boy and strong also, still he was not selected for the marathon race in the school. (B, S, M)
17. If rain falls steadily for several days and the river overflowed its banks, then the terrified villagers would abandon their homes and would fly to the higher grounds. (F, O, A, G)
18. Either it is false that monsoon failed and tanks become empty or grain could not be sown and famine is feared. (M, T, G, F)
19. If an author is genius, then he suffers the penalty of being a genius and if he has talent, then various cares and worries make his life extremely miserable. (G, S, T, M)
20. The Suez Canal can neither be obstructed nor closed, if treaty is signed among the principal nations of Europe. (O, C, S)
21. Either French and Italian languages are diferent forms of Latin or it is false that they have different origin. (F, I, O)
22. If I stay at home and watch the late show, then either I do not do my homework or I do not sleep well. (S, W, H, D)

23. Arti will get job only if Veena does not, but it is not the case both Arti and Veena get jobs. (A, V)
24. If the weather is pleasant and there is a holiday, then either we go for picnic or we go for movie. (P, H, G, M)
25. If Sita goes to the party if and only if Radha goes to the party, then either both will go to the party or neither will. (S, R)

4. Symbolize the following arguments:-

   1. If John is healthy, then he is active. He is healthy. Therefore John is active. (H, A)
   2. This fellow is either a fool or a coward. He is not a fool. Therefore he is a coward. (F, C)
   3. The universe is either contingent or self-explanatory. But the universe is not self-explanatory. Therefore, the universe is contingent (C, E)
   4. Unless a person believes that everything makes for the best, he is not an optimist. A person either believes that everything makes for the best, or he does not believe in that. Hence, a person is either optimist or he is not. (B, O)
   5. If a child is interested in studies, then he will pay attention and will enjoy it. If a child does not pay attention in studies, then he will not learn. The purpose of teaching is defeated if the child does not learn. So if the child does not enjoy studies, then the purpose of teaching is defeated. (S, A, E, L, D)
   6. If the police obeys the laws, then they will put an end to smuggling. But if they are corrupt, then they will not put an end to smuggling. Thus, they either do not obey the laws or are not corrupt. (L, S, C)
   7. It is false that species of animals are fixed in number and that new species are not formed. But we know

that they are not fixed. It implies that new species are formed. (S, F)

8. If the doctor knew that the speed limit is fifty kilometre per hour, then he would not have been driving at sixty. He was driving at sixty kilometre per hour and was caught by the traffic police. Hence either the doctor did not know the speed limit is fifty kilometre per hour, or he was not caught by the traffic police. (F, S, C)

9. If the invigilators are alert and government makes strict anticopying laws, then the malaise from the education sector can be rooted out. But neither the invigilators are alert nor the strict anticopying laws are there. Hence, the malaise from the education sector cannot be rooted out. (A, L, M)

10. If X's passing the examination implies that he is lucky then he must not have worked hard. If X gets good marks, then he must have worked hard. Therefore, if X passed the examination then if he got good marks, then he must have worked hard. (P, L, G, W)

Chapter 11

Truth Function

WE have seen in the previous chapter symbols like '•', '⊃', 'v', '≡' are very important. They connect simple propositions to form compound propositions. They are thus called logical connectives. Compound propositions using these logical connectives are truth functionally compound. Truth functional logic is called "logic of statement connections". 'Conjunction', 'disjunction', 'implication', 'bi-conditional', etc. are logical connectives, for they connect two simple propositions.

In the elementary symbolic logic seven types of truth functions are r-0ecognized. They are:

1. Negative
2. Conjunctive
3. Disjunctive
4. Alternative
5. Implicative or conditional
6. Equivalent or bi-conditional
7. Stroke.

Before each one of them is discussed in detail, let us first understand the meaning of function and truth function. The word 'function' is a familiar notion in mathematics. When the value of an expression depends on the value of its constituents, then the expression is said to be function of its constituents. For example, in the expression:

y = 4x + 8

the value of 'y' depends on the value of 'x'. The moment 'x' is given a value, the value of 'y' becomes known. If 'x' is 3 then:

$y = 4x + 8$

$y = 12 + 8$

$y = 20$

If the value of 'x' changes then value of 'y' also changes subsequently. In that case 'y' is called function of 'x'.

In the expression

$z = 3x + 2y + 5$

'z' is function of 'x' and 'y'. The value of variable 'z' depends on the values of two variables 'x' and 'y'.

In logic the word 'function' is used exactly in the same sense as in mathematics. But instead of using word 'function', the logicians preferred 'truth function'. There is a reason for this. The logicians are interested in the truth value of expressions and validity of arguments. The logicians are looking for truth conditions of statements and statement forms.

A proposition is called truth functionally compound when its value depends on the truth value of its components and connectives. For example, the value of the expression 'p•q' depends on the value of 'p', 'q' variables. Thus, 'p•q' is truth function of 'p', 'q'. The truth value of the proposition "Ram is honest and Ram is hard-working" depends on the truth value of "Ram is honest" and "Ram is hard-working".

Let us examine the seven types of truth functions one by one in detail.

Negative Function

The negation of a proposition is another proposition whose value depends on the original proposition. The negation of the proposition "Cats are mammals" is "Cats are not mammals". If the former proposition is true, the latter is false. In other words, if p is true, then not p is false; if p is false, then not p is true. To deny a proposition is to affirm another proposition known as the negation N or contradictory of the first.

p	~p
T	F
F	T

Since the value of ~P depends on the value of p variable, ~p is truth function of p. Double negating a proposition means to affirm a proposition. ~ ~p = p.

Negative function is very important for the interdefinability of truth functions (logical constants). Later in the chapter this is discussed in detail.

Conjunctive Function

Two simple propositions when combined by 'and' makes a compound proposition called conjunctive proposition. For example, "It is very hot and it is very humid" is a compound proposition having a conjunctive sign.

Symbolically a conjunctive proposition is written like 'p•q'. The truth value of a conjunctive proposition depends on its constituents. The truth value of the proposition 'p•q' depends on the value of 'p' 'q' and '•'. Since the value of 'p•q' depends on the variable 'p', 'q' and the characteristics of '•', it is called conjunctive function.

The constituents of conjunctive proposition 'p', 'q' are called conjuncts. A conjunctive proposition is true when all its conjuncts are true. A conjunctive proposition is false if one of the conjuncts is false.

p	q	p•q
T	T	T
T	F	F
F	T	F
F	F	F

The table shows conjunctive function 'p•q' is true when both of its conjuncts 'p', 'q' are true. If either of conjuncts 'p', 'q' is false, then conjunction becomes false.

Let us see some solved examples here:

1. New Delhi is capital of India and Dr. Rajendra Prasad was the first President of free India.

   T and T
   T•T
   T

2. Cats are mammals and fish are also mammals.

   T and F
   T•F
   F

3. Mrs. Gandhi was 5th President of India and India is the biggest democratic country in the world.

   F and T
   F•T
   F

4. 'Children are voters in India' and 'India is in Australian Continent'

   F and F
   F•F
   F

Sometimes values of the variables are given, and on that basis the value of the expression can be worked out. For example, if 'A', 'B' are given as false, then the following expression is true.

$$\begin{aligned} & \sim (A \bullet B) \\ = & \sim (F \bullet F) \\ = & \sim F \\ = & \;\; T \end{aligned}$$

Conjunctive function has other important characteristics also which can be explained by using 'mathematical jargons'. Conjunctive function is *commutative, associative* as well as *idempotent.*

$p \bullet q \equiv q \bullet p$	Commutative property
$p \bullet (q \bullet r) \equiv (p \bullet q) \bullet r$	Associative property
$p \bullet p \equiv p$	Idempotent property

In certain cases, the value of one conjuct or more conjuncts are unknown. As for instance if 'p' is unknown then the values of the following expressions are as such:

(i) $p \bullet T = p$

(ii) $p \bullet F = F$

(iii) $p \bullet {\sim}p = F$

Here the value of 'p' variable is not known, yet in some cases one can find the truth value of conjunctive compound propositions. The truth value of the expression (i) 'p•T' depends on 'p'. If 'p' is true then 'p•T' is true; similarly if 'p' is false, 'p•T' is false. That is why 'p•T' is equivalent to 'P'.

The truth value of the expression (ii) 'p•F' is false. For a conjunctive function is true when all conjuncts are true. Here one of the conjuncts is false, hence 'p•F' is false.

Similarly, the truth value of the expression (iii) 'p•~p' is false because whatever may be the value of 'p, ~p' is the contradictory of it. Hence one of the conjuncts (either p or ~p) will be false. Thus the expression 'p•~p' is false.

Disjunctive Function

Two simple propositions when combined by 'either or' makes disjunctive proposition. "Either Sohan is ill or he is involved in some important matter" is disjunctive proposition symbolized as I v M. Both 'I' and 'M' are disjuncts.

The truth value of a disjunctive proposition 'p v q' depends on the values of its disjuncts 'p, q' and the characteristic of 'v'. Thus, the proposition 'p v q' is truth function of 'p', 'q'.

A disjunctive proposition is true when at least one of the disjuncts is true. When all the disjuncts are false, then the disjunctive proposition is false.

p	q	pvq
T	T	T
T	F	T
F	T	T
F	F	F

Some solved expressions are given below. If p is true and q is false, then the value of the following expressions are worked out as follows:

1. ~ (p v q)
   = ~ (T v F)
   = ~ T
   = F

2. (p v q) v (p • q)
   = (T v F) v (T • F)
   = T v F
   = T

3. ~ (p•q) v (p v q)
   = ~ (T•F) v (T v F)
   = ~ (F) v T
   = T v T
   = T

4. ~ (p v ~q) v (q• ~ q)
   = ~ (T v ~F) v (F• ~ F)
   = ~ (T v T) v (F•T)
   = ~T v F
   = F v F
   = F

5. ~ (p • p)• ~ (q v p)
   = ~ (T • T) • ~ (F V T)
   = ~ (T) • ~ (T)
   = F • F
   = F

Like conjunctive function, disjunctive function also has certain mathematical properties. Disjunctive function has *commutative, associative* as well as *idempotent* properties.

$p \vee q \equiv q \vee p$	Commutative property
$p \vee (q \vee r) \equiv (p \vee q) \vee r$	Associative property
$p \vee p \equiv p$	Idempotent property

Besides, the value of disjunctive propositions in certain cases can be known even if all the disjuncts are not known. For instance if p is unknown the value of following statement forms are as follows:

(i) $p \vee T = T$

(ii) $p \vee F = p$

(iii) $p \vee \sim p = T$

The value of p variable is not known, yet in certain cases the truth value of disjunctive compound propositions can be determined. The truth value of (i) expression 'p v T' is true for a disjunction is true even if one of the disjuncts is true. The truth value of (ii) expression 'p v F' is 'p'. Whatever will be the value of 'p', 'p v F' expresion will have that value. If 'p' is true, 'pvF' is true and, on the other hand, if 'p' is false 'pvF' is false. The truth value of (iii) expression 'pv~p' is true, for whatever may be the value of 'p', one of the disjuncts in 'pv~p' will be true. Thus 'pv~p' in any case will be true only.

Both conjunctive and disjunctive functions resemble certain mathematical binary operations like addition and multiplication (but not substraction and division) in the sense that they have associative and commutative properties.

However, the relationship of 'either or' is not a simple one. In logic this relationship is interpreted in two different ways: one is disjunction and the other is alternation. The following examples may help to see the difference:

A mother asked her daughter: choose one of the dresses which I selected for you. Either take dress 'A' or 'B'. The mother obviously intends the child should pick up one and reject another. But she is not surprised when the daughter says I will take both. The example shows one can accept both the options 'A' and 'B'. This is disjunctive sense of 'either or'.

Take yet another set of example: suppose there is a guest and I ask him what will you take, tea or coffee? I am certainly surprised if the guest says both. Here 'either or' is used in the alternative sense. The guest is given option to choose one out of two alternatives. If a professor asks a student what do you want to do? You want to study or you want a job. The professor is quite comfortable when the student says I want to do both. This is the use of 'either' or in disjunctive sense.

Alternative Function

In the alternative function, if one of the alternates is true and the other is false, only then it (alternative function) is true.

p	q	p ∧ q
T	T	F
T	F	T
F	T	T
F	F	F

Let us compare alternative function with disjunctive function.

<u>*Disjunctive function*</u> (inclusive sense of 'or')

p	q	pvq
T	T	T
T	F	T
F	T	T
F	F	F

<u>*Alternative function*</u> (exclusive sense of 'or'")

p	q	p^q
T	T	F
T	F	T
F	T	T
F	F	F

The difference between disjunctive and alternative interpretations of 'either or' lies in the first row. Whereas the disjunctive function allows all the disjuncts to be true, the alternative function does not allow all the alternates to be true. Disjunction is weaker and inclusive sense of 'either or' whereas alternation is stronger, strict and exclusive sense of 'either or'.

However, while symbolizing the arguments in the elementry symbolic logic, only disjunctive function is used for 'either or' relationship although in our daily life, we use 'either or' in both the senses.

Implicative Function (Conditional Function)

In an implicative function two simple propositions are combined by 'if then' relationship. For example, "If it is pleasant, then we shall go for picnic" is a conditional proposition. It is symbolized as 'P ⊃ G'. Here 'P' is antecedent and 'G' is consequent. The truth value of 'p ⊃ q' depends on the truth value of antecedent 'p' and consequent 'q'. Thus 'p ⊃ q' is truth function of 'p' and 'q'.

p	q	p ⊃ q
T	T	T
T	F	F
F	T	T
F	F	T

Let us see some solved examples:

If 'p' is true and 'q' is false, the values of the following expressions are worked as follows:

1. (p ⊃ q) v p
   = (T ⊃ F) v T
   = F v T
   = T

2. $q \supset (p \bullet \sim q)$

$= F \supset (T \bullet \sim F)$

$= F \supset (T \bullet T)$

$= F \supset T$

$= T$

3. $\sim (p \bullet q) \supset \sim q$

$= \sim (T \bullet F) \supset \sim F$

$= \sim F \supset T$

$= T \supset T$

$= T$

Implicative (conditional) statement is true if it satisfies the following conditions:

(i) A true antecedent must have a true consequent.

(ii) a false consequent must have a false antecedent.

This interpretation of 'if then' relation has generated a serious debate in the field of logic. The main question is: "Does truth functionally compound implicative relation where true antecedent must have true consequent and false consequent must have false antecedent represent all the various interpretations of implicative relations?" The answer is No. Modern logicians' interpretation of implicative (conditional) statements in terms of truth functionally compound statement is merely a sub set of a more comprehensive set of different other interpretations of conditional statements. In simple words, 'if then' relationship is used in many senses and truth functionally implicative relationship is just one of them. This is the reason why the latter relationship of 'if then' is given a name of material implication and is symbolized by using horseshoe sign '$\supset$'.

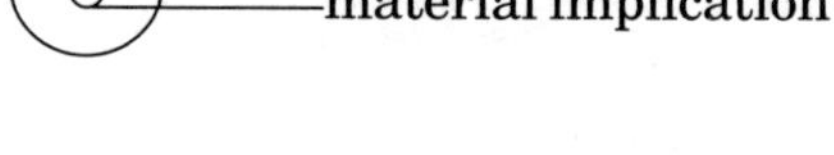

The results of material implication that "a false proposition implies any proposition and a true proposition is implied by any proposition" is not compatible with common-sense use and other uses of 'if then' relationship. A common man relates two propositions by 'if then' only if the meanings of the propositions are also related. For example, the proposition "If Ram has killed Ravan, then 2+2 = 4" is neither true nor false; rather it is a meaningless, a pseudo expression because the meanings of the propositions are not related. Antecedent is mythical statement but consequent is arithmetical. Besides, a common man expects consequent to follow from the antecedent. For example, in the proposition "If is rains, then we shall go for picnic", 'our going' depends and follows from the proposition 'it rains'. The common-sense understanding presupposes "some sort of connection" between the antecedent and the consequent, whereas there is no such requirement in the material implication. "Thus for a common man two simple propositions are related by conditional relation of 'if then' only when their meanings are related and also when the consequent follows from the antecedent. But for the logicians (who advocate material implication) any two simple propositions can be combined by 'if then' whether their meanings are related or not, provided antecedent should not be true if consequent is false. He is interested only in the logical properties of an implicative relation and not in the meaning and relationship of its constituents.

The truth conditions of material implicative statements have generated paradoxical situation. There are twofold paradoxes which are called 'Paradoxes of Material Implication" The paradoxes are results of material implicative truth conditions which can be summarized as:

(i) A false proposition implies any proposition (true or false)

(ii) A true proposition is implied by any propostion (true or false)

PARADOX OF MATERIAL IMPLICATION

The truth value of material implication is as follows:

p	⊃	q
T	T	T
T	F	F
F	T	T
F	T	F

The first row states that a true proposition implies a true proposition.

The third row states that a false proposition can also imply a true proposition.

Two together state: A proposition true or false can imply a true proposition. In other words: any proposition, true or false, can imply a true proposition. This is the outcome of the logical properties of a material implication. But to a common man this (that any proposition, true or false, can imply a true proposition) is unacceptable. A true proposition implying true proposition is accepted; a false proposition implying false proposition is also accepted. But how can any proposition (true or false) imply any true proposition? This is paradoxical situation.

Let us see how the second paradox occurred.

The third row states that a true proposition is implied by false proposition.

The fourth row states that a false proposition is implied by false proposition.

Together they state: Any proposition (true or false) is implied by a false proposition. This is the logical outcome but again to a common man this is unacceptable. A false proposition implied by false proposition is accepted; but how can any proposition (true or false) be implied by any false proposition?

Common man is interested in first row

$T \supset T \Rightarrow T$

and in second row

$T \supset F \Rightarrow F$

Third and fourth row seem to be 'irrelevant' to him. He unconsciously accepts the truth of antecedent and then expects the truth of consequent. For the logicians if antecedent is false, then whatever may be consequent the material implicative proposition will be true. But to an ordinary person both of these propositions cannot be true at the same time. See the following example:

"If I catch the plane, then tomorrow I will attend the meeting"

"If I catch the plane, then tomorrow I will not attend the meeting"

If the antecedent that "I catch the plane" is false, then according to the truth conditions of material implication both the propositions will be true. But an ordinary person asks how can they both be true because they are inconsistent propositions. That probably is the reason why material implication cannot be considered as the representative of all types of conditional propositions. One way to solve and desolve these paradoxes is to keep separate the truth conditions of material implication from the truth conditions of other conditional (implicative) propositions.

Equivalent Function (bi-conditional)

Two propositions or expressions are equivalent if they have same truth value. If both the propositions are true then they are equivalent and similarly if both the propositions are false then also they are equivalent. However, if one proposition is true and the other is false, then they are not equivalent. The truth value of equivalent proposition can be framed with the help of ordinary understanding of the word equivalent.

p	q	p ≡ q
T	T	T
T	F	F
F	T	F
F	F	T

Since the truth value of 'p ≡ q', depends on the truth values of 'p', 'q' the expression 'p ≡ q' is truth function of its constituents 'p', 'q'.

Let us see some solved examples. If p is true and q is false, then values of the following expressions are worked as follows:

1. $p \supset (q \equiv p)$
   $= T \supset (F \equiv T)$
   $= T \supset F$
   $= F$
2. $\sim p \equiv (p \supset p)$
   $= \sim T \equiv (T \supset T)$
   $= F \equiv T$
   $= F$
3. $(p \supset q) \equiv (\sim p \vee q)$
   $= (T \supset F) \equiv (\sim T \vee F)$
   $= F \equiv (F \vee F)$
   $= F \equiv F$
   $= T$

After studying the various truth functions, a student may get an impression that all uses of words like 'and', 'either or', etc. make truth functionally compound propositions. But this is not so. There are non-truth functional compound propositions also. The following propositions, for example, are not truth functionally compound:

Radha and Rama are sisters
Mohan and Gopal are friends
Sita and Gita are twins
He believes that he is right

A compound statement or a compound proposition is truth functionally compound if and only if its (compound proposition's) truth value depends on the truth value of its components or constituents. In other words, a truth functional statement is that statement whose truth value depends on words like 'not', 'and', 'either' or 'if then', etc.

INTERDEFINABILITY OF TRUTH FUNCTIONS (CONSTANTS)

Some of the truth functions are basic while some others have merely theoretical value. Basic truth functions are ., ~, ⊃, v whereas ≡, ∧, / (stroke) are mainly for the theoretical purposes. Each truth function has its own special characteristics, yet they can be reduced and defined into each other. A conjunction, for example, can be defined into other functions, such as '~' and 'v', '~' and '⊃'. Disjunction can similarly be defined into other functions. **Defining and reducing the truth functions or constants into one another is called "interdefinability of the constants".** In other words, functions like ~, •, v, ⊃ ≡ are dispensable signs. This can be shown by defining one function into other functions. However, while defining one truth function (or constant) into other truth functions (constants), the meaning of the expression should not be changed or destroyed.

Conjunctive function can be defined into:

(i) '~' and 'v'

'(p•q)' = df '~ (~ p v ~ q)'

(ii) '~' and '⊃' as

'(p•q)' = df '~ (p ⊃ ~ q)'

The truth value of (p•q) is same as of (~ p v ~ q) or ~ (p ⊃ ~ q).

Ram is intelligent and Ram is hard-working can be defined in two ways:

1. It is false that either he is not intelligent or he is not hard-working.

2. It is false that if he is intelligent then he is not hardworking.

Disjunctive function can be defined into:

(i) '~' and '•'

'(pvq)' = df '~(~p•~q)'

(ii) '~' and '⊃'

'(pvq)' = df '~ p ⊃ q'

The truth value of pvq is same as that of ~(~p•~q) or (~p ⊃ q).

Either the opposition demands are met or they will boycott President's address, can be defined in two ways.

(1) It is false that neither opposition demands are met nor they boycott the President's address.

(2) If the opposition demands are not met, then they boycott the President's address.

Implicative function can be defined into:

(i) '~' and 'v'

'(p ⊃ q)' = df '(~pvq)'

(ii) '~' and '•'

'(p ⊃ q)' = df '~ (p• ~q)'

If it rains, then the harvest will be good can be defined in two ways:

(1) Either it does not rain or the harvest will be good.

(2) It is false that it rains and the harvest is not good.

Equivalent function can be defined into:

(i) '.' and '⊃'

'(p ≡ q)' = df '(p⊃q)'• (q ⊃ p)'

(ii) '~' and '•' and 'v'

'p≡q' =df '(p•q) v (~p• ~q)'

The opposition attends the session, if and only if their demand of inquiry is accepted, can be expressed in two ways:

(1) If the opposition attends the session, then their demand for inquiry is accepted, and if their demand for inquiry is accepted, then they will attend the session.

(2) Either the opposition attends the session and their demand for inquiry is accepted or neither the opposition attends the session nor their demand for inquiry is accepted.

Alternative function can be defined into:

(i) 'p∧q' = df '(pvq)• ~(p•q)'

(ii) 'p∧q' = df '(pvq) • (~pv~q)'

Both equivalent and alternative functions are not basic functions, but they can be defined in terms of basic functions.

Stroke Function

Five logical constants (truth functions) • v ⊃ ≡ ∧ are defined into one and another with the help of '~'. The question arises how can '~' as a constant be defined? The interdefinability of truth functions is possible only with the help of negation. But none of the constants • ⊃ v ≡ helps in defining 'not'. **Thus in order to define negation, another new logical function was introduced by Sheffer in 1913. It is called stroke function.** The primary aim of the stroke function was to define negative function. Later on all other logical functions were also reduced into this single function of stroke. Stroke is symbolized as '/' and is true if and only if at least one of its components is false.

p	q	p/q
T	T	F
T	F	T
F	T	T
F	F	T

The table shows that if both p and q are true, then p/q is false and if either of the variable is false, then p/q is true.

Let us see how other functions are defined in terms of stroke function.

1. ~p is defined as p/p.
   '~p' = df 'p/p'.
2. p•q is defined as (p/q)/(p/q)
   'p•q' = df '(p/q)/(p/q)'
3. pvq is defined as (p/p)/(q/q)
   'pvq' = df '(p/p)/(q/q)'
4. p ⊃ q is defined as p/(q/q)
   'p ⊃ q' = df 'p/(q/q)'
5. 'p ≡ q' is defined as:
   'p/(q/q)/q/(p/p)/p/(q/q)/q/(p/p)'

Exercises

1. If A, B, C are true statements and X, Y, Z are false, determine the truth value of the following propositions:
   1. (X ⊃ Z) ⊃ ~Y
   2. (A ⊃ ~ B) v ~ C
   3. (B v X) ⊃ (B • Y)
   4. (A v B) • (Z • C)
   5. (C • Y) v (Z v B)
   6. (~ B v ~ X) ⊃ (B v X)
   7. (C • B) ⊃ (~ Z • ~ X)
   8. ~ (A • B) v ~ (X v Y)
   9. ~ (C ⊃ ~ B) ⊃ ~ (~ X ⊃ ~ Y)
   10. ~ (Z V A) ⊃ (~ X • ~ A)
   11. (A • B) ⊃ (~ Z • ~ X)
   12. (X ⊃ Y) ⊃ (~ Z ≡ ~ A)
   13. [(C • X) ⊃ Y] ⊃ (~A ⊃ ~Y)
   14. [(A ⊃ B) v C] ≡ (X ⊃ A)
   15. [B ⊃ (X • Y)] ⊃ [(X • Z) v B]

16. $[(C \bullet X) \supset C] \supset [(A \supset X) \supset C]$
17. $[(A \bullet B) \bullet C] \supset [(A \vee X) \vee Y]$
18. $[(A \supset C) \supset Y] \supset \sim (X \bullet \sim Y)$
19. $[(\sim B \bullet Y) \supset B)] \supset [A \supset (B \supset X)]$
20. $[B \supset (A \vee X)] \supset [(C \supset A) \supset Y]$
21. $[(A \vee X) \supset C] \bullet [(X \bullet Z) \vee (A \vee Y)]$
22. $[(X \bullet Y) \supset B] \vee [(Y \bullet Z) \vee (A \bullet Y)]$
23. $[A \supset (X \bullet Y)] \bullet [(A \supset X) \vee (A \supset Y)]$
24. $[(B \supset B) \supset X] \supset [(X \supset \sim Y) \supset Z]$
25. $\sim[(\sim C \vee Z) \vee (\sim Z \vee B)]$
26. $\sim [\sim (A \supset B) \vee \sim (\sim X \vee \sim Y)]$
27. $\sim [(B \supset \sim A) \vee \sim C] \supset (A \equiv B)$
28. $[(A \vee Y) \bullet \sim B] \vee [(A \bullet B) \vee (Z \bullet C)]$
29. $[\sim B \supset (Y \bullet Z)] \supset \sim [(A \bullet X) \supset (C \bullet X)]$
30. $[(C \bullet X) \supset Y] \equiv [(B \supset Y) \bullet (C \supset Z)]$
31. $[(B \bullet X) \vee (\sim A \bullet \sim X)] \bullet [(A \supset X) \bullet (X \supset A]$
32. $\sim [(\sim A \bullet \sim X) \vee A] \vee [(A \supset \sim X) \bullet (\sim B \supset \sim Y)]$
33. $[(A \supset C) \supset (X \bullet \sim Y)] \supset \sim [(- X \vee Y) \supset (A \vee X)]$
34. $\sim [(C \supset B) \bullet (X \supset Y)] \equiv [(A \vee X) \supset (B \supset Y)]$
35. $\sim [(X \supset A) \bullet (Y \vee B)] \vee \sim [(X \vee A) \bullet (Y \vee B)]$

2. A and B are known to be true, and X and Y are known to be false, but the truth values of P and Q are not known, determine the truth values of the following expression:

   1. $X \bullet P$
   2. $Y \supset Q$
   3. $\sim A \supset P$
   4. $P \supset \sim Y$
   5. $P \bullet \sim P$
   6. $P \vee \sim P$

7. $P \supset P$
8. $\sim P \supset \sim P$
9. $X \equiv (P \bullet Y)$
10. $A \equiv (B \vee Q)$
11. $P \equiv P$
12. $P \supset (X \vee B)$
13. $B \supset (Q \supset B)$
14. $\sim (Q \bullet Y) \supset X$
15. $(P \vee A) \supset X$
16. $(A \vee P) \supset (P \bullet X)$
17. $Q \vee \sim (\sim B \vee Y)$
18. $(X \bullet Y) \supset (P \supset A)$
19. $[\sim (A \bullet B) \vee (X \bullet Y)] \supset P$
20. $(P \supset A) \supset (B \supset X)$

3. Define the following expressions into stroke function:
   1. $\sim p \bullet q$
   2. $p \vee \sim q$
   3. $\sim (p \supset q)$
   4. $(p \supset q) \vee r$
   5. $p \vee (q \bullet r)$
   6. $(p \supset q) \bullet r$
   7. $(p \supset q) \supset r$
   8. $(p \vee r) \supset q$
   9. $p \supset (q \supset p)$
   10. $\sim p \supset (q \bullet r)$
   11. $p \supset (p \bullet q)$
   12. $(\sim p \vee q) \bullet q$
   13. $(p \supset q) \vee p$

14. $(p \bullet q) \supset (p \vee q)$
15. $(p \bullet q) \bullet r$
16. $\sim p \vee (p \supset \sim q)$
17. $(p \bullet q) \supset r$
18. $p \equiv q$
19. $(p \vee q) \bullet (q \supset p)$
20. $(\sim p \supset \sim q) \supset r$

4. Define the following expressions into '~' and 'v'.
   1. $(\sim p \supset q)$
   2. $(p \bullet q) \vee r$
   3. $p \bullet (\sim q \vee p)$
   4. $(p \supset q) \supset p$
   5. $\sim p \supset (\sim q \bullet r)$
   6. $(\sim p \supset \sim q) \vee r$
   7. $(p \bullet q) \supset r$
   8. $p \supset (q \supset r)$
   9. $(p \bullet q) \supset (p \vee q)$
   10. $\sim (p \bullet q) \vee (q \supset p)$

5. Define the following expressions into '~' and '•'.
   1. $\sim p \vee q$
   2. $p \supset \sim q$
   3. $\sim (p \vee q)$
   4. $(p \bullet q) \vee r$
   5. $p \vee (\sim q \supset p)$
   6. $(p \supset q) \supset p$
   7. $\sim p \supset (\sim q \vee r)$
   8. $(p \vee q) \supset r$
   9. $(\sim p \supset \sim q) \vee (p \bullet r)$
   10. $p \equiv q$

6. What do you understand by truth function? Explain four basic truth functions with the of help of examples.
7. Explain with suitable examples 'inclusive' and 'exclusive' meaning of 'either or' relation.
8. Define material implication. Explain with examples the 'Paradox of Material Implication'.
9. Define stroke function. What is its utility in logic? Discuss.
10. What do you understand by interdefinability of truth functions? In this context examine the role of Stroke function.

Chapter 12

Truth Table Method as Decision Procedure

As we have seen in the last two chapters, the aim of symbolic logic is twofold — firstly to symbolize the arguments and expressions, and secondly to evaluate them. This chapter deals with the latter objective. In the logic of propositions there are many methods to test the validity of arguments and argument forms, and also to examine whether statements or statement forms are tautologous or not. These methods are called **decision procedures,** for they help in taking a decision whether an argument is valid or invalid, and also whether statement is tautologous or not. Some standard decision procedures in the logic of propositions are:

(1) Truth table method

(2) Shorter truth table method (*reductio ad absurdum*)

(3) CNF (Conjunctive Normal Form)

(4) DNF (Disjunctive Normal Form)

(5) Truth tree method.

The present chapter, however, deals with the truth table method only.

Truth Table Method

Truth table method is the most basic and perhaps the most popular method to examine the validity of arguments as well as logical status of statements. Let us see how the method is applied. First of all the numbers of simple propositions in the argument are counted. If a simple proposition is repeated in the argument or in the expression, then it is counted only once. In the expression p ⊃ (p v q), the numbers of propositional variables are 2, since p occurs twice, it will be considered only once. In the expression ~q v [q v (r.p)], the numbers of propositional variables are 3, since q is repeated, it will be considered only once.

In the following argument form:

p ⊃ q

q ⊃ r

~s • ~ p ∴ p

the propositional variables are 4.

After knowing the numbers of propositional variables, the numbers of rows are decided. This depends on the numbers of propositional variables. If the numbers of propositional variables is 3, the numbers of rows are $2^3 = 2 \times 2 \times 2 = 8$ and if the propositional variables are 4, then the numbers of rows are $2^4 = 2 \times 2 \times 2 \times 2 = 16$.

The base is always 2 because we are dealing with two-valued logic only. A proposition has two values, true or false. The power of 2 or the exponent of 2 is according to the numbers of propositional variables an argument form or an expression has. In the expression ~ p v [q v (r v p)] since the numbers of propositional variables are 3, the numbers of rows are $2^3 = 2 \times 2 \times 2 = 8$.

(p ⊃ q) • (r ⊃ t) has 4 variables, so the rows are $2^4 = 2 \times 2 \times 2 \times 2 = 16$. In the argument form:

p ⊃ q

r ⊃ s

s • t / ∴(q ⊃ r)

since the propositional variables are 5, the numbers of rows are $2^5 = 32$.

After counting the numbers of variables and deciding the numbers of rows, the truth table is constructed. Here some examples are given which show how the truth table is constructed.

(1) (p	⊃ q)	v	p
T	T		T
T	F		T
F	T		F
F	F		F
1	2		3

In the above statement form, there are two propositional variables and hence total numbers of rows are $2^2 = 2 \times 2 = 4$. Under the first propositional variable two Ts, two Fs occur, total 4 times. Under the second variable one T and one F occur, total 4 times. Since p is repeated, the same value of p (two Ts and two Fs) is substituted.

(2) $[(p \supset q) \bullet (r \supset p)] \supset q$

Here, the numbers of propositional variables are 3, so numbers of rows are $2^3 = 2 \times 2 \times 2 = 8$. Under first variable four Ts, four Fs occur total 8 times. Under the second variable, two Ts, two Fs occur 8 times, and under the third variable one T and one F total 8 times.

The rule is: under the first variable half of the total numbers of rows are Ts and half are Fs. Under the second variable half of the first variable Ts and half of the first variable Fs are assigned. Under the third variable half of the second variable's Ts and half of the second variable's Fs are assigned.

[(p ⊃	q) •	(r ⊃	p)] ⊃	q
T	T	T	T	T
T	T	F	T	T
T	F	T	T	F
T	F	F	T	F
F	T	T	F	T
F	T	F	F	T
F	F	T	F	F
F	F	F	F	F

(3) (~p • p) v p

Number of propositional variable = 1

Number of rows are 2^1 =2

(~p •	p)	v p
T	T	T
F	F	F

(4) ~(~ p • ~ q) ≡ (p v q)

Number of propositional variables = 2

Number of rows = $2^2 = 2 \times 2 = 4$

~ p •	~ q)	≡	(p	v q)
T	T		T	T
T	F		T	F
F	T		F	T
F	F		F	F

(5) {(p v q) • (q ⊃ r)} ⊃ (p ⊃ r)

Number of propositional variables are 3

Number of rows = $2^3 = 2 \times 2 \times 2 = 8$

{(p	v q)	• (q	⊃ r)}	⊃ (p	⊃ r)
T	T	T	T	T	T
T	T	T	F	T	F
T	F	F	T	T	T
T	F	F	F	T	F
F	T	T	T	F	T
F	T	T	F	F	F
F	F	F	T	F	T
F	F	F	F	F	F

After constructing truth table, the variables are joined using the properties of constants. First brackets are solved. Let us see some solved examples.

Example 1:

(p ⊃ q) v p

Number of propositional variables = 2

Number of rows = $2^2 = 2 \times 2 = 4$

(p	⊃	q)	v	p
T	T	T	T	T
T	F	F	T	T
F	T	T	T	F
F	T	F	T	F
1	3	2	5	4

Just as in mathematical expressions, here also first the brackets are considered. In this example 'p ⊃ q' is in bracket, so it is solved first. We know an implication (⊃) is false when the antecedent is true and consequent is false. After solving the bracket, the other part of the expression is solved. A disjunction is true when at least one of the disjuncts is true. The main column is under 5. **If under the main column there are all Ts then the expression form is *tautology*.** This statement form is tautologous, for there are all Ts under the main column.

Example 2 :

(p v q) ⊃ (q • p)

Number of propositional variables = 2

Number of rows = $2^2 = 2 \times 2 = 4$

(p	v	q)	⊃	(q	•	p)
T	T	T	T	T	T	T
T	T	F	F	F	F	T
F	T	T	F	T	F	F
F	F	F	T	F	F	F
1	3	2	7	4	6	5

The main column (No. 7) contains some Ts and some Fs. Hence this statement form is *contingent.*

(3) (p ⊃ q) • ~ (p ⊃ q)

Number of prepositional variables = 2

Number of rows = $2^2 = 2 \times 2 = 4$

(p	⊃	q)	•	~	(p	⊃	q)
T	T	T	F	F	T	T	T
T	F	F	F	T	T	F	F
F	T	T	F	F	F	T	T
F	T	F	F	F	F	T	F
1	3	2	8	7	4	6	5

The main column (No. 8) contains all Fs, therefore, the above statement form is self-contradictory or contradictory.

A proposition, a propositional form, a statement, a statement form or an expression is either *tautology* or *contingent* or *self-contradictory.* A propositional form is tautology when under the main column there are all Ts; it is contingent when under the main column there are both Ts and Fs, and it is self-contradictory when under the main column there are all Fs. In other words, the logical status of a propositional form is either tautologous or contingent or self-contradictory.

Illustrated Statement forms

Test by truth table which of the following statement forms are tautologous, contingent or self-contradictory:

or

Examine the logical status of the following propositional forms.

(1) (p	⊃	q)	v	(~	p	v	~	r)
T	T	T	T	F	T	F	F	T
T	T	T	T	F	T	T	T	F
T	F	F	F	F	T	F	F	T
T	F	F	T	F	T	T	T	F
F	T	T	T	T	F	T	F	T
F	T	T	T	T	F	T	T	F
F	T	F	T	T	F	T	F	T
F	T	F	T	T	F	T	T	F
1	3	2	9	5	4	8	7	6

Since the main column (9) contains both Ts and Fs, the statement form is contingent.

(2) (p	•	q)	⊃	[(p	v	q)	•	p]
T	T	T	T	T	T	T	T	T
T	F	F	T	T	T	F	T	T
F	F	T	T	F	T	T	F	F
F	F	F	T	F	F	F	F	F
1	3	2	9	4	6	5	8	7

Since there are all Ts in the main column (9), therefore, the above statement form is tautologous.

(3) (p	v	q)	•	(~	p	•	~	q)
T	T	T	F	F	T	F	F	T
T	T	F	F	F	T	F	T	F
F	T	T	F	T	F	F	F	T
F	F	F	F	T	F	T	T	F
1	3	2	9	5	4	8	7	6

Since there are all Fs in the main column (9), the expression form is self-contradictory.

The truth table method can also be used to examine the bi-conditional of the propositional forms. Propositional forms are equivalent if their truth tables are same.

Illustrated examples:

(1)

(p	⊃	q)	≡	(~	p	v	q)
T	T	T	T	F	T	T	T
T	F	F	T	F	T	F	F
F	T	T	T	T	F	T	T
F	T	F	T	T	F	T	F
1	3	2	8	5	4	7	6

Since the truth tables of both the expressions (column 3 and 7) are same, they are equivalent. The column number 8 contains all Ts which further confirms that both the expressions are bi-conditional.

(2)

(p	⊃	q)	≡	(~	p	•	~	q)
T	T	T	F	F	T	F	F	T
T	F	F	T	F	T	F	T	F
F	T	T	F	T	F	F	F	T
F	T	F	T	T	F	T	T	F
1	3	2	9	5	4	8	7	6

Since the truth tables of both the expressions are different (columns 3 and 8 have different truth tables), the above expressions are not bi-conditional.

(3)

(p	•	q)	≡	(p	v	q)
T	T	T	T	T	T	T
T	F	F	F	T	T	F
F	F	T	F	F	T	T
F	F	F	T	F	F	F
1	3	2	7	4	6	5

Not bi-conditional.

Exercises

1. Use truth table method to find out which of the following propositional forms are tautologous, contingent or self-contradictory:

    1. $p \supset (p \supset q)$
    2. $(p \bullet q) \supset r$
    3. $p \supset (p \vee q)$
    4. $(p \bullet p) \supset p$
    5. $(p \vee p) \supset \sim p$
    6. $p \supset (\sim p \supset \sim q)$
    7. $p \supset (q \supset \sim q)$
    8. $p \supset (q \supset \sim r)$
    9. $(p \vee \sim p) \vee q$
    10. $(p \bullet \sim p) \supset q$
    11. $\sim (p \vee q) \vee \sim r$
    12. $(\sim p \bullet \sim q) \bullet r$
    13. $p \supset \sim (q \supset \sim r)$
    14. $(p \supset q) \supset \sim (p \bullet r)$
    15. $(\sim p \vee q) \supset (\sim p \bullet \sim p)$
    16. $(p \supset q) \supset (\sim p \bullet \sim q)$
    17. $(p \vee \sim p) \supset (p \bullet \sim p)$
    18. $\sim (p \bullet q) \bullet (q \supset p)$
    19. $(p \bullet \sim p) \vee (p \bullet \sim p)$
    20. $[q \equiv (p \supset q)] \supset p$

2. Use truth table method to determine logical status of the following expressions:

    1. $[(p \supset q) \bullet \sim p] \supset \sim q$
    2. $[(p \supset q) \bullet p] \supset q$
    3. $p \supset \sim [p \supset (p \bullet q)]$

4. $[(p \lor q) \supset r] \supset (p \supset r)$
5. $[\sim p \bullet (q \lor r)] \supset (q \lor r)$
6. $\sim [p \supset (q \bullet r)] \lor [(p \lor q) \supset r]$
7. $[(p \supset (q \supset r)] \supset [(p \lor q) \supset r]$
8. $(\sim p \supset \sim r) \supset \sim (\sim p \bullet \sim q)$
9. $p \supset [(p \supset q) \supset (\sim q \lor \sim q)]$
10. $[(p \supset q) \supset (q \sim r)] \supset [p \supset (q \bullet r)]$
11. $[(p \bullet q) \supset r] \lor [\sim p \supset (q \supset r)]$
12. $(p \lor q) \supset [(\sim p \supset r) \bullet (\sim q \supset r)]$
13. $(p \lor q) \supset [(\sim p \bullet r) \lor (\sim q \bullet r)]$
14. $[p \supset (q \supset r)] \supset [(p \bullet q) \supset r]$
15. $[(\sim p \supset \sim q) \supset \sim r] \supset \sim [p \supset (q \supset r)]$
16. $(p \supset q) \supset [(r \supset p) \supset (r \supset q)]$
17. $(p \lor q) \supset [(\sim p \supset r) \bullet (\sim q \bullet r)]$
18. $(p \lor q) \supset [(\sim p \bullet r) \lor (\sim q \lor r)]$
19. $[(p \supset q) \bullet (q \supset r)] \supset (\sim p \lor r)$
20. $(\sim p \equiv q) \equiv [(\sim p \supset q) \bullet (q \supset \sim p)]$

3. Examine by truth table method which of the following are bi-conditional:

1. $(p \supset q) \equiv (\sim p \supset \sim q)$
2. $(p \bullet q) \equiv \sim (p \lor \sim q)$
3. $(\sim p \supset q) \equiv (\sim q \supset p)$
4. $(p \bullet q) \equiv \sim (p \lor q)$
5. $(p \bullet q) \equiv (\sim p \lor \sim q)$
6. $(\sim p \bullet \sim q) \equiv \sim (p \lor q)$
7. $(p \bullet q) \equiv \sim (\sim p \lor \sim q)$
8. $(p \bullet q) \equiv (\sim q \supset \sim p)$
9. $\sim (p \bullet q) \equiv (\sim p \bullet \sim q)$
10. $\sim (p \supset q) \equiv (p \lor q)$

11. $\sim (p \bullet \sim q) \equiv (q \vee \sim p)$
12. $\sim (p \vee q) \equiv (\sim p \bullet \sim q)$
13. $(\sim p \vee q) \equiv \sim (p \bullet q)$
14. $\sim (p \bullet q) \equiv (p \supset q)$
15. $[(p \bullet q) \vee r] \equiv q$
16. $p \equiv [(p \supset (p \bullet q)]$
17. $(p \supset q) \equiv [p \supset (p \supset q)]$
18. $[\sim (p \vee q) \supset r] \equiv \sim (p \vee q)$
19. $\sim (p \vee q) \equiv [(p \vee q) \supset p]$
20. $[(p \bullet (q \vee r)] \equiv \sim r$

Testing the Validity/Invalidity of the Argument Forms and Arguments by Truth Table Method

Whereas a statement form is either tautologous, contingent or self-contradictory, an argument form is evaluated as valid or invalid. In a valid argument form all the premisses jointly imply the conclusion. A valid argument form cannot have all true premisses if the conclusion is false. We can test the validity of arguments and argument forms by truth table method. The procedure of constructing truth table is the same and the logical constants have the same properties.

All the premisses of the argument form are combined by conjunction and conclusion is replaced by '⊃' sign. Look at the following illustrated argument forms:

Example 1:

(1) $p \supset q$

$p \mathbin{/} \therefore q$

is rewritten as

$[(p \supset q) \bullet p] \supset q$

after combining premisses and conclusion.

In this argument form there are two premisses 'p ⊃ q'and 'p'. They together imply the conclusion 'q'.

[(p	⊃	q)	•	p]	⊃	q
T	T	T	T	T	T	T
T	F	F	F	T	T	F
F	T	T	F	F	T	T
F	T	F	F	F	T	F
1	3	2	5	4	7	6

Since the main column (number 7) contains all Ts, hence the above argument form is valid.

Example 2:

p ⊃ q

q ⊃ r / ∴ p

[(p	⊃	q)	•	(q	⊃	r)]	⊃	p
T	T	T	T	T	T	T	T	T
T	T	T	F	T	F	F	T	T
T	F	F	F	F	T	T	T	T
T	F	F	F	F	T	F	T	T
F	T	T	T	T	T	T	F	F
F	T	T	F	T	F	F	T	F
F	T	F	T	F	T	T	F	F
F	T	F	T	F	T	F	F	F
1	3	2	7	4	6	5	9	8

Since the main column (number 9) contains Fs, the above argument form is invalid. One F in the main column makes an argument form invalid.

Example 3:

p • q / ∴ ~ p

There is only one premiss and that premiss does not imply the conclusion. Let us see how:

(p	•	q)	⊃	~	p
T	T	T	F	F	T
T	F	F	T	F	T
F	F	T	T	T	F
F	F	F	T	T	F
1	3	2	6	5	4

Invalid argument form.

Example 4:

(p ⊃ q) / ∴ ~ (~ q ⊃ ~ p)

(p	⊃	q)	⊃	~	(~	q	⊃	~	p)
T	T	T	F	F	F	T	T	F	T
T	F	F	T	T	T	F	F	F	T
F	T	T	F	F	F	T	T	T	F
F	T	F	F	F	T	F	T	T	F
1	3	2	10	9	5	4	8	7	6

Since the main column contains Fs, the above argument form is invalid.

Example 5:

~ (p ⊃ q)

p / ∴ q

[~	(p	⊃	q)	•	p)]	⊃	q
F	T	T	T	F	T	T	T
T	T	F	F	T	T	F	F
F	F	T	T	F	F	T	T
F	F	T	F	F	F	T	F
4	1	3	2	6	5	8	7

Invalid argument form.

Example 6:

p v q

~p / ∴ q

[p	v	q)	•	~	p]	⊃	q
T	T	T	F	F	T	T	T
T	T	F	F	F	T	T	F
F	T	T	T	T	F	T	T
F	F	F	F	T	F	T	F
1	3	2	6	5	4	8	7

Valid argument form.

Example 7:

p ⊃ q

q ⊃ r / ∴ p ⊃ r

[(p	⊃	q)	•	(q	⊃	r)]	⊃	(p	⊃	r)
T	T	T	T	T	T	T	T	T	T	T
T	T	T	F	T	F	F	T	T	F	F
T	F	F	F	F	T	T	T	T	T	T
T	F	F	F	F	T	F	T	T	F	F
F	T	T	T	T	T	T	T	F	T	T
F	T	T	F	T	F	F	T	F	T	F
F	T	F	T	F	T	T	T	F	T	T
F	T	F	T	F	T	F	T	F	T	F
1	3	2	7	4	6	5	11	8	10	9

Valid argument form.

Example 8: If A wins the first prize then either B wins the second prize or C is disappointed. B wins the second prize. Therefore, either C is disappointed or A wins the first prize.

A ⊃ (B v C)

B

∴ C v A

{[A	⊃	(B	v	C)]	•	B}	⊃	(C	v	A)
T	T	T	T	T	T	T	T	T	T	T
T	T	T	T	F	T	T	T	F	T	T
T	T	F	T	T	F	F	T	T	T	T
T	F	F	F	F	F	F	T	F	T	T
F	T	T	T	T	T	T	T	T	T	F
F	T	T	T	F	T	T	F	F	F	F
F	T	F	T	T	F	F	T	T	T	F
F	T	F	F	F	F	F	T	F	F	F
1	5	2	4	3	7	6	11	8	10	9

Invalid argument.

Example 9: If it does not rain, then the harvest will be destroyed and inflation will increase. It is false that if it rains then inflation will increase. The harvest will be destroyed. Therefore, inflation will increase.

~ R ⊃ (D • I)

~(R ⊃ I)

D/ ∴ I

{[~	R	⊃	(D	•	I)]	•	~	(R	⊃	I)	•	D}	⊃	I
F	T	T	T	T	T	F	F	T	T	T	F	T	T	T
F	T	T	T	F	F	T	T	T	F	F	T	T	F	F
F	T	T	F	F	T	F	F	T	T	T	F	F	T	T
F	T	T	F	F	F	T	T	T	F	F	F	F	T	F
T	F	T	T	T	T	F	F	F	T	T	F	T	T	T
T	F	F	T	F	F	F	F	F	T	F	F	T	T	F
T	F	F	F	F	T	F	F	F	T	T	F	F	T	T
T	F	F	F	F	F	F	F	F	T	F	F	F	T	F
2	1	6	3	5	4	11	10	7	9	8	13	12	15	14

Invalid argument.

Example 10: If Mr. X is late, then he will miss the plane. If he misses the plane, then the captain will not be pleased. It is false that either captain is pleased or Mr. X will not miss the plane. Mr. X will miss the plane. Therefore, Mr. X will be late.

Symbolization:

L ⊃ M

M ⊃ ~ P

~ (P v ~ M)

M

∴ L

[(L	⊃	M)	•	(M	⊃	~	P)	•	~	(P	v	~	M)	•	M]	⊃	L
T	T	T	F	T	F	F	T	F	F	T	T	F	T	F	T	T	T
T	T	T	T	T	T	T	F	T	T	F	F	F	T	T	T	T	T
T	F	F	F	F	T	F	T	F	F	T	T	T	F	F	F	T	T
T	F	F	F	F	T	T	F	F	F	F	T	T	F	F	F	T	T
F	T	T	F	T	F	F	T	F	F	T	T	F	T	F	T	T	F
F	T	T	T	T	T	T	F	T	T	F	F	F	T	T	T	F	F
F	T	F	T	F	T	F	T	F	F	T	T	T	F	F	F	T	F
F	T	F	T	F	T	T	F	F	F	F	T	T	F	F	F	T	F
1	3	2	8	4	7	6	5	14	13	9	12	11	10	16	15	18	17

Invalid argument.

Exercises

1. Construct the truth table of the following argument forms and determine their validity/invalidity:

   1. p • q

      p / ∴ q

   2. ~ p ⊃ q

      ~ p / ∴ q

   3. p v q

      ~ p / ∴ ~ q

4. $p \supset q$

   $p \vee r \quad / \therefore (q \vee r)$

5. $\sim (p \supset q)$

   $p \vee r \quad / \therefore q \vee r$

6. $p \supset \sim q$

   $\sim q \supset r \quad / \therefore r \supset \sim p$

7. $(p \supset q)$

   $\sim (q \supset r) \quad / \therefore \sim r$

8. $(p \supset q)$

   $q \vee r \quad / \therefore \sim (p \supset q)$

9. $p \equiv \sim q \quad / \therefore p \supset \sim q$

10. $p \supset (q \bullet r) \;/ \therefore (q \bullet r) \supset \sim p$

11. $\sim p \supset q$

    $\sim r \vee q \quad / \therefore r \supset p$

12. $p \supset q$

    $\sim p \supset r \quad / \therefore q \vee r$

13. $\sim p \supset q$

    $\sim p \vee r \quad / \therefore p \bullet q$

14. $(p \supset q) \bullet (p \supset r) \;/ \therefore q \vee r$

15. $p \supset (q \supset r)$

    $p \supset q \quad / \therefore (p \supset r)$

16. $\sim (p \vee q)$

    $p \supset q \quad / \therefore p \bullet \sim q$

17. $(p \vee q) \supset (p \bullet q)$

    $/ \therefore p \vee q$

18. $p \vee (q \bullet \sim q)$

    $p \supset \sim q \quad / \therefore q \bullet \sim p$

19. $\sim p \supset q$

    $\sim p \supset r$

$\sim r$ $/ \therefore p$

20. $p \supset (q \vee r)$

    $p \supset \sim q$ $/ \therefore p \vee r$

2. Symbolize the following arguments and determine their validity/invalidity by truth table method:
   1. If children do not eat protein, then they do not have powerful bones. But children have powerful bones. Therefore, they eat protein. (P, B)
   2. Either Sachin is a good player or he is lucky. Playing in several test matches implies he is a good player. Hence, he is not lucky. (G, L, T)
   3. If it rains, then Sita drinks tea. If it does not rain, then she takes cold drinks. Therefore, if Sita does not drink tea, then she will take cold drinks. (R, T, C)
   4. If dragons are not fearful of fire, then unicorns are not fighters. It is true that dragons are fearful of fire. Thus, unicorns are fighters. (D, U)
   5. If the football team wins, then it does not boast its victory. If the football team does not win, then it is not ashamed of its defeat. It follows that football team neither boasts its victory nor is ashamed of its defeat. (W, B, A)
   6. If Mohan is late, then he will miss the plane. If he misses the plane, then his boss will not be pleased. Either his boss is pleased or Mohan will not miss the plane. Therefore, Mohan will not be late. (L, M, P)
   7. If peacock is bird and it has feathers, then it is not a mammal. It is false that peacock is bird but does not have feathers. Thus, it implies that peacock is certainly not a mammal.
   8. The Congress party cannot win the election unless it brings down the prices of essential commodities. If the new economic policies are implemented, then the

prices of essential commodities will come down. It follows either the Congress party does not win the election or the new economic policies are not implemented. (W, P, N)

9. Either the police chief does not know the truth or he is hiding something in the interest of country. If he is hiding something in the interest of country, then the Parliament should provide him necessary security. Therefore, it is not the case that the police chief knows the truth and the Parliament will not provide him the necessary security. (K, H, S)

10. If the demand stays constant and the prices are lowered then the business will increase. If the lowering of the prices implies business to increase, then people will be happy. Demand will stay constant. Thus, people will be happy. (D, P, I, H)

Chapter 13

Shorter Truth Table Method (Reductio ad absurdum or Indirect Method)

In the previous chapter you had noticed that the truth table method is an easy and simple decision procedure to test the validity of arguments, and to evaluate the expressions as tautologous. This is a mechanical[1] method and can be applied to a large number of arguments. But sometimes this method becomes very lengthy and it takes long to work it out. When the number of variables are considerably more, the number of rows subsequently increases and the truth table becomes quite big. In order to avoid this, there is another method which is shorter, and can be applied to all those cases where truth table is applicable. This new decision procedure is shorter truth table method or indirect method which is sometimes called *reductio ad absurdum* method also.

In this method we start by assuming that the argument form is invalid. By assuming it to be invalid, if we *do not meet any inconsistency* (while working the entire argument) then that argument form is actually *invalid.* But if by assuming it to be invalid we *do meet* any inconsistency, then the argument form is proved valid. In other words, if the thesis is reduced to absurdity by assuming it to be wrong, then indirectly it is valid. On the

1. The truth table method is a mechanical procedure because there is one fixed *modus operandi* in applyng this method. Whenever the truth method is applied, its procedure is exactly the same. No new strategy has to be formed for evaluating the validity/invalidity of each argument or argument form. In this sense and only in this sense the method is mechanical.

other hand, if the thesis is not reduced to absurdity by assuming it to be wrong, then indirectly it is invalid. The method of *reductio ad absurdum* consists in establishing the truth of a thesis by showing that the consequence of the truth of its contradictory is an inconsistency or self-contradictory.

Shorter truth table method is in a way backward counting of truth table method. In the truth table method one reaches to the main column in the end, but in the shorter truth table method one starts with the main column. The method can best be explained with the help of examples.

Example 1:

6	2	7	1	4	3	5
(p	⊃	q)	⊃	(q	⊃	p)
F	T	T	F	T	F	F

We begin by assuming the argument form to be invalid. It is assumed that there is at least one F in the main column. In the above example, the main column can have F only when the antecedent (p ⊃ q) is true and consequent (q ⊃ p) is false. We can proceed further either from the antecedent or from the consequent. But in the present case, it is better if we proceed with consequent (q ⊃ p), for it is false only in one case (that is when antecedent is true and consequent is false), whereas p ⊃ q is true in three cases. Further q ⊃ p being false means q is true and p is false. We got the value of p as F and q as T. The value of these variables are assigned in p ⊃ q. After assigning these values (in p ⊃ q) we find there is no inconsistency in the expression (p ⊃ q) ⊃ (q ⊃ p). So at least one F under the main column is justified and the argument form is invalid.

Example 2:

p ⊃ q

q / ∴ p

As in the case of truth table method, in shorter truth table method also, all the premisses are combined with conjunction to form the expression like:

6	4	7	2	5	1	3
[(p	⊃	q)	•	q]	⊃	p
F	T	T	T	T	F	F

Invalid argument form.

We start by assuming argument form to be invalid. After assuming it to be invalid, we find no error or inconsistence in working out the entire expression, therefore, the argument form is invalid.

Example 3:

~ (q • p)

~ q / ∴ p

After joining the premisses and the conclusion the argument form is changed into the following expression:

4	8	7	9	2	5	6	1	3
[~	(q	•	p)	•	~	q]	⊃	p
T	F	F	F	T	T	F	F	F

Since there is no inconsistency, no error in assigning the values of variables, therefore, the argument form is invalid.

Example 4:

p ⊃ q

q ⊃ r /∴ p ⊃ r

10	6	11	2	9	7	8	1	4	3	5
[(p	⊃	q)	•	(q	⊃	r]	⊃	(p	⊃	r)
T	T	F	T	F	T	F	F	T	F	F
	F									
	12									

We started by assuming the entire argument form as invalid. From p ⊃ r we got the values of p and r as T, F respectively. By substituting the value of r in q ⊃ r, we got q as F. By substituting the values of variables p, q, (p ⊃ q) becomes false whereas it had to be true according to our assumption. How can the same expression (p ⊃ q) be true and false together? Thus, there is inconsistency, and this inconsistency is because of assuming F under the main column. The inconsistency can be removed if there is no F under the main column. Therefore, the argument form is valid.

Note: In q ⊃ r, q can only be F, for 'q ⊃ r' is T and since value of r is F, q can only be F.

Indirect method or *reductio ad absurdum* method when applied to arguments or argument form is a complete decision procedure. It can evaluate an argument form as valid or invalid. One F under the main column justifies the invalidity of the argument form, and no F under the main column means argument form is valid.

Let us now apply the method to a statement form in order to evaluate whether they are tautologous or not. The procedure here is exactly the same as we have done in the case of argument forms.

Example 1:

7	9	8	2	10	12	11	1	3	5	4	6
{(p	⊃	q)	•	(q	⊃	r)}	•	~	(p	⊃	r)
T	T	T	F	T	F	F	F	T	T	F	F

Since there is no error, no inconsistency in assuming one F under the main column, therefore, the statement form is *not tautologous*.

But a non-tautologous expression can be either contingent or self-contradictory. How do, then, we know whether the above expression is contingent or self-contradictory? There is a way to do it. Let us see how it can be done. We will assume the expression has at least one T in the main column instead of F[2].

2. The process is same whether we substitute T or F under the main column. By assuming either T or F if no inconsistency is met then the assumption (whether T or F) is correct.

9	7	10	2	11	8	12	1	3	5	4	6
{(p	⊃	q)	•	(q	⊃	r)}	•	~	(p	⊃	r)
T	T	T	T	T	T	F	T	T	T	F	F
					F						
					13						

By keeping one T in the main column there is inconsistency in working out (q ⊃ r). So the main column cannot have even one T. Hence, the above expression cannot be contingent; it is self-contradictory.

Example 2:

2	1	4	3	6	5	8	7
p	⊃	[p	⊃	(q	•	~	q)]
T	F	T	F	T	F	F	T

Since no inconsistency, no error, so the above expression is not tautology.

Now to prove whether it is contingent or self-contradictory, we will apply the method of *reductio ad absurdum* once again but instead of assuming F under the main column, we will assume one T.

2	1	4	3	6	5	7	8
p	⊃	[p	⊃	(q	•	~	q)]
F	T	F	T	T	F	F	T

By keeping one T under the main column no inconsistency is found, so the above expression has at least one T in the main column. The above expression thus is *contingent.*

Let us confirm this by truth table method:

1	8	2	7	3	6	5	4
p	⊃	[p	⊃	(q	•	~	q)]
T	F	T	F	T	F	F	T
T	F	T	F	F	F	T	F
F	T	F	T	T	F	F	T
F	T	F	T	F	F	T	F

The above expression is further confirmed contingent by applying truth table.

When an expression is proved non-tautologous by *reductio ad absurdum* method, then to determine whether that non-tautologous expression is contingent or self-contradictory, once again the *reductio ad absurdum* method is to be applied. But now instead of assuming the expression to be false, it is assumed to be true. By the same mechanism, if by substituting T in the main column, no inconsistency is met, then it means at least one T is justified in the main column, and hence the expression is contingent.

Exercises

1. Examine by shorter truth table method which of the following expressions are tautologous:

   1. (p ⊃ q) ⊃ (p v q)
   2. (p • q) ⊃ (p ⊃ q)
   3. (p v q) ⊃ (p ⊃ ~ q)
   4. (p • q) ⊃ (~ q ⊃ p)
   5. (p v q) ⊃ ~(p • q)
   6. (p v q) v (~ p ⊃ ~ q)
   7. (p • q) v (~ p ⊃ ~ q)
   8. (p ≡ q) ⊃ (~ p v ~ q)
   9. (p ⊃ q) ⊃ ~ (p • ~ q)
   10. (~ p • q) v ~ (~ q • ~ p)

11. $(p \vee \sim q) \supset \sim (p \bullet q)$
12. $(\sim p \supset \sim q) \supset \sim (p \bullet \sim q)$
13. $\sim (p \vee q) \supset (p \supset q)$
14. $\sim (p \supset q) \supset \sim (p \vee q)$
15. $p \supset (p \equiv q)$

2. Examine by shorter truth table method which of the following expressions are tautologous:
   1. $[(p \supset q) \bullet (q \supset r)] \supset (p \supset r)$
   2. $(p \supset q) \supset [(r \supset p) \supset (r \supset q)]$
   3. $(p \supset q) \supset [(q \supset r) \supset (p \supset r)]$
   4. $[(p \supset q) \supset r] \supset [(p \supset q) \supset (p \supset r)]$
   5. $[p \supset (q \supset r)] \supset [(p \supset q) \supset (p \supset r)]$
   6. $(p \supset q) \supset [(\sim p \supset r) \supset (p \supset (q \supset r))]$
   7. $[(p \bullet q) \supset r] \supset [p \supset (q \supset r)]$
   8. $[(p \supset q) \supset r] \supset (p \supset r)$
   9. $[p \supset (q \bullet r)] \supset [(p \supset q) \supset r]$
   10. $[p \supset (q \bullet r)] \supset [p \supset (q \supset r)]$
   11. $[(p \vee q) \supset p] \supset \sim q$
   12. $[p \supset (q \supset r)] \supset [(p \bullet q) \supset r]$
   13. $[(p \supset q) \supset r] \supset [p \supset (q \supset r)]$
   14. $[(p \supset q) \bullet (r \supset s) \bullet (p \vee r)] \supset (q \supset s)$
   15. $[(p \supset q) \supset r] \supset [\sim p \supset (\sim q \supset \sim r)]$

3. Examine by *reductio ad absurdum* method the validity/invalidity of the following argument forms:
   1. $p \supset q \quad / \therefore q \supset \sim p$
   2. $\sim (p \vee q) \quad / \therefore \sim (p \bullet \sim q)$
   3. $p \supset q$

      $p \vee q \quad / \therefore \sim (p \bullet q)$

4. $p \supset q$

   $\sim q$ / $\therefore p \supset r$

5. $p \vee q$ / $\therefore \sim(\sim p \bullet \sim q)$

6. $p \supset q$

   $\sim q$ / $\therefore \sim p \vee q$

7. $p \supset q$

   $\sim p$ / $\therefore \sim q$

8. $p \supset q$ / $\therefore (q \bullet q) \supset \sim p$

9. $p \supset (q \supset r)$ / $\therefore (p \bullet q) \supset r$

10. $p \supset q$

    $q \supset r$ / $\therefore \sim p \vee r$

11. $(p \vee q) \supset \sim r$ / $\therefore r$

12. $p \vee \sim q$

    $p \bullet q$ / $\therefore \sim(p \supset q)$

13. $p \supset q$ / $\therefore (\sim p \vee q) \vee r$

14. $p \supset q$

    $p \supset r$ / $\therefore p \vee r$

15. $\sim p \supset q$

    $q \supset r$ / $\therefore \sim r \supset \sim p$

4. Examine by shorter truth table method the validity/invalidity of the following argument forms:

   1. $p \supset (q \supset r)$

      $p \supset q$ / $\therefore p \supset r$

   2. $p \supset (q \supset r)$

      $r \supset \sim p$ / $\therefore r \supset \sim q$

   3. $(p \supset q) \supset r$

      $p \vee q$ / $\therefore q \vee r$

   4. $(p \supset q) \supset r$

      $\sim r$ / $\therefore \sim p \vee q$

5. $(p \supset q)$

   $q \supset r \qquad / \therefore p \vee r$

6. $p \supset \sim q$

   $p \vee r$

   $r \equiv p \qquad / \therefore \sim (p \bullet q)$

7. $p \supset (q \supset r)$

   $p \supset q \qquad / \therefore p \supset r$

8. $p \supset (q \supset r)$

   $q \supset (p \supset r) \; / \therefore (p \bullet q) \supset r$

9. $p \supset (q \supset r)$

   $r \supset \sim p \qquad / \therefore r \supset \sim q$

10. $p \supset q$

    $r \supset t$

    $p \vee r \qquad / \therefore q \vee t$

11. $q \supset (p \bullet r)$

    $r \supset \sim q \qquad / \therefore q \vee \sim r$

12. $p \equiv q$

    $q \equiv (r \bullet p)$

    $p \qquad / \therefore r \bullet p$

13. $p \supset (q \bullet \sim r)$

    $(\quad q \vee r) \supset t$

    $p \qquad / \therefore t$

14. $(p \vee q) \supset (p \bullet q)$

    $\sim p \supset \sim q \quad / \therefore \sim (p \bullet q)$

15. $(p \bullet q) \supset r$

    $\sim r \qquad / \therefore \sim (\sim p \vee \sim q)$

Chapter 14

Formal Proof of Validity

FORMAL proof of validity is a decision procedure. But it is a half decision procedure because if we are able to construct a formal proof, then that argument is valid. But if, on the other hand, we are not able to construct its formal proof, then either the argument is invalid or we are not able to construct its formal proof. It is quite possible that the argument is valid but we are not able to form its formal validity. It is also possible that the argument may, in fact, be invalid and in that case howsoever hard we may try we can never construct its formal proof of validity. For the invalid arguments formal proof of validity can never be constructed. Thus there is a need for another decision procedure which can establish its validity or invalidity for sure.

Let us see how formal proof of validity is constructed. Constructing a formal proof of validity is like solving a puzzle. It is like a rat chasing cheese and it is a detective's hunt to solve mystery. In order to reach the target, one has to form a strategy. The detective too makes a planning to achieve the targeted aim.

Formal proof of validity is *not* a mechanical process. Unlike truth table method or any other decision procedure, the formal proof of validity does not have fixed *modus operandi*. Each argument needs different strategy. There is no master strategy which can solve all the mysteries. A swimmer negotiates each and every wave while swimming even though he is efficient swimmer. A driver also has to manipulate each turn while driving a vehicle. A good batsman assesses and examines each and every ball he faces. Each ball is challenge to him. Similarly in order to construct formal proof of validity one has to treat every argument differently.

There are nine Rules of Inference (and ten Rules of Replacement*) which help in constructing formal proof of validity. These rules are tautological and hence are valid forever. They are self-evident and thus are the basis of validity though they themselves are beyond proof. A set of nine rules serves like *tool kit* in constructing formal proof of validity.

In formal proof of validity some premisses are given and on that basis, conclusion is deduced with the help of these **Rules**. It resembles the geometrical process where in order to prove a certain theorem, the geometrician begins with certain given facts and axioms. He *starts* with some given statements and with the help of certain self-evident rules, he *deduces* the conclusion. This method is called *Deductive Method*. Thus within a defined system, a geometrical theorem is formally proved valid. Exactly in the same way in the formal proof of validity certain premisses are *given* and with the help of Rules of Inference conclusion is drawn from them.

The nine *Rules of Inference* are as follows:

Modus Ponens (M.P.)

$$\begin{array}{c} p \supset q \\ p \\ \hline \therefore q \end{array}$$

Modus Ponens means affirming the antecedent and on that basis affirming the consequent.

For example, the following two arguments are valid by this rule:

(i) If Ram is graduate, then he is eligible for the job.

Ram is graduate.

∴ He is eligible for the job.

---

* This book deals only with the Rules of Inference.

(ii) If I stay in the city, then I will have no peace of mind.
I stay in the city.
∴ I will have no peace of mind.

All the following are *valid* forms of Modus Ponens:

(i) $p \supset q$
p
$\therefore q$

(ii) $\sim p \supset \sim q$
$\sim p$
$\therefore \sim q$

(iii) $(p \cdot q) \supset r$
$p \cdot q$
$\therefore r$

All the following are *invalid* forms of Modus Ponens:

(i) $\sim p \supset q$
p
$\therefore q$

(ii) $p \supset q$
$\sim p$
$\therefore \sim q$

Modus Tollens (M.T.)

$$\begin{array}{c} p \supset q \\ \sim q \\ \hline \therefore \sim p \end{array}$$

Modus Tollens means denying the consequent and hence denying the antecedent. For example, the following arguments are valid by Modus Tollens:

(i) If it rains, then we shall go for picnic.
We shall not go for picnic.
∴ It does not rain.

(ii) If there is storm tonight, then the nights will be cool.
The nights are not cool.
∴ There is no storm tonight.

(iii) If I win the case, then I will not have to pay penalty.
I pay the penalty.
∴ I will not win the case.

All the following are *valid* forms of Modus Tollens:

(i)
$$\frac{\begin{array}{c} p \supset q \\ \sim q \end{array}}{\therefore \sim p}$$

(ii)
$$\frac{\begin{array}{c} p \supset \sim q \\ q \end{array}}{\therefore \sim p}$$

(iii)
$$\frac{\begin{array}{c} p \supset (q \bullet r) \\ \sim (q \bullet r) \end{array}}{\therefore \sim p}$$

All the following are *invalid* forms of Modus Tollens:

(i)
$$\frac{\begin{array}{c} \sim p \supset q \\ q \end{array}}{\therefore \sim p}$$

(ii)
$$\frac{\begin{array}{c} p \supset \sim q \\ \sim q \end{array}}{\therefore \sim p}$$

Disjunctive Syllogism (D.S.)

$$\frac{\begin{array}{c} p \vee q \\ \sim p \end{array}}{\therefore q}$$

In Disjunctive Syllogism two options are given. If one option is denied then the other option is to be accepted. For example, the following arguments are valid because of Disjunctive Syllogism.

(i) Either the support is strong or we lose the election.
The support is not strong.

∴ We loose the election.

(ii) Either we play football or we eat hat dogs.
We will not play football.

∴ We eat hot dogs.

Yet another example:

(iii) Either he is fool or he is knave.
He is not fool.

∴ He is knave.

All the following are *valid* forms of disjunctive syllogism:

(i) $p \vee q$
$\sim p$

$\therefore q$

(ii) $\sim p \vee q$
p

$\therefore q$

(iii) $\sim p \vee \sim q$
p

$\therefore \sim q$

(iv) $(p \bullet q) \vee r$
$\sim (p \bullet q)$

$\therefore r$

All the following are *invalid* forms of Disjunctive Syllogism:

(i) $p \vee q$
p

$\therefore \sim q$

(ii) $\sim p \vee q$
$\sim p$

$\therefore \sim q$

(iii) $\sim p \vee q$

$\sim p$

$\therefore q$

(iv) $\sim p \vee \sim q$

$\sim p$

$\therefore q$

(v) $p \vee q$

q

$\therefore \sim p$

Hypothetical Syllogism (H.S.)

$$\begin{array}{c} p \supset q \\ q \supset r \\ \hline \therefore p \supset r \end{array}$$

In this rule of inference both the premisses are conditional statements and they have one common component. The common component is antecedent in one premiss and consequent in another premiss. It can best be understood with the help of examples:

(i) If she studies humanities, then she prepares to earn a good living.

If she prepares to earn a good living, then her college days are well spent.

∴ If she studies humanities, then her college days are well spent.

(ii) If x is a politician, then x is interested in securing votes.

If x is interested in securing votes, then x must be attentive to the needs of the people.

∴ If x is a politician, then x must be attentive to the needs of the people.

The following are *valid* forms of Hypothetical Syllogism:

(i) $p \supset q$

$q \supset r$

$\therefore p \supset r$

(ii) $q \supset r$

$p \supset q$

$\therefore p \supset r$

(iii) $p \supset \sim q$

$\sim q \supset r$

$\therefore p \supset r$

(iv) $\sim p \supset \sim q$

$\sim q \supset \sim r$

$\therefore \sim p \supset \sim r$

The following are *invalid* forms of Hypothetical Syllogism:

(i) $p \supset q$

$r \supset q$

$\therefore p \supset r$

(ii) $p \supset q$

$p \supset r$

$\therefore q \supset r$

(iii) $p \supset q$

$p \supset r$

$\therefore r \supset q$

The rule states that in the Hypothetical Syllogism the common term should be antecedent in one premiss and consequent in the other premiss.

Constructive Dilemma (C.D.)

$$(p \supset q) \bullet (r \supset s)$$

$$p \vee r$$

$$\therefore q \vee s$$

Every dilemma has two conditional propositions (as its major premiss). In the Constructive Dilemma the major premiss is one having two different antecedents, both leading to the different consequent. Look at the following examples:

(i) If a man is rationalist, then he must forgo the enjoyment of many pleasures; and if he is a hedonist, he must often neglect his duty. A man is either a rationalist or a hedonist.

∴ Either he will forgo the enjoyment of many pleasures or he must often neglect his duty.

Look at another famous example of Constructive Dilemma:

(ii) If I do justice then God will love me and if I am unjust then politician will love me.

Either I do justice or I am unjust.

∴ Either God will love me or politician will love me.

All the following are *valid* forms of Constructive Dilemma:

(i) $(p \supset q) \bullet (r \supset s)$

$p \vee r$

$\therefore q \vee s$

(ii) $(\sim p \supset q) \bullet (\sim r \supset s)$

$\sim p \vee \sim r$

$\therefore q \vee s$

All the following are *invalid* forms of Constructive Dilemma:

(i) $(p \supset q) \bullet (r \supset s)$

$q \vee s$

$\therefore p \vee r$

(ii) $(p \supset q) \bullet (r \supset s)$

$p \vee s$

$\therefore q \vee r$

Conjunction (Conj.)

$$\frac{\begin{array}{c} p \\ q \end{array}}{\therefore p \bullet q}$$

This rule states that all the premisses are joint together by using Conjunction. This device we had used earlier also in Truth Table Method and Shorter Truth Table Method. This rule can be expanded. See the following example:

$$\frac{\begin{array}{c} p \\ q \\ r \end{array}}{\therefore p \bullet q \bullet r}$$

Simplification (Simp.)

$$\frac{p \bullet q}{\therefore p}$$

This rule is just the opposite of the earlier rule. If in the premiss Conjunction is the main sign, then the *first conjunction* can be inferred.

Following are *valid* forms of simplification:

(i) $\frac{p \bullet q}{\therefore p}$

(ii) $\frac{\sim p \bullet q}{\therefore \sim p}$

(iii) $\frac{(p \vee q) \bullet r}{\therefore p \vee q}$

Following are *invalid* forms of simplification:

(i) $\frac{(p \bullet q) \vee r}{\therefore p}$

(ii) $\frac{p \supset (q \bullet r)}{\therefore q}$

Addition (Add.)

$$\frac{p}{\therefore p \vee q}$$

This rule states one can add any variable or variables to the premiss with the help of wedge (v). The following are *valid* forms of Addition:

(i) $$\frac{p}{\therefore p \vee q}$$

(ii) $$\frac{p}{p \vee (q \bullet r)}$$

(iii) $$\frac{p}{\therefore p \vee \sim p}$$

(iv) $$\frac{p}{\therefore p \vee (q \vee (p \bullet r))}$$

The following are *invalid* forms of Addition:

(i) $$\frac{p}{\therefore p \bullet (q \vee p)}$$

(ii) $$\frac{p}{\therefore p \supset (p \vee r)}$$

Absorption (Abs.)

$$\frac{p \supset q}{\therefore p \supset (p \bullet q)}$$

In this rule, consequent carries (and absorbes) antecedent in the conclusion as stated above.

SOME SOLVED EXAMPLES

Construct Formal Proof of validity of the following argument forms and arguments:

(i)

1	$p \supset q$	
2	$q \supset s$	
3	p	$/ \therefore s$
4	$p \supset s$	1st and 2nd by H.S.
5	s	4th and 3rd by M.P.

(ii)

1	$N \supset M$	
2	$M \supset D$	
3	$M \supset P$	
4	$\sim P$	
5	$N \vee M$	$/ \therefore D$
6	$\sim M$	3rd and 4th by M.T.
7	$\sim N$	1st and 6th by M.T.
8	M	5th and 7th by D.S.
9	D	2nd and 8th by M.P.

(iii)

1	$(p \vee q) \supset r$	
2	$s \vee p$	
3	$\sim s$	$/ \therefore r$
4	p	2nd and 3rd by D.S.
5	$p \vee q$	4th by Add.
6	r	1st and 5th by M.P.

(iv)

1	$p \supset q$	
2	$r \supset s$	
3	$p \vee r$	
4	$(q \vee s) \supset t$	$/ \therefore t$
5	$(p \supset q) \bullet (r \supset s)$	1st and 2nd by Conj.
6	$q \vee s$	5th and 3rd by C.D.
7	t	4th and 6th by M.P.

(v)

1	$p \supset q$	
2	$q \supset r$	
3	$\sim p \supset (s \vee t)$	
4	$\sim r$	$/ \therefore s \vee t$
5	$p \supset r$	1st and 2nd by H.S.
6	$\sim p$	5th and 4th by M.T.
7	$s \vee t$	3rd and 6th by M.P.

(vi)
1 ~ P v (I v E)
2 P • R
3 ~ I — / ∴ E
4 P — 2nd by Simp.
5 I v E — 1st and 4th by D.S.
6 E — 5th and 3rd by D.S.

(vii)
1 p ⊃ ~ q
2 ~ q ⊃ r
3 r ⊃ s
4 (p • s) ⊃ u — / ∴ p ⊃ u
5 p ⊃ r — 1st and 2nd by H.S.
6 p ⊃ s — 5th and 3rd by H.S.
7 p ⊃ (p • s) — 6th by Abs.
8 p ⊃ u — 7th and 4th by H.S.

(viii)
1 p ⊃ q
2 q ⊃ (s v r)
3 r ⊃ t
4 t ⊃ u
5 s ⊃ y
6 p
7 ~ y — / ∴ u
8 p ⊃ (s v r) — 1st and 2nd by H.S.
9 s v r — 8th and 6th by M.P.
10 ~ s — 5th and 7th by M.T.
11 r — 9th and 10th by D.S.
12 r ⊃ u — 3rd and 4th by H.S.
13 u — 12th and 11th by M.P.

(ix) If it rains in time, there will be good crops. If there is good crops, then prices of essential commodities will not increase. It rains in time. Therefore the prices of essential commodities will not increase.

1 R ⊃ C
2 C ⊃ ~ I

3 R $/ \therefore \sim I$

4 C 1st and 3rd by M.P.

5 ~ I 2nd and 4th by M.P.

(x) If the students protest hike in fees then either the college will withdraw extra facilities or the government will have to spend more. The students will protest hike in fees. The college will not withdraw extra facilities. Therefore the government will have to spend more.

1 $S \supset (F \vee G)$

2 S

3 ~ F $/ \therefore G$

4 F v G 1st and 2nd by M.P.

5 G 4th and 3rd by D.S.

Exercises

1. Construct formal proof of validity for each of the following argument forms by adding 1 step more.

1. $p \bullet q$ $/ \therefore p$
2. p $/ \therefore p \vee q$
3. $\sim p \supset q$
   $\sim p$ $/ \therefore q$
4. $(p \supset q) \supset r$
   $\sim r$ $/ \therefore \sim (p \supset q)$
5. $p \supset q$
   $q \supset \sim r$ $/ \therefore p \supset \sim r$
6. $\sim p \supset q$
   $\sim p$ $/ \therefore q$
7. $(\sim s \supset t) \supset (\sim t \supset s)$
   $\sim s \supset t$ $/ \therefore \sim t \supset s$
8. $p \supset (q \equiv r)$
   $(q \equiv r) \supset s$ $/ \therefore p \supset s$

9. $\sim s \supset t$

   $t \supset \sim s$ $\quad / \therefore \sim s \supset \sim s$

10. $(\sim p \supset \sim q) \bullet (r \supset s)$

    $\sim p \vee r$ $\quad / \therefore \sim q \vee s$

2. Construct formal proof of validity for each of the following argument forms by adding 2 steps more.

   1. $p \supset q$

      p $\quad / \therefore q \vee s$

   2. $p \supset q$

      $p \bullet q$ $\quad / \therefore q$

   3. $p \supset q$

      $q \supset s$

      p $\quad / \therefore s$

   4. $(p \vee q) \supset r$

      p $\quad / \therefore r$

   5. $p \supset q$

      $q \supset r$

      $r \supset s$ $\quad / \therefore p \supset s$

   6. $p \supset q$

      $q \supset \sim r$

      r $\quad / \therefore \sim p$

   7. $p \supset (q \bullet r)$

      $r \supset \sim (q \bullet r)$

      r $\quad / \therefore \sim p$

   8. $p \supset q$

      $r \vee p$

      $\sim r$ $\quad / \therefore q$

   9. $p \supset q$

$q \supset r$
$\sim r \qquad / \therefore \sim p$

10. $\sim p \supset \sim q$
$q \vee r$
$\sim p \qquad / \therefore r$

11. $p \supset (q \vee r)$
p
$\sim q \qquad / \therefore r$

12. $p \supset q$
$q \supset r$
$\sim r \qquad / \therefore \sim p$

13. $p \supset (q \vee r)$
$s \supset p$
$s \qquad / \therefore q \vee r$

14. $p \supset \sim q$
$\sim q \supset r \qquad / \therefore p \supset (p \bullet r)$

15. $\sim p \supset q$
$\sim p$
$\sim r \supset \sim q \qquad / \therefore \sim \sim r$

16. $p \supset (q \supset r)$
p
$\sim r \qquad / \therefore \sim q$

17. $p \supset (p \bullet q)$
$\sim (p \bullet q) \qquad / \therefore \sim p \vee s$

18. $(p \supset q) \bullet (r \supset s)$
$s \supset (p \vee r)$
$s \qquad / \therefore q \vee s$

19. $(p \supset q) \bullet (r \supset s)$

$p \vee r$

$\sim q \qquad / \therefore s$

20. $r \vee [\, q \supset (p \supset s)]$

$\sim r$

$q \qquad / \therefore p \supset s$

3. Construct formal proof of validity of the following argument forms by adding three steps:

1. $p \supset q$

$q \supset r$

$r \supset s \qquad / \therefore p \supset t$

$s \supset t$

2. $(p \bullet q) \supset \sim s$

$\sim s \supset t$

$r \vee \sim t \qquad / \therefore \sim (p \bullet q)$

$\sim r$

3. $p \vee (\, q \bullet r)$

$r \supset \sim q \qquad / \therefore \sim r$

$\sim p$

4. $(p \supset q) \bullet (s \supset t)$

$r \vee p$

$\sim r \qquad / \therefore q$

5. $q \vee p$

$r \vee \sim p$

$\sim q$

$\sim r \qquad / p \bullet \sim p$

6. $p \vee \sim q$

$r \supset q$

$\sim r \supset s$

$\sim p \qquad / \therefore s$

7. $p \supset q$

   $q \supset \sim r$

   $r \vee s \qquad / \therefore s$

   p

8. $p \supset q$

   $q \supset r$

   $s \vee \sim r$

   $\sim s \qquad / \therefore \sim p$

9. $p \vee \sim \sim q$

   $\sim p$

   $r \supset \sim q \qquad / \therefore \sim r \vee t$

10. $p \supset (q \supset r)$

    $p \bullet t$

    $r \supset s \qquad / \therefore q \supset s$

4. Construct formal proof of validity of the following arguments and argument forms by adding four or more steps:

   1. $[(p \vee q) \bullet (r \vee s)] \supset t$

      p

      $r \qquad / \therefore t$

   2. $p \supset (q \bullet r)$

      $q \supset (s \supset p)$

      $p \qquad / \therefore s \supset (s \bullet p)$

   3. $p \supset q$

      $q \supset r$

      $r \supset s$

      $p \vee q \qquad / \therefore q \vee t$

      $\sim s$

   4. $(F \bullet \sim T) \supset G$

$U \supset F$

$B \supset \sim T$

U

$B \qquad / \supset \therefore G$

5. $C \supset D$

$E \vee \sim D$

$\sim E \bullet A$

$(A \bullet \sim B) \supset C$

$(A \bullet \sim B) \vee B \qquad / \therefore B$

5. Construct formal proof of validity of the following arguments:

   1. If the market drops, Simon will borrow more money. Simon does not borrow more money. Therefore, the market does not drop (M, B).

   2. If the witness is honest, he will speak truth. He is known to be honest person. Therefore, he will speak truth (W, S).

   3. If there is a drought, then grain will be dearer. Grains will not be dearer. Therefore, there is no drought (D, G).

   4. If the support is not strong, then we do not win the election. The support is not strong. Therefore, we do not win the election (S, E).

   5. If we are aggressive, then we are accused of hostile acts and if we are passive, then we are threatened by disaster. Either we are aggressive or we are passive. Therefore, either we are accused of hostile acts or we are threatened by disaster (A, H, P, T).

   6. If a man goes to university, then he has a chance to develop his natural intelligence. If a man has inquisitive mind, then he will go to university. He never got a chance to develop his natural intelligence.

Therefore, either he does not have inquisitive mind or he was not lucky (G, D, I, L).

7. If a manager makes an important decision, then if he wants to implement it, then he must be courageous. The manager makes an important decision. It is false that the manager is courageous. Therefore, the manager will not implement his decision (M, I, C).
8. A doctor cannot diagnose the disease, unless he has experience in the tropics. If the doctor has experience in the tropics, then the patient will not be very ill. The doctor can diagnose the disease. Therefore, the patient will not be very ill (D, T, L).
9. If the minority is not willing to accept the majority decision, there can be no democracy. If the majority does not respect the rights of the minority, then minority will not be willing to accept the majority decision. The majority does not respect the rights of the minority. Therefore, there cannot be democracy (W, D, R).
10. If taxes rise, then the cost of living rises, and if inflation continues, then wages are permitted to rise. Either the taxes rise or the inflation continues. The cost of living will not rise. If wages are permitted to rise, then the public will not be agitated. Therefore, neither the cost of living will rise nor the public will be agitated (T, L, I, W, A).

Chapter 15 — Section A

Predicate Calculus

GEORGE BOOLE in the mid-nineteenth century was the first logician to start calculus in logic. In the *Mathematical Analysis of Logic* and *An Investigation of the Laws of Thought*, he has given the precise idea of logical calculus. His logic of algebra can be divided into two parts: the calculus of classes and the calculus of proposition. So far what you have read in the previous few chapters of this book was a part of propositional calculus.

In propositional calculus proposition is taken as basic unit. In this branch of knowledge, subject matter of a proposition is not considered. The logicians are concerned only with the essential features common to all the propositions, namely truth and falsehood. These twin values are usually called truth-values. In the propositional calculus, logicians focus on the various combinations of simple propositions. Since atomic or simple proposition is the smallest unit, they can be combined in various ways. This process makes truth functionally compound propositions such as 'p • q', 'p v q', 'p ⊃ q', 'p ≡ q', etc. possible about which you have already read in the previous chapters.

There are, however, certain limitations of the propositional calculus. While symbolizing the propositions, their qualities (affirmation or negation) are shown whereas the quantities (universality or particularity) of the propositions are not made explicit. For example, all the following propositions.

1a. All voters are citizens.

1b. Some voters are citizens.

1c. Ram being a voter is citizen.

are symbolized as C as if they are same. But we all know they are different. Whereas (1a) is A proposition, (1b) is I proposition and (1c) is singular proposition.

Take another example. Both of the following propositions

2a. All men are wise
 and
2b. Some men are wise

are symbolized as M. But the above two propositions are different because whereas (2a) is universal affirmative A proposition, (2b) is particular affirmative I proposition.

Similarly,

3a. No man is perfect
 and
3b. Some men are not perfect

are treated symbolized as ~ P.

But the above two propositions are different because the former proposition is E and the latter is O.

Thus, in order to make this point clear another calculus was introduced which is called **Predicate Calculus,** sometimes it is referred as **Propositional Function.** This new calculus makes the "internal structure" of the propositions clear. Both qualities (affirmation and negation) and quantities (universality and particularity) of the propositions are made clear. Predicate calculus gives more information about the internal structure of the propositions.

In the predicate calculus, as the name suggests, weightage is given to the predicates of the propositions. The predicate may be assigned to the subject (affirmative propositions) or it may be denied to the subject (negative propositions). Also the predicate may be assigned (or denied) to all members such as in universal propositions; or to some members like particular propositions; or to a singular object like singular proposition.

It also further reveals that same predicate is assigned to two different subjects such as in the proposition "Ram and Mohan both are students of this college"; or different predicates are assigned to the same subject like in the proposition "Ram is intelligent and he is hard-working." In predicate calculus, subject and predicate of a proposition are viewed as properties, characteristics or attributes. For example: "All men are mortal" is analysed as: If there is a thing which has the characteristics of a man, then it necessarily has the property of being mortal. The proposition "All leaves are green," suggests that the quality of green is a 'part' of the quality of leaves. This statement in the predicate calculus is explained as: "If a thing is leaf, then it has the property of being green." Here the **logicians are not concerned with characteristics but with the things that have characteristics.**

But at the same time it is wrong to think that predicate calculus is totally different from propositional calculus. Rather the predicate calculus takes many things from the propositional calculus; but it goes beyond Predicate calculus gives more information about the "internal structure" of the propositions. Basson and O' Connor states:

> We may thus regard the calculus of predicate as a branch of logic which includes not only the calculus of proposition but also goes beyond it. It includes it in the sense that, if any formula is valid in the calculus of proposition, the corresponding predicate formula will be valid in the predicate calculus. And goes beyond it in the sense that it makes the **structure** of its propositional material more explicit. And because of this it is able to deal with forms of argument which, on account of their complexity, are beyond the scope of the propositional calculus.[1]

The basic symbols frequently used in the predicate calculus are as follows:

1. 'x', 'y', 'z' are individual variables.

---

1. A.H. Basson, and D.J. O'Connor, *Introduction to Symbolic Logic*, p. 107.

2. 'a', 'b', 'c' are individual constants for proper names.
3. 'F', 'G', 'H' stand for predicates, characteristics and attributes.
4. The auxiliary for a universal proposition is small x within parentheses like it (x). It is read as "for all values of x"...
5. The auxiliary symbol for a particular proposition is (∃ x) and it is read as "there is at least one object x such that"...

Let us see how the categorical propositions are analysed and symbolized in the predicate calculus.

Universal affirmative A proposition "All cats are mammals" is analysed as:

⇒ (Whatever x may be) (If x is cat then it is mammal)

⇒ (x) (If x is C, then x is M)

⇒ (x) (Cx ⊃ Mx)

(x) stands for the universal quantity of the proposition. All universal propositions are symbolized by using the (x) or equivalent like (y), etc. which is known as Universal Quantifier, because it reveals universal quantity of the proposition.

E proposition "No child is voter" is analysed and symbolized as:

⇒ (Whatever x may be) (If x is a child then x is not a voter)

⇒ (x) (If x is a child, then x is not a voter)

⇒ (x) (If x is C, then x is ~V)

⇒ (x) (Cx ⊃ ~ Vx)

Turning now to particular propositions which are also called existential propositions, let us begin with 'I' proposition:

"Some students are Indian."

⇒ (There is something x) (This x is a student and this x is Indian)

⇒ (∃x) (This x is S and This x is I)

⇒ (∃x) (Sx • Ix)

'∃x' is read as 'Ex' and is called existential quantifier. It represents particular propositions and in modern logic particular propositions are called existential propositions because they have existential import.

Proposition 'O' "Some students are not voters" is analysed and symbolized in the similar way such as:

⇒ (There is something x) (This x is a student and this x is not a voter)

⇒ (∃x) (This x is S and This x is not V)

⇒ $(\exists x)\ (Sx \bullet \sim Vx)$

The traditional four categorical propositions, A, E, I and O in the predicate calculus are symbolized as:

A: All S in P

⇒ $(x)\ (Sx \supset Px)$

E: No S is P

⇒ $(x)\ (Sx \supset \sim Px)$

I: Some S is P

⇒ $(\exists x)\ (Sx \bullet Px)$

O: Some S is not P

⇒ $(\exists x)\ (Sx \bullet \sim Px)$

The above symbolization brings out clearly the internal structure of the propositions. Both quantities and qualities of the propositions are made explicit. At the same time more information is given about the characteristics whether they are applied to the same individual or to different people.

The traditional four categorical propositions are symbolized in many ways in the history of logic from time to time. Look at the following four different ways in which these propositions are symbolized.

Proposition	*Traditional Accounts*	*George Boole*	*Venn Diagram*	*Predicate Calculus*
A	All S is P	$S\bar{P} = 0$		$(x)(Sx \supset Px)$
E	No S is P	$SP = 0$	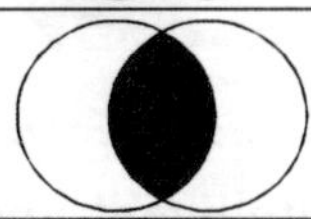	$(x)(Sx \supset \sim Px)$
I	Some S is P	$SP \neq 0$	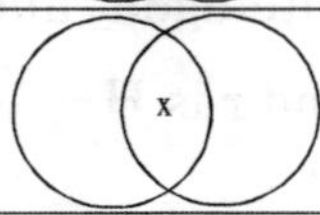	$(\exists x)(Sx \bullet Px)$
O	Some S is not P	$S\bar{P} \neq 0$	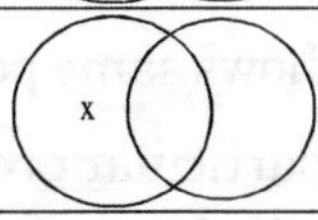	$(\exists x)(Sx \bullet \sim Px)$

Singular Propositions

A singular proposition is that which does not contain truth functional connectives like $\bullet$, $\supset$, v, $\equiv$, etc. and also singular propositions do not have words like 'all' or 'Some' or their equivalents. Subjects in a singular proposition is either a proper name like "Mohan is student of this college" or is a definite descriptive subject like "The present Prime Minister of India." Such propositions are symbolized in different ways.

Note: Small letters like 'a', 'b', 'c' are used for the individuals. Attribute symbol is used towards the left of individual.

Look at the following examples:

1. Ramesh is an engineer

   $\Rightarrow$ r is E

   $\Rightarrow$ Er

2. New Delhi is Capital of India

   $\Rightarrow$ n is C

   $\Rightarrow$ Cn

3. Rohit is graduate

   $\Rightarrow$ r is G

   $\Rightarrow$ Gr

4. Asha is a player

 ⇒ a is P

 ⇒ Pa

5. This boy is tall

 ⇒ b is T

 ⇒ Tb

6. Radha is intelligent and she is hard-working

 ⇒ r is I and r is H

 ⇒ Ir • Hr

 (This shows same person has two different attributes)

Universal and particular propositions are symbolized by using quantifiers and variables:

7. All students are literates

 ⇒ (Whatever x may be) (If x is a student, then x is literate)

 ⇒ (x) (Sx ⊃ Lx)

8. No crow is purple

 ⇒ (Whatever x may be) (If x is a crow, then x is not purple)

 ⇒ (x) (Cx ⊃ ~ Px)

9. Some voters are women

 ⇒ (There is something x) (This x is a voter and this x is a woman)

 ⇒ (∃x) (Vx • Wx)

10. Some applicants are not Indians

 ⇒ (There is something x) (This x is an applicant and this x is not an Indian)

 ⇒ (∃x) (Ax • ~ Ix)

Note: In order to symbolize propositions using quantifiers and variables, it is important that you first reduce the proposition in a standard form, like you had done earlier in Chapter 3A.

11. Who is not wise after the event? Standard form proposition is "All persons are wise after the event."

    ⇒ (Whatever x may be) (If x is a person then x is wise after the event)

    ⇒ (x) (Px ⊃ Wx)

12. He who hesitates fails. Standard form proposition is "All those who hesitate are those who fail."

    ⇒ (Whatever x may be) (If x hesitates then x fails)

    ⇒ (x) (Hx ⊃ Fx)

13. None of the doctors in the city could save him.

    ⇒ No doctor in the city is a person who could save him.

    ⇒ (Whatever x may be) (If x is a doctor in the city then x is a person who could not save him)

    ⇒ (x) (Dx ⊃ ~ Sx)

14. Only brave are winners.

    ⇒ All those who are winners are brave.

    ⇒ (Whatever x may be) (If x is a winner then x is a brave).

    ⇒ (x) (Wx ⊃ Bx)

15. Not all people love cricket.

    ⇒ Some people are not cricket lovers.

    ⇒ (There is something x) (This x is people and this x is not cricket lover)

    ⇒ (∃x) (Px • ~ Cx)

There are propositions where the subject or predicate has more than one characteristic such as:

1. All students and teachers are members of library. Then one propositions is symbolized as:

    ⇒ (Whatever x may be) (If x is either a student or x is a teacher, then x is member of library)

    ⇒ (x) (If x is S or x is T, then x is M)

    ⇒ (x) [(Sx v Tx) ⊃ Mx]

Here 'and' between student and teacher is deceptive. The meaning of the above proposition is that x is either a student or x is teacher, but x is not both student and teacher.

Take another example:

2. All brave soldiers were given medals. This is symbolized as:

   ⇒ (Whatever x may be) (If x is soldier and x is brave, then x is given medal)

   ⇒ $(x) [(Sx \bullet Bx) \supset Mx)]$

   Here soldiers and brave go together and hence joined by '•'

3. "Boys who are athletes are strong":

   ⇒ (Whatever x may be) (If x is a boy and x is a athlete, then x is strong)

   ⇒ $(x) [(Bx \bullet Ax) \supset Sx]$

4. Mobile phones that are expensive are lost quickly.

   ⇒ (Whatever x may be) (If x is a mobile phone and x is expensive, then x is lost quickly)

   ⇒ $(x) [(Mx \bullet Ex) \supset Lx]$

These are propositions where both subject and predicate have more characteristics.

5. All professional athletes are healthy and strong.

   ⇒ (Whatever x may be) (If x is an athlete and x is professional, then x is healthy and x is strong)

   ⇒ $(x) [(Ax \bullet Px) \supset (Hx \bullet Sx)]$

6. Children who eat protein are strong and active.

   ⇒ (Whatever x may be) (If x is a child and x eats protein then x is strong and x is active)

   ⇒ $(x) [(Cx \bullet Px) \supset (Sx \bullet Mx)]$

7. It is false that some books are expensive.

   ⇒ ~ (There is something x) (This x is a book and this x is expensive)

⇒ $\sim (\exists x)(Bx \bullet Ex)$

8. It is false that every book is expensive.

⇒ ~ (Whatever x may be) (If x is a book then x is expensive)

⇒ $\sim (x)(Bx \supset Ex)$

Exercises

1. Symbolize the following propositions using quantifiers and suggested variables.
    1. Carrots are nutritious.
       (Cx, x is Carrot; Nx, x is nutritious)
    2. A few diamonds are blue.
       (Dx, x is diamond; Bx, x is blue)
    3. No unicorns eat oats.
       (Ux, x is unicorn; Ox, x eats oats)
    4. Some dragons do not breathe fire.
       (Dx, x is dragon; Bx, x breathes fire)
    5. All cars are useful.
       (Cx, x is car; Ux, x is useful)
    6. All Kangaroos are introvert.
       (Kx, x is Kangaroo; Ix, x is introvert)
    7. Most of the dogs are intelligent.
       (Dx, x is dog; Ix, x is intelligent)
    8. Every soldier serves his country.
       (Sx, x is soldier; Cx, x serves his country)
    9. The envious are never happy.
       (Ex, x is envious; Hx, x is happy)
    10. Rivers generally run into the sea.
        (Rx, x is river; Sx, x runs into the sea)
    11. Every man is fallible.
        (Mx, x is man; Fx, x is fallible)

12. No horse is bipeds.

    (Hx, x is horse; Bx, x is bipeds)

13. Whales are mammals.

    (Wx, x is whales; Mx, x is mammal)

14. Majority of the students of this institute are not Indians.

    (Sx, x is student of this institute; Ix, x is an Indian)

15. Every scientist is a serious thinker.

    (Sx, x is a scientist; Tx, x is a serious thinker)

16. No angels are mortal.

    (Ax, x is angel; Mx, x is mortal)

17. All socialists are not communists.

    (Sx, x is a socialist; Cx, x is a communist)

18. Actors are generally hard workers.

    (Ax, x is an actor; Hx, x is hard worker)

19. Every student of this class can do this question.

    (Sx, x is a student of the class; Dx, x can do this question)

20. A few professors are not strict.

    (Px, x is a professor; Sx, x is strict)

21. Crows are black.

    (Cx, x is crow; Bx, x is black)

22. Only ungrateful people blame.

    (Ux, x is ungrateful people; Bx, x blames)

23. No men is reptile.

    (Mx, x is a man; Rx, x is a reptile)

24. All horses are animals.

    (Hx, x is a horse; Ax, x is an animal)

25. Not every man can swim.

    (Mx, x is a man; Sx, x can swim)

26. Only philosophers are scholars.
    (Px, x is a philosopher; Sx, x is a scholar)
27. No leopards are gentle.
    (Lx, x is a leopard; Gx, x is gentle)
28. Each bird is bipeds.
    (Bx, x is a bird; Px, x is biped)
29. Only ticket holders are permitted.
    (Tx, x is ticket holder; Px, x is permitted)
30. Every giraffe is herbivorous.
    (Gx, x is a giraffe; Hx, x is herbivorous)

2. Symbolize the following propositions using quantifiers and suggested notation:
    1. A triangle is bounded by three straight lines.
       (Tx, x is triangle; Bx, x is bounded by three straight lines)
    2. Vices never bring happiness.
       (Vx, x is vice; Bx, x brings happiness)
    3. Only those who are unselfish are happy.
       (Ux, x is unselfish; Hx, x is happy)
    4. Not all schemes of social reform are feasible.
       (Sx, x is scheme of social reform; Fx, x is feasible)
    5. A few voters are literate.
       (Vx, x is a voter; Lx, x is literate)
    6. Every rectangle is a parallelogram.
       (Rx, x is rectangle; Px, x is parallelogram)
    7. Only intelligent persons are scholars.
       (Ix, x is an intelligent person; Sx, x is a scholar)
    8. All racists are insecure.
       (Rx, x is racist; Bx, x is insecure)
    9. Every triangle is a polygon.

(Tx, x is a triangle; Px, x is a polygon)

10. Fat people are happy.

(Fx, x is a fat person; Hx, x is happy)

11. Few men are cultured.

(Mx, x is a man; Cx, x is cultured)

12. Mice are rodents.

(Mx, x is mice; Rx, x is rodent)

13. All snakes are not poisonous.

(Sx, x is snake; Bx, x is poisonous)

14. No poachers are law-abiding

(Px, x is a poacher; Lx, x is law-abiding)

15. At least some officers are not corrupt.

(Ox, x is an officer; Cx, x is corrupt)

16. All acids are compounds.

(Ax, x is acid; Cx, x is compound)

17. Every unwanted plant is weed.

(Ux, x is unwanted plant; Wx, x is weed)

18. All those who are happy on earth are virtuous.

(Wx, x is one who is happy on earth; Vx, x virtuous)

19. Few people are scholars.

(Px, x is people; Sx, x is scholar)

20. All sailors are adventurous people.

(Sx, x is sailor; Ax, x is adventurous people)

21. None but healthy persons are recruited in army.

(Hx, x is healthy person; Rx, x is recruited in army)

22. A tiger is not a domestic animal.

(Tx, x is a tiger; Dx, x is a domestic animal)

23. Almost all antibiotics are remedies.

(Ax, x is antibiotics; Rx, x is remedy)

24. None but communists are radicals.

(Cx, x is communist; Rx, x is radical)

25. All living things are perishable.

    (Lx, x is living thing; Px, x is perishable)

26. Whales are mammals.

    (Wx, x is a whale; Mx, x is a mammal)

27. All peace-loving persons hate war.

    (Px, x is peace-loving person; Hx, x hates war)

28. All models are attractive.

    (Mx, x is a model; Ax, x is attractive)

29. No computers are animated objects.

    (Cx, x is computer; Ax, x is animate object)

30. Every college student is adult.

    (Cx, x is college student; Ax, x is adult)

31. Not every octopus has a bad temper.

    (Ox, x is octopus; Bx, x has bad temper)

32. Some Americans are not materialists.

    (Ax, x is American; Mx, x is materialist)

33. Only elephants have trunks.

    (E, x is elephant; Tx, x has trunk)

34. A few men are optimistic.

    (Mx, x is a man; Ox, x is optimistic)

35. Ram is graduate.

    (Gx, x is graduate, r is for Ram)

3. Symbolize the following propositions using quantifiers and variables:

   1. Nothing which perishes is divine.

      (Px, x perishes; Dx, x is divine)

   2. All employees are eligible for social security benefits.

      (Ex, x is employee; Sx, x is eligible for social security benefits)

3. A few physicians are humanitarians.

   (Px, x is physician; Hx, x is humanitarian)

4. White diamonds are expensive.

   (Dx, x is diamond; Wx, x is white; Ex, x is expensive)

5. All football players are active and disciplined.

   (Fx, x is football player; Ax, x is active; Dx, x is disciplined)

6. The Cheetahs are the fastest runner.

   (Cx, x is cheetah; Fx, x is fastest runner)

7. Girls and women are both delicate and pretty.

   (Gx, x is girl; Wx, x is woman; Dx, x is delicate; Px, x is pretty)

8. Some cold-blooded animals are not mammals.

   (Ax, x is animal; Cx, x is cold-blooded; Mx, x is mammal)

9. Only ambitious people are successful.

   (Ax, x is ambitious; Px, x is people; Sx, x is successful)

10. All floods in the valley are either due to heavy rain or melting snow.

    (Fx, x is flood in the valley; Hx, x has heavy rain; Mx, x is due to melting snow)

11. Every eligible person is graduate.

    (Px, x is person; Ex, x is eligible; Gx, x is graduate)

12. Many well-tried old methods are best remedies.

    (Mx, x is method; Wx, x is well-tried; Ox, x is old; Bx, x is best remedies)

13. A few men and women are learned and wise.

    (Mx, x is a man; Wx, x is woman; Lx, x is learned; Sx, x is wise)

14. Most of the employed students are optimistic and forward looking people.

(Sx, x is student; Ex, x is employed; Ox, x is optimistic; Fx, x is forward looking; Px, x is people)

15. Every good law is just.

    (Lx, x is law; Gx, x is good; Jx, x is just)

16. Few happy men are rich.

    (Hx, x is happy; Mx, x is man; Rx, x is rich)

17. All happy men are healthy and contented.

    (Hx, x is happy; Mx, x is man; Ex, x is healthy; Cx, x is contented)

18. All citizens who are eligible to vote are above eighteen years old.

    (Cx, x is citizen; Ex, x is eligible; Ax, x is above eighteen years old)

19. Every benign tumor is not curable.

    (Tx, x is tumor; Bx, x is benign; Cx, x is curable)

20. A well-fed animal is healthy.

    (Wx, x is well-fed; Ax, x is animal; Hx, x is healthy)

21. Birds and fishes are vertebrates.

    (Bx, x is bird; Fx, x is fish; Vx, x is vertebrates)

22. Some workers are neither skilful nor hard-working.

    (Wx, x is worker; Sx, x is skilful; Hx, x is hard-working)

23. A few students are both intelligent and hard-working.

    (Sx, x is student; Ix, x is intelligent; Hx, x is hard-working)

24. Many scientific theories have become obsolete.

    (Tx, x is theory; Sx, x is scientific; Ox, x obsolete)

25. Several good things of life are free of cost.

    (Tx, x is things of life; Gx, x is good; Fx, x is free of cost)

26. Some books are neither expressive nor informative.

    (Bx, x is book; Ex, x is expressive; Ix, x is informative)

27. Every faculty member is well-informed person.

    (Fx, x is faculty member; Wx, x well-informed; Px, x is people)

28. Sonu and Monu are both intelligent students and good sportsmen.

    (Ix, x is intelligent student; Gx, x is good sportsman; s is for Sonu, m is for Monu)

29. No scholar who is in the military has academic freedom.

    (Sx, x is scholar; Mx, x is in military; Ax, x has academic freedom)

30. Mountains and rivers are perceptible.

    (Mx, x is mountain; Rx, x is river; Px, x is perceptible)

31. Murders are committed and regretted.

    (Mx, x is murder; Cx, x is committed act; Rx, x is regretted act)

32. Evening colleges are useful but troublesome.

    (Ex, x is evening; Cx, x is college; Ux, x is useful; Tx, x is troublesome)

33. Genuine foods contain hydrogen and oxygen.

    (Fx, x is food; Gx, x is genuine; Hx, x is hydrogen; Ox, x is oxygen)

34. Every graduate is either intelligent or hard-working.

    (Gx, x is graduate; Ix, x is intelligent; Hx, x is hard-working)

35. A politician who is elected as MLA is public servant.

    (Px, x is politician; Ex, x is elected as MLA; Sx, x is public servant)

Chapter 15 — Section B

Validity

FORMAL validity of an argument in the predicate calculus is examined in the similar way as has been done in the previous chapter of the formal proof of validity. Rules of Inference are applied here also. But in addition to those rules four more rules are introduced to test the validity of arguments falling in the predicate calculus. These four rules felicitate in reducing the predicate calculus argument in the framework of propositional calculus. The rules are as follows:

1. Universal Instantiation (UI)
2. Existential Instantiation (EI)
3. Universal Generalization (UG)
4. Existential Generalization (EG)

What is meant by Instantiation? This is something which was stated by the traditional logicians in the form of *Dictum de omni et nullo*, that is, whatever is predicated (affirmatively or negatively) universally or particularly to any class, it may be predicated (affirmatively or negatively) to its individuals. For instance, if "All men are mortal" is true then "Ram is mortal" is also true. Similarly if "No men are immortal" is true, then "Ram is not immortal" is also true.

Existential Instantiation means that if "Some students are voters" is true, then at least one student says "Ram is a voter" is also true. Similarly if "Some students are not employed" is true, then there is at least one student says "Ram who is not employed" is also true.

In order to test the validity of argument and argument form by formal proof of validity in Predicate Calculus, first of all the premisses are to be reduced in the format of propositional calculus by shaking off the quantifiers. 'x' which is *individual variable* (in the argument) is to be replaced by individual constant, say, 'a'. This can be done by using rules of Universal Instantiation (UI) and Existential Instantiation (EI). The reason — is that if an argument (in the matrix of propositional calculus) is proved valid, then its corresponding argument in predicate calculus will also be valid.

Three strategies are used in predicate calculus to prove its formal validity. **First strategy is**: if an argument has a singular proposition as one of the premisses, then that constant will replace that 'individual variable'. See the following example.

All students are optimists $\Rightarrow$ (x) (Sx $\supset$ Ox)
Ram is a student $\Rightarrow$ Sr

Therefore, Ram is opitimist $\Rightarrow$ Or

Solution:

1.	(x) (Sx $\supset$ Ox)	
2.	Sr	/ Or
3.	Sr $\supset$ Or	1st by UI
4.	Or	3rd and 2nd by M.P.

See another example:

All human beings are mortal $\Rightarrow$ (x) (Hx $\supset$ Mx)
Govind is human being $\Rightarrow$ Hg

Therefore, Govind is mortal $\Rightarrow$ Mg

Solution:

1.	(x) (Hx $\supset$ Mx)	
2.	Hg	/ Mg
3.	Hg $\supset$ Mg	1st by UI
4.	Mg	3rd and 2nd by M.P.

Second strategy: If the argument has particular proposition as one of the premisses, then the solution be will be as follows:

1.	(x) (Sx ⊃ ~ Px)	
2.	(∃x) (Px)	/ (∃x) (~ Sx)
3.	Pa 2nd	EI
4.	Sa ⊃ ~ Pa	1st by UI
5.	~ Sa	4th and 3rd by M.T.
6.	(∃x) (~ Sa)	5th EG

First particular premiss (or premisses) are to be replaced by individual constant because it is appropriate to take limited generalization (or propositions with limited scope) first. After that universal propositions are to be replaced by individual constant by using UI.

Take another example:

1.	(x) (Px ⊃ Rx)	
2.	(∃x) (Px)	/ (∃x) (Rx)
3.	Pa	2nd by EI
4.	Pa ⊃ Ra	1st by UI
5.	Ra —	4th and 3rd by M.P.
6.	(∃x) (Rx)	5th EG

Third strategy: If all the propositions (premiss and conclusion) are universal, then yet another strategy is applied to test the formal validity of an argument. For example the following argument is treated differently:

(x) (Fx ⊃ Gx)

(x) (Gx ⊃ Hx)

(x) (Fx ⊃ Hx)

The reasoning here is if an argument is valid for one individual variable 'x' then it is valid for any other individual variable say 'y' as well. But this strategy is applied to only those arguments where all the propositions (premisses and conclusion) are universal propositions. The solution of the above agrument will be like this:

1.	(x) (Fx ⊃ Gx)	
2.	(x) (Gx ⊃ Hx)	/ (x) (Fx ⊃ Hx)
3.	Fy ⊃ Gy	1st by UI
4.	Gy ⊃ Hy	2nd by UI
5.	Fy ⊃ Hy	3rd and 4th by H.S.
6.	(x) (Fx ⊃ Hx)	5th by UG

Exercises

1. Construct formal proof of validity for each of the following arguments:

1. (x) (Px ⊃ Sx)
   (∃x) ~ Sx   / ∴ (∃x) (~ Px)

2. (x) (Lx ⊃ Mx)
   (x) (Mx ⊃ Sx)   / ∴ (x) (Lx ⊃ Sx)

3. (∃x) (Px•Sx)
   (x) (Px ⊃ Hx)   / ∴ (∃x) (Hx)

4. (x) [(Px•Mx) ⊃ Sx]
   (x) (Px•Mx)   / ∴ (x) Sx

5. (x) [Px ⊃ (Mx•Hx)]
   (x) ~ (Mx•Hx)   / ∴ (x) ~ Px

6. (x) Fx
   (x) Mx   / ∴ (x) (Fx•Mx)

7. (x) (Px ⊃ Qx)
   Pa   / ∴ Qa

8. (x) (Px v Mx)
   (x) (~ Px)   / ∴ (x) (Mx)

9. (∃x) (Px)
   (x) (Px ⊃ Hx)   / ∴ (∃x) (Hx v Lx)

10. $(x) [(Fx \supset Gx) \bullet (Hx \supset Lx)]$
    $(x) (Fx \lor Hx)$ $/ \therefore (x) (Gx \lor Lx)$

11. $(x) (Px \supset Sx)$ $/ \therefore (x) [Px \supset (Px \bullet Sx)]$

12. $(x) [Fx \supset (Gx \bullet Hx)]$
    Fa $/ \therefore Ga$

13. $(x) (Sx \supset Tx)$
    $(x) (Tx \supset Rx)$
    $(x) (Rx \supset Gx)$ $/ \therefore (x) (Sx \supset Gx)$

14. $(x) [Rx \supset (Tx \lor Sx)]$
    $(x) [Sx \supset (Ux \supset Wx)]$
    $(\exists x) (\sim Tx \bullet Rx)$
    $(x) Rx$
    $\therefore (\exists x) (Ux \supset Wx)$

15. $(x) (Mx \supset Hx)$
    $(x) (Gx \supset Mx)$
    $(x) (Lx \supset Gx)$ $/ \therefore (x) (Lx \supset Hx)$

2. Construct formal proof of validity for each of the following arguments using suggested notations:

   1. All physicians are college graduates.
      All surgeons are physicians.
      Therefore, all surgeons are college graduates.
      (Px, x is physician; Cx, x is college graduate; Sx, x is surgeon).

   2. All good lawyers read fine print in contracts.
      Rohit is a good lawyer.
      Therefore, Rohit reads fine print in contracts.
      (Lx, x is good lawyer; Rx, x reads fine prints in contracts; r is for Rohit).

   3. All Indians are peace-loving people.
      Gujrati's are Indians.
      Therefore, Gujratis are peace-loving people.
      (Ix, x is Indian; Px, x is peace-loving people; Gx, x is Gujrati)

4. All prisoners are captives.
   No captives are happy.
   Therefore, No prisoners are happy.
   (Px, x is prisoner; Cx, x is captive; Hx x is happy person).
5. All iron objects are metallic.
   All metals conduct electricity.
   So all iron objects conduct electricity.
   (Ix, x is iron object; Mx, x is metallic or metal; Cx, x conducts electricity).
6. All mammals have heart.
   All horses are mammals.
   Therefore, all horses have heart.
   (Mx, x is mammal; Hx, x has heart; Rx, x is horse).
7. All researchers are dedicated.
   Some researchers are insurance persons.
   Some insurance persons are secure.
   Therefore, some insurance persons are dedicated persons.
   (Rx, x is researcher; Dx, x is dedicated; Ix, x is insurance person; S, x is secure).
8. All models are attractive.
   Some models are active in civil right movement.
   All attractive persons are envied persons.
   Therefore, some attractive persons are envied persons.
   (Mx, x is model; Ax, x is attractive; Cx, x is active in civil rights movements; Ex, x is an envied persons).
9. All sailors are travellers.
   All travellers are knowledgeable.
   All knowledge persons are broadminded.
   All broadminded people are confident. Therefore, all sailors are confident.
   (Sx, x is sailor; Tx, x is traveller; Kx, x is knowledgeable; Bx, x is broadminded; Cx, x is confident).
10. An animal is substance.
    All quadruped is an animal.

A horse is a quadruped.
All bucephalus are horses.
Thus all bucephalus are substance.
(Ax, x is animal; Sx, x is substance; Qx, x is quadruped; Bx, x is bucephalus; Hx, x is horse).

Chapter 15 – Section C

Invalidity

THE invalidity of arguments in the predicate calculus is proved in the similar way as has been done in the propositional calculus proving invalidity by assigning truth values. By using rules of UI and EI the argument is proved invalid for the individual. For instance the invalidity of the following argument is proved in the following manner:

(x) (Fx ⊃ Gx)

(x) (Mx ⊃ Gx) / ∴ (x) (Fx ⊃ Mx)

By applying UI, the argument is reduced to propositional calculus formate.

Fa ⊃ Ga

Ma ⊃ Ga / ∴ Fa ⊃ Ma

Keeping in sequence it is written as follows:

8	6	10	2	9	7	11	1	4	3	5
[(Fa	⊃	Ga)	•	(Ma	⊃	Ga)]	⊃	(Fa	⊃	Ma)
T	T	T	T	F	T	T	F	T	F	F

No error, no inconsistency found, hence the above argument is proved invalid in the propositional calculus. Therefore it is proved invalid in the predicate calculus as well.

2. Take another example:

(x) (Fx ⊃ Gx)

(x) (~ Fx) / ∴ (x) (~ Gx)

After applying UI, we get the following sequence:

8	5	9	2	6	7	1	3	4
[(Fa	⊃	Ga)	•	(~	Fa)]	⊃	(~	Ga)

F T T T T F F F T

No error hence proved invalid.

3. Take yet another example:

(x) (Px ⊃ ~ Mx)

(∃x) (Px) / ∴ (x) (Mx)

replacing the above argument by using individual constant we get the following sequence:

6 4 8 7 2 5 1 3

[(Pa ⊃ ~ Ma) • Pa] ⊃ Ma

T T T F T T F F

No error hence proved invalid.

4. See another example:

(x) (Px ⊃ Gx)

(x) (Gx ⊃ Mx)

(x) (Mx ⊃ Lx) / ∴ (x) (Lx ⊃ Px)

After applying UI, we get the following sequence:

11 7 12 2 13 8 14 3 15 9 10 1 5 4 6

[(Pa ⊃ Ga) • (Ga ⊃ Ma) • (Ma ⊃ La)] ⊃ (La ⊃ Pa)

F T T T T T T T T T T F T F F

The above argument is proved invalid by assigning truth values. Hence its corresponding predicate calculus argument will also be invalid.

5. (x) (Fx ⊃ Gx)

(∃x) (Gx • Lx)/ ∴ (∃x) (Lx•Fx)

After reducing this argument into propositional calculus sequence by replacing individual variable x by individual constant 'a' with the help of UI and EI, we get the following sequence:

11 6 10 2 8 7 9 1 4 3 5

[(Fa ⊃ Ga) • (Ga • La)] ⊃ (La • Fa)

F T T T T T T F T F F

The above argument is proved invalid by assigning truth values in propositional calculus. Hence its corresponding predicate calculus argument is also proved invalid.

Exercises

1. Prove the invalidity of the following argument forms:

1.
(x) (Fx v Gx)
(x) (Gx ⊃ Hx)
∴ (∃x) (Hx ⊃ Fx)

2.
(x) (Fx ⊃ Gx)
(∃x) (~ Gx)
∴ (∃x) (Fx)

3.
(x) (Gx ⊃ ~ Hx)
(∃x) (Fx • ~ Gx)
∴ (∃x) (Hx • ~ Fx)

4.
(∃x) (Lx v Mx)
(x) (Mx ⊃ Px)
∴ (∃x) (Px)

5.
(x) (Px ⊃ Qx)
(x) (Rx ⊃ Qx)
∴ (x) (Px ⊃ Rx)

6.
(x) (Fx ⊃ Gx)
(x) (Gx ⊃ Hx)
(x) (Px ⊃ Hx)
(∃x) (Fx • Tx)
∴ (∃x) (Px • Tx)

7.
(x) (Px ⊃ Qx)
(x) (Qx ⊃ Rx)
(x) (Rx ⊃ ~Tx)
(x) ~ Px / ∴ (∃x) ~ Tx

8.
(x) (Mx ⊃ Nx)
(x) (Nx ⊃ Lx)
(x) (Hx ⊃ Mx)

$(\exists x)\ (Lx)$
$(\exists x)\ (Mx)\quad / \therefore (x)\ (Nx \supset Hx)$

9. $(x)\quad [(Px \supset Qx) \bullet (Rx \supset Sx)]$
$(x)\quad (Px \supset Rx)$
$(\exists x)\ (\sim Px \bullet Rx)$
$(x)\quad (Mx \supset Sx)$
$(\exists x)\ (Qx)\quad / \therefore (x)\ (Mx \supset Px)$

10. $(\exists x)\ (Hx)$
$(x)\quad (Hx \supset \sim Lx)$
$(\exists x)\ (\sim Lx)$
$(x)\quad [(Lx \supset (Hx \bullet Px)]$
$(x)\quad (Px \supset Lx)\ / \therefore (x)\ (Hx \supset Lx)$

2. Prove the invalidity of the following arguments using suggested notations:

1. All men are mortal.
All professors are mortal.
∴ All professors are men.
(Mx, x is man; Tx, x is mortal; Px, x is professor).

2. All students are intelligent persons.
Some intelligent persons are voters.
∴ Some voters are students.
(Sx, x is student; Ix, x is intelligent person; Vx, x voter)

3. All capitalists are critical of communists.
Some critical of communists are intellectuals.
Therefore, some intellectuals are capitalists.
(Cx, x is capitalist; Rx, x is critical of communists; Ix, x is intellectual).

4. All socialists believe in nationalization.
All communists believe in nationalization.
Therefore, all socialists are communists.
(Sx, x is socialist; Nx, x believes in nationalization; Cx, x is communist).

5. All scientists are researchers.

Some scientists are not well paid.
Therefore, some well paid are not researchers.
(Sx, x is scientist; Rx, x is researcher; Wx, x is well paid).

6. Some acts of civil disobedience are not violent.
All violent acts are morally unsound.
Therefore, some morally unsound acts are acts of civil disobedience.
(Cx, x is act of civil disobedience; Vx, x is violent act; Mx, x is morally unsound).

7. All materialists are atheists.
Some Hindus are not atheists.
Therefore, all Hindus are materialists.
(Mx, x is materialist; Ax, x is atheist; Hx, x is Hindu).

8. All doctors are psychoanalysts because all psychiatrists are psychoanalysts and all psychiatrists are doctors.
(Px, x is psychiatrist; Dx, x is doctor; Ax, x is psychoanalyst).

9. No military men are expert in social legislation for all for those who trained for war are military men and some of those who are trained for war are expert in social legislation.
(Mx, x is military men; Ex, x is expert in social legislation; Tx, x is trained for war).

10. Since all poets live in the world of dreams and they all are ignorant of the evils of reality, so all those who live in the world of dreams are ignorant of the evils of reality.
(Px, x is poet; Ix, x is ignorant of the evils; Dx, x lives in the world of dreams.)

Reference

Basson, A.H. and D.J. O'Connor, *Introduction to Symbolic Logic*.

Part III

Chapter 16

Induction

INDUCTION like deduction is a form of reasoning; it is a type of inference in which from some observed instances a conclusion is drawn about the unobserved instances of the same kind. Though the premisses do not necessarily imply the conclusion in induction, yet the premisses are good reason for drawing the conclusion. No empirical science, natural or social, which aims to describe nature, world, or society, can do without induction. In fact all sciences, except pure mathematics and formal logic, are making extensive use of inductive inferences.

In induction, on the basis of some observed instances, a conclusion about the unobserved instances is drawn. For instance, on the basis of observed crows found to be black, one draws a conclusion that "All crows (observed as well as unobserved) are black". From observing Ram is mortal, Mohan is mortal, Sita is mortal and so on, one concludes "All men are mortal". The formal structure of this type of inductive reasoning can be symbolically expressed as:

x_1, x_2, x_3 . . ., have the characteristics of A. Therefore probably all xs have the characteristics of A.

The above cited examples of inductive reasoning can be elaborated logically as follows:

(1) Crow x was observed and it was black.

" y " " "

" z " " "

! ! ! ! !

Therefore, probably all crows are black.

(2) Ram is mortal.
Mohan is mortal.
Sita is mortal.
! !
!

Therefore, probably all men are mortal.

From this, one may get the impression that induction is a logical process in which a universal conclusion is supported on the basis of some observed and limited number of instances. But this is not always true. Traditionally, it was understood that a deductive inference (reasoning) goes from general premisses to the particular conclusion, and an inductive inference (reasoning) goes from the particular premisses to the general conclusion. Look at the following illustrations:

Deductive reasoning:
All men are mortal.
Ram is a man.

Therefore, Ram is mortal.

Inductive reasoning:
Metal x expanded on heating.
Metal y expanded on heating.
Metal z expanded on heating.

Therefore, probably all metals expand on heating.

Though this distinction between deduction and induction (that is, in deduction particular conclusion is drawn from universal premisses and in induction universal conclusion is drawn from particular premisses) holds good in some cases (for instance in forming empirical inductive generalizations like "All men are mortal", "All crows are black", where we move from particular evidences to universal truths), but there are instances both in deduction as well as in induction where this 'traditional dichotomy' does not 'fit'. In deductive inferences, there are instances where universal conclusions are inferred from the universal premisses. For example:

All men are mortal.

All employees are men.

Therefore, all employees are mortal.

In induction also sometimes we move from particular to particular. For instance:

x is a citizen and a voter in Indian general election.

x is a citizen and a voter in Indian general election.

z is a citizen.

Therefore, probably z is a voter in Indian general election.

The most acceptable difference between deduction and induction, nowadays, is that deductive is "necessary" or demonstrative inference, whereas inductive inference is merely "probable". The conclusion "is claimed to follow" necessarily from the premisses in deductive inference, whereas in inductive inference, the conclusion is not "claimed to follow" necessarily (but only with some degree of probability) from the evidences.

The formal sciences like pure mathematics and formal logic are often described as deductive in nature. The reasoning that goes on in pure mathematics and in formal logic is purely deductive. The empirical sciences like physics, chemistry, biology, etc. (all natural sciences), and also political science, economics, history, psychology, etc. (all social sciences) are often described as inductive, for the reasoning involved in them is inductive in nature. But this is wrong. The empirical sciences whether natural or social are not purely inductive. The deductive reasoning also occurs in the empirical sciences as well. The scientists move from empirical data to theories and laws. It is, thus, wrong to think that empirical sciences are totally inductive in nature. Even theoretical sciences (for instance pure physics) cannot do away with sense data. There is an empirical cushion at their back. They need empirical dimension or matrix to verify the theories. Arthur Pap says, "there is no other way of testing an empirical hypothesis — especially one of highly theoretical character, such as the hypothesis of universal gravitation, or the atomic hypothesis, or the gene theory of biology — than by deducing from it directly testable consequences."[1] This shows that "purely inductive sciences" are not possible, though there are "purely deductive sciences" (pure mathematics and formal logic). All inductive sciences (empirical sciences based on experiences and sense data) make use of inductive as well as deductive processes.

Before we go further, let us see what exactly is meant by induction and what is an inductive inference? According to J.S. Mill, "Induction is the name given to the operation of the mind, by which we infer that what we know to be true in particular case or cases, will be true in any other case or cases of a similar kind. . . ."[2] In other words induction is a process by which we conclude that what is true of certain individuals of a class is true of the whole class, or that what is true at certain times will be true in similar circumstances at all times.

Induction is "concatenated" process in the sense that the results of induction that have already proved successful become the criteria of soundness of inductions yet to come. There is then an 'inductive leap' in this logical process because we move from one level to another level, from observed to unobserved instances. One jumps from one level of quantity to another level of quantity, from one platform to another platform. That is why the results of inductive inferences are only probable though the degree of probability may be very high in certain cases. The relation between evidences and conclusion is not of necessity but rather of suggestion.

An inductive logician has twofold tasks:

(i) to collect evidences (premisses) or sense data from experiences and observations, and

(ii) to draw a conclusion from these evidences (premisses).

---

1. Arthur, Pap, *An Introduction to the Philosophy of Science*, p. 139.
2. J.S. Mill, *A System of Logic*. Appendix A, "Of the various grounds of Induction", p. 1103.

In deductive logic, on the other hand, a logician undertakes just one task, that of drawing the conclusion from the given premisses in accordance with the logical rules. A deductive logician does not hunt for the premisses. They are given to him. He is not even bothered about the actual logical status (truth value) of the premisses either. A deductive logician takes for granted the truth value of the premisses. He is interested merely in the fact that from the given premisses what necessarily follows. He is thus interested only in the 'formal consistency'.

An inductive logician, however, is not so fortunate. He gathers the evidences through experiences and observations. The observed instances serve as evidences (premisses) and from that he draws the conclusion. Moreover, in induction all the premisses are materially true because they are experienced instances whereas in deduction valid reasoning may even have false premisses. The form of an argument is the sole factor in deciding the validity of an argument in deductive reasoning. The material truth of the propositions has little role to play. In inductive reasoning, however, the evidences as well as the conclusion are materially true. Both form and matter of an inference play equal role in the evaluation of an inductive argument.

No inductive argument, however, is 'valid' or 'invalid'. The evaluative notions of validity and invalidity are applied to deductive arguments only. A deductive inference is assessed as either valid or invalid. An inductive inference is neither of them. An inductive argument is evaluated by degrees such as weaker or stronger, appealing or non-appealing, convincing or non-convincing, etc. depending on the strength of the evidences.

The soundness of an inductive argument depends on the strength of the evidences in relation to the conclusion. For example "90 per cent of alcoholics have an unhappy family life, and that x is an alcoholic, therefore, it is highly probable to infer that x has an unhappy family too" has a very high 'truth frequency'. The argument thus is strong and sound. On the other hand, in the inference "45 per cent of post-graduate students miss their classes and x is a postgraduate student, therefore, x misses his classes too", the 'truth frequency' is very low. The inference thus is weak, less appealing and less convincing. It is quite possible that x is a postgraduate student and still not missing classes. **There is no contradiction in accepting true premisses and false conclusion in inductive inferences. But in the deductive inferences it is impossible to have all true premisses and a false conclusion.**

The inductive procedures (which the twentieth-century logicians have accepted) originated from Francis Bacon[3] in sixteenth century, and because of this Bacon is called "Founder of Modern Inductive Philosophy". He is of the opinion that deductive procedures of Aristotelian syllogism cannot be applied to the principles of sciences. It is in the inductive procedures the scientific methodology is to be justified. J.S. Mill,[4] in the nineteenth century, further contributed to the modern inductive logic, initiated by Bacon three hundred years back. The experimental methods of causation (about which you will learn in later chapters) are formulated by J.S. Mill.

The relationship of induction and deduction always remained a favourite topic for the logicians of all ages. Aristotle and Scholastic logicians saw induction as antithetical to syllogism and to deduction. The formal logicians like Stanlay Jevons,[5] in the

---

3. Francis Bacon (1561–1626) was English statesman and philosopher of science. Though strictly speaking he himself was not a scientist, he had no laboratory and he made no new discoveries, yet he was "the prophet of modern science" for he gave method and inspiration to it.
4. John Stuart Mill (1806–1873) was the most influential philosopher in the English-speaking world during the nineteenth century. He was an economist, and an administrator too. He is generally held to be one of the most effective spokesmen for the liberal view of man and society.
5. William Stanley Jevons (1835–1882) was a British logician and an economist. He has written many books on logic. His most important contribution to scientific methodology is an account of his "celebrated logical machine".

nineteenth century, tried to prove the supremacy of deduction over inductive procedures while the informal or material logicians such as Francis Bacon and J.S. Mill thought the inductive procedure is more fundamental than deductive ones. Jevons calls induction and deduction as the "inverse process" (induction is the converse of deduction). Francis Bacon calls "induction as ascending process" and "deduction as a descending process".

The inductive logicians tried to prove the supremacy of induction while the deductive logicians were advocating just the opposite. But induction and deduction should not be viewed as to which is more fundamental between them, rather they should be seen as various parts of the same game. They are not antithetical, contradictory or opposed to each other but supplementary and complimentary to each other. Just as in a relay race, the starting point of one player is a terminus for another, similarly induction and deduction differ in their "starting point". The terminus of induction (generalizations) serves as the starting point for deduction. Race seems to be started by induction, and deduction takes over later on. The conclusion of induction serves as the premisses in the deductive reasoning. Both induction and deduction, however, investigate and provide rules to evaluate whether the premisses are adequate evidences to support the conclusion or not.

Types of Induction

Inductive inferences occur in a large variety of forms. Out of them four types of inductive inferences are recognized in the elementary logic. They are:

(1) Induction by simple enumeration.

(2) Induction by complete enumeration.

(3) Induction by analogy

(4) Scientific induction.

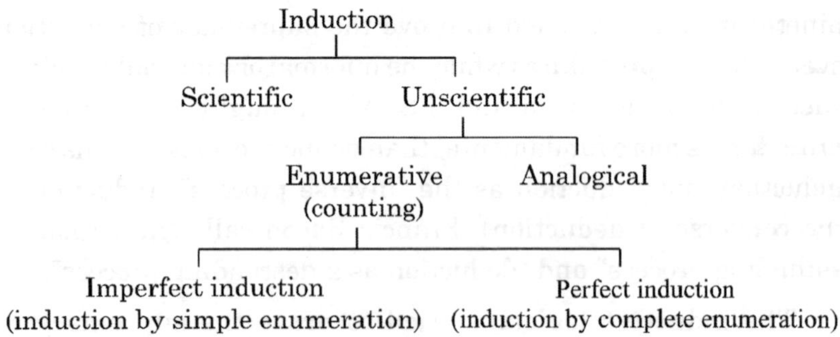

1. *Induction by simple enumeration*: The simplest and most popular form of induction is induction by simple enumeration. Here generalizations are inferred or made simply on the basis of observed instances. The observed instances are found to possess a particular quality and on that basis we infer that the unobserved instances also possess the same quality. For instance, the crows are observed to be of black colour and men are observed to possess the quality of mortality, from that the conclusions "All crows are black" and "All men are mortal" are drawn, respectively. However, no connection or relation is established between being a crow and of black colour, man and mortality. Our past experiences and observations serve as the evidences, they serve as the good reasons to accept the generalizations.

The larger number of conformable or favourable instances, and absence of any contradictory, unconformable, or unfavourable instance is the criteria of dependable induction in this kind of reasoning. "Random Sampling" of the phenomena under investigation increases the reliability of the conclusion. There is a tendency, a 'natural impulse' in a man to expect that if certain phenomenon is occurring repeatedly, then the same phenomenon will occur in the same circumstances in future also. The more are the number of instances, the greater is the probability of induction provided no negative or contrary instance is found. "All crows are black" is true as long as no crow of any other colour is found.

There are, however, many drawbacks in the induction by simple enumeration. Since the induction of this type is based on simple counting of instances alone, there is a possibility of committing a fallacy of 'hasty generalization'. A single negative instance is enough to destroy the hard earned generalization. One non-black coloured crow is enough to make the generalization "All crows are black" a false generalization. Thus a generalization cannot be proved with certainty by innumerable finite instances. That is why Francis Bacon thought, induction by simple enumeration is puerile [childish], for it is always exposed to the danger of contrary instances.

In spite of all that, the number of observed instances are somehow treated as a mark of reliability in common induction, the more the instances the better or more reliable is the conclusion. However, in certain cases a very large number of instances are not enough to establish a reliable generalization whereas in some other cases a very few instances are enough to establish a reliable generalization. For example, to learn that fire burns and hurts, one dares not to have put his hand in fire again and again. No one knows why and how in some other cases, a few instances are enough to establish a generalization. An experimental physicist who has established through one or two samples of a certain metal melting at such and such a temperature under standard pressure confidently generalizes that all samples of that metal have the same melting point. But a naturalist will not generalize with the same confidence that all members of a given species of birds have the same colour as the one or two observed birds.

2. *Induction by complete enumeration*: An induction by complete enumeration or "perfect induction" as is termed by Aristotle, is a type of reasoning in which every instance or every event has been observed and examined, and then the conclusion is drawn. For example, the conclusion "All the students of this class are Indian citizens" is drawn after examining each and every student of the class. Also the conclusions like "All books of this library are stamped and labelled", "All apples of this container are rotten", "All ladies of this family are educated" are instances of induction by complete enumeration.

Induction by complete enumeration, however, is possible in those cases where the total number of instances can be counted or observed. It is clear that induction of this type is applicable only in few cases. Most of the inductive reasoning done by a common man and by a scientist is not of this type. It is thus of little use to a logician also. He is interested in "incomplete induction" where unobserved conclusion is drawn from a few observed instances. There is an "inductive leap", a jump from observed instances to unobserved conclusion in an incomplete induction which is missing in "perfect induction". The conclusion of a complete induction is like a total "summary of the facts".

3. *Induction by Analogy*: Most of our daily arguments are in the form of analogy. Analogy is a form of inference in which similarity of characteristics possessed by the evidences (premisses) is the basis of the conclusion. Analogy can best be understood with the help of examples. For instance, I had read three books, say A, B and C written by an author, say, X. I enjoyed reading all of them. Next time when I want to read a book, I will most probably pick up a book, say, D by the same author hoping I will enjoy reading the next book also. But it may be possible that the new book D turns out to be totally boring and uninteresting. Thus the results of analogical arguments are not certain. They are merely probable. Like induction by simple enumeration, an analogical argument is neither totally correct nor totally incorrect. They are rather stronger or weaker, appealing or non-appealing.

Look at another illustration of the use of analogical argument. Four girl students, say, X, Y, Z and K resemble in respect of having good academic record (R), good personality (P) and good conversational ability (C). X, Y, Z all cleared MBBS entrance test. From the above two premisses it follows that K will also clear the MBBS entrance test. The student K resembles X, Y, Z students in all relevant aspects and these resemblances are the basis to predict that the girl K will qualify for the MBBS test. But it may be possible the girl K may not qualify the test at all in spite of having a good academic record and good personality.

Analogical arguments are widely used by the common people in daily life. A scientist also makes use of analogical arguments very often in discovering casual relationships among events and state of affairs. There are many scientific laws and theories which were discovered and suggested by the analogy. For instance, the function of human body served as the modal for making several machines. The analogy established between the anatomy of frog and anatomy of human body helped doctors to find the causes of various diseases. The planet Mars resembles the earth in certain respects, say, X, Y, Z, etc. The earth has an additional characteristic of inhabitation also, therefore, probably Mars too has the characteristic of inhabitation.

Besides this there are other uses of analogy also. A poet makes use of analogy to describe beautiful landscape in order to make his description more lively. A scientist also makes use of analogy to explain some unintelligible phenomenon. Scientist's use of analogy is explanatory. A logician, however, is interested in the analogy neither as description nor even as explanation. He is interested in the analogy only as an argument.[6]

Symbolically an analogical argument can be expressed as:

A, B, C, D are entities having the characteristics X_1 X_2 X_3 X_4.

A, B, C have another characteristic say X_5.

Therefore, probably D also has the characteristic X_5.

Let us express the example of reading books given above in the argumental form. A, B, C, D are entities or objects among whom the analogy is established. In the present case analogy is established among four entities, that is, four books.

Four books (A, B, C D) have the characteristics of X_1, X_2, X_3, X_4.

A, B, C have another characteristics X_5.

Therefore, D also has the characteristics of X_5.

6. Cf. Irving M. Copi, and Carl Cohen, *An Introduction to Logic*, (Ninth Edition), p. 454.

X_1 - being a book

X_2 - written by a particular author

X_3 - being a detective novel

X_4 - published by a particular publisher

X_5 - interesting book that gave me a feeling of good reading.

Like induction by simple enumeration, an analogy is more reliable and stronger if the number of similarities among things or objects are more. But similarities between the instances should be important and relevant. For instances, if I establish analogy among books (which I liked reading) on the basis of their cover and binding, then this is a irrelevant similarity. For, I enjoyed reading books A, B, C, D because of their style and content, and not because of their appearances and bindings. The force of an argument from Analogy depends "on the character of identity and not on the amount of similarity." We must weight "the points of resemblance rather than count them." Thus in analogical argument, like induction by simple enumeration, "number is not safe guide." The similarity among the entities should be relevant and one relevant similarity is far superior than many irrelevant similarities. But the important question is, how do we know that a similarity is relevant or irrelevant? The characteristics by themselves do not carry tags suggesting relevant or irrelevant characteristics. A fallacy in analogical reasoning often occurs due to the confusion between essential and non-essential characteristics, between relevant and irrelevant characteristics. A good and sound analogical argument is that in which the conclusion is drawn on the basis of sound, careful and comprehensive comparison of the points of resemblances among objects and events.

The relevance of characteristics is to be explained in terms of causation though the argument by analogy itself does not establish a causal relationship between the events or phenomena. And in this respect analogical induction remains at the level of unscientific induction. Analogy like induction by simple enumeration can suggest a causal relationship between phenomena, and thus is useful for scientific research. It is, "a guidepost pointing out" the direction in which more rigorous investigations should be prosecuted. Analogy is thus an important source of making hypothesis on which scientific researches are based. It is, therefore, a milestone in the direction of scientific induction.

4. *Scientific induction*: This is the best and most reliable form of induction. The aim of scientific induction is to establish natural universal laws on the basis of observations and experiments. It does so by establishing a causal relation between the two phenomena or facts. A scientific induction does all that what an induction by simple enumeration does but it goes further. It establishes a cause and effect relationship between events and facts. If induction by simple enumeration is stamped with causation, it becomes scientific induction. Thus establishing the causal relation between phenomena is the distinguishing mark of scientific induction.

A scientist, and also a person with scientific bend of thinking, always inquires why two facts, say, A and B always occur together. He answers the queries like why two particular phenomena, say, A and B always occur together, why with increase in heat, the mercury rises. A scientist looks and hunts for a causal order in the nature, whereas a common man hardly bothers to know why two phenomena A and B occur together. For instance, an experienced and old farmer on the basis of his experiences and observations states that climate A is good for the crop X; but young agricultural engineer says this on the basis of his knowledge of causal relationship. He explains that the climate A is good for crop X because climate A is cause or part of cause of good harvesting of crop X.

Thus, whereas the causal relationship is the essence of scientific induction, induction by simple enumeration is satisfied with observations and samplings alone. A scientist aims to produce ordered, and organized systems of nature and society. The facts are put in the order of cause and effect. From this, however, one should not gather the idea that a scientist can do without samplings and conformable instances. But whereas in induction by simple enumeration number of observed instances is criteria of its reliability, in the natural sciences the situation is different. Sciences like chemistry or physics do not so heavily depend on the adequate number of instances. The social sciences, on the other hand, require a substantial number of observed instances. Many times you come across the social researchers collecting data by giving questionnaires to people and asking the required information from them. This they do to get the samples, or the data, for drawing conclusions in the form of generalizations.

It is very wrong to think that induction by simple enumeration is of no use to a scientist. It seems that the race in the inductive reasoning is started with induction by simple enumeration and is completed by scientific induction. In other words, both scientific induction and induction by simple enumeration started race together, from the same starting point, but whereas the latter stops in the midway, the former goes further and establishes the causal relationship between phenomena. Induction by simple enumeration though inferior than the scientific induction, yet it is a 'stepping stone' for the scientific induction. The scientific induction does everything what induction by simple enumeration does, but it does something more. It establishes a causal relationship among the phenomena. Induction based on the causal relationship becomes more reliable and the probability of its conclusion increases subsequently.

Though the induction by simple enumeration and induction based on analogy are not forms of scientific induction, yet they suggest a direction in which more serious and fruitful researches can be carried out by the scientists. In this sense, non-scientific inductions are assets to scientists.

However, the aim of every type of induction is to establish a real, and materially true proposition. Real propositions are fruits of knowledge and they are opposed to verbal analytical propositions. The propositions like "All bachelors are unmarried", "The sum of all angles of a triangle is equal to 180°", are analytical propositions. The predicates of such propositions do not give any new information. They are only formal generalizations and are of a priori nature. But the propositions like "All solid objects are heavy", "All metals when heated expand" provide some new information, some new knowledge. An inductive reasoning thus provides empirical, factual, materially true synthetical propositions.

The main question which worries the logicians about induction is, how are we justified in stating that since X has worked in past, it will also work in future? Since all the metals when heated got expanded, how are we justified in saying that in future metals when heated will expand. It seems there is no formal ground on which inductive inferences can be justified. They, however, can be justified in the matrix of '**uniformity of nature**' and '**universal law of causation**' which are informal grounds of inductive reasoning. 'Uniformity of nature' and 'Universal law of Causation' are necessary postulates presupposed by every inductive reasoning. Mill, Keynes, David Hume and other eminent empirical philosophers assert that inductive inferences are possible only on the assumption of these general postulates.

The law of 'uniformity of nature' broadly states that if certain phenomenon behaves or acts in a certain manner in the past, then in future the same phenomenon will behave exactly in the same way. If water quenched our thirst or fire burns us, then in future water will quench our thirst and fire will burn us; though it is **not rational** to believe so, but it is certainly **reasonable** to do so.

The scientific induction is based on the axiom of the uniformity of nature that the "same" cause is always and everywhere followed by "same" effect. If a set of certain conditions p, q, r has been followed by an effect X, then the same set of conditions is followed by X anywhere anytime. Besides the uniform occurrences of cause and effect events, **there is an assumption in all scientific reasonings that every event has a cause**. The scientists have taken for granted that nothing occurs by chance. Every change in the universe is due to some cause.

What puzzles the logicians most is how are these postulates of the "uniformity of nature" and the "universal law of causation" acquired? What is the logical status of these postulates? Are they self-evident and a priori, or are they empirical generalizations? These postulates are neither self-evident nor a priori analytical propositions because the truth of analytical propositions is determined by the meaning of the terms used in the propositions. The significance and truth of these postulates are not based on the meaning of the terms used in these postulates either. Only through experience and observation we know nature acts in uniform order. Similarly, it is only by experience and observation we know that every event has a cause. These postulates then are justified through the uniform occurrences of phenomena; but earlier we have seen uniform occurrences of phenomena is justified in terms of postulates. It seems we are reasoning in circle and commit the fallacy of *petitio principii*.

This may compel us to think that induction is unjustified process of reasoning. But the situation is not that hopeless. Induction can be justified in terms of our mental faculty of accepting that future resembles the present. There is a "natural impulse" in a man to expect that future behaves like the present and past, though at the same time it is wrong to aspire for hundred per cent certainty in this prediction.

Exercises

1. Explain the nature of inductive inference? Discuss its role in natural sciences.
2. "There is a distinction between deduction and induction, but there is no opposition between them; they supplement each other." Explain.

3. Explain induction by simple enumeration? Is it useful for a scientist? Elaborate your answer.
4. Explain the nature of scientific induction. In what way you think this is the best of all the other types of inductions? Discuss.
5. Explain the importance of analogical arguments in natural sciences.
6. "'Uniformilty of nature' and 'Universal laws of causation' are necessary postulates presupposed by every inductive reasoning." Explain.

Chapter 17

Causation

To establish a causal relationship is the distinguishing mark of scientific induction. So naturally a question arises what is a cause? There is no one definition of causation. Philosophers, scientists, logicians and also common man define causation according to their requirements. Philosophers deal with that aspect of causation which answers the question, "Why events happen the way they occur"? For them the concept of causality is related with the problem of determinism and free will Determinism states that strict causal laws govern all natural events and human actions and behaviour.

A logician, on the other hand, looks to cause and effect relationship as reasoning in disguise. Cause or parts of a cause are premisses, and effect is taken as a conclusion. A logician investigates the legitimacy and sufficiency of the premisses with respect to the conclusion. He thus investigates and tries to answer two questions:

(i) What is meant by a cause? In other words, how to define a cause?

(ii) How is a causal connection established?

The present chapter deals with the first of these questions and following chapter with the second.

Causal connection is a relation of invariable succession and hence stronger and stricter connection than any other relation. Causal relationship implies succession in time. Cause is antecedent, and hence precedes the effect. Effect is consequent, and hence follows the cause. In the time sequence, it is the cause which occurs first and the effect later on. The time interval between cause and effect may be very less but the gap none the less is there. Because of this a cause is different from co-existence.

Though cause is antecedent event, but not every antecedent event is the cause or part of the cause of an effect. If x is cause of y, then certainly x precedes y; but to say that since x precedes y, therefore, x is definitely cause of y, is wrong. This kind of thinking leads to the fallacy of *post hoc; ergo propter hoc* about which you will study in the last chapter of the book. For example, to say that since the sun was shining hot when the house was burnt, therefore, the sun is the cause of burning the house is wrong. For the house can burn in night also when there is no sun. Thus only invariable and unchangeable antecedent can be the cause of an effect. But mere invariability of antecedent is also not enough to be a cause of an effect. Day is invariable antecedent of night, and similarly night is invariable antecedent of day, but neither day is cause of night nor night is cause of day. Rather they (day and night) are effect of the rotation of the earth around the sun.

Cause must be invariable as well as unconditional antecedent of an effect. Unconditionality of antecedent event means the antecedent is self-sufficient to produce an effect. The antecedent event when capable enough to give rise to effect by itself, then it is called unconditional, for it does not need anything more to give birth to effect. Besides being unconditional and invariable, cause must also be immediate or proximate antecedent of an effect. Scientists and logicians are not interested in the remote causes. The conditions which precede cause and which have indirect bearing upon the effect are called "remote, mediate or predisposing causes". For instance in the following case:

A is cause of B.
B is cause of C.
C is cause of D.
D is cause of E.
Therefore, A is cause of E.

A is remote cause of E; B and C are also remote causes of E, though less remote than A. Only D is immediate or proximate cause of E. Logicians and scientists are interested only in proximate causes. **Cause, thus, is defined as invariable, unconditional, immediate antecedent of an effect.**

It is truistic to say that scientists aim to discover the causal connections. To a scientist the principle of causality is a 'guiding principle', and because of this his conception of cause is very precise and exact. A scientist asserts exact propositions of the form "Whenever A occurs in the presence of $C_1 \bullet C_2 \ldots$, A is followed by B".[1]

To a scientist, cause means conditions, factors, components responsible for producing an effect. There is a fundamental assumption in the study of natural and social phenomena that events just do not occur, they occur only under certain conditions. Cause thus is defined in terms of conditions by the scientists. Two types of conditions, necessary and sufficient, are recognized by them. P is necessary condition for Q, if Q never occurs in the absence of P. P is sufficient condition of Q, if every occurrence of P is accompanied by the occurrence of Q.

A necessary condition is that whose absence can prevent the effect to occur, but its presence cannot guarantee the effect to occur. Necessary or positive conditions are present when the effect occurs but mere presence of one necessary or few necessary conditions are not enough to produce the effect. To follow I.M. Copi's example of fire,[2] the presence of oxygen, fuel and ignition are three necessary conditions but presence of any one, or two do not ensure the effect to occur. For instance oxygen is present here, fuel is also present but there is no fire here because third necessary condition, that is, ignition is missing.

Sufficient condition is the sum total of all necessary conditions. Conjunction of all necessary conditions imply sufficient condition. As soon as the sufficient conditions occur, the effect event also follows without any fail. For instance, fire takes place only when

1. Arthur Pap, op. cit., p. 260.
2. Irving M. Copi, and Carl Cohen, op. cit., p. 480.

all the three necessary conditions oxygen, fuel and ignition are present at the same time at the same place.

A scientist defines 'cause' in terms of necessary conditions when he wants to prevent something unpleasant. In order to extinguish fire at an undesired place, it is not required that all the necessary conditions (for fire to take place) are to be withdrawn. Even if one of the necessary conditions is removed, the effect vanishes. When the wells of oil were burning in Kuwait, (when Iraq attacked Kuwait in early 1990s), the supply of oxygen was stopped in and around the oil wells to extinguish fire. By stopping the supply of oxygen to the wells, fire was extinguished though other two conditions fuel and ignition were there.

A scientist defines cause in terms of sufficient condition when his aim is to produce something desirable. The presence of sufficient condition ensures the presence of effect. Wherever and whenever fire is required and desired, oxygen, fuel and ignition all should be there.

Necessary and sufficient conditions are not isolated. They are related to each other as parts to whole. Whereas sufficient condition should be treated as a whole, a necessary condition is merely a part of the whole.

The circle represents whole and hence stands for sufficient condition. Parts of the circle represent necessary conditions. One

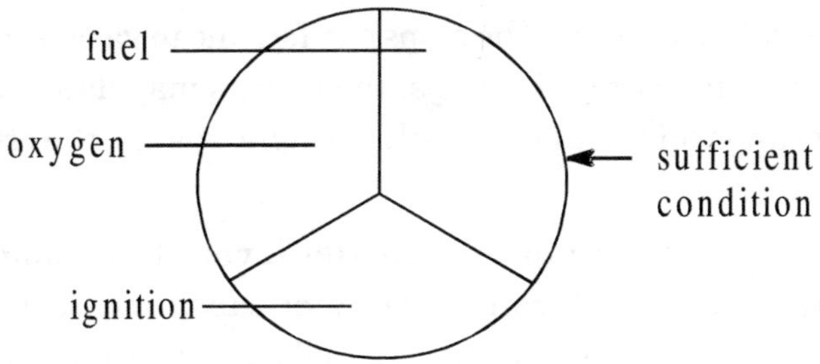

can equate cause with the sufficient condition, but one cannot equate a cause with necessary condition.

The relation between cause and condition is of peculiar type. If by condition we mean sufficient condition, then cause can be equated with condition. But if, on the other hand, by condition we mean a necessary condition, then cause cannot be equated with condition. It is very simple; whole is equated with whole and part with part; whole cannot be equated with part.

Plurality Theory of Causation

The scientific interpretation of causation (discussed above) has an important characteristic that the 'same' cause produces the 'same' effect. A slight change in the cause event makes similar change in the effect event. This scientific interpretation of causation that the 'same' cause produces 'same' effect, however, differs from the views held by certain logicians, like J.S. Mill, who thinks there can be *more than one cause* which produce the *same effect*. There can be several causes, "several logically independent sufficient conditions" which produce the 'same' effect. This theory is called plurality theory of causation. "Many causes may produce mechanical motion; many causes may produce some kinds of sensation; many causes may produce death."[3]

The causes of unnatural death are several such as accident, illness, bullet injury, poison, burns, etc. The effect remains the same. Take another example, there are many sources of light, say, sun, moon, fire, electricity. Take yet another example of poor cultivation of crops. The crops can fail due to various reasons. The floods can destroy the crops, the insects may damage it, the drought can spoil it, but the result is single, that is, the crops had failed.

For a common man and on the level of common-sense understanding the plurality theory of causation seems to be correct and acceptable. But if we analyse the situation a little further and go in depth, then the plurality theory of causation

---

3. J.S. Mill, *A System of Logic*, bk. 3, ch. 10, sec. 1.

will be found incorrect and unattainable. In all the examples cited above, the causes were analysed and separated but effect events were not analysed properly. The causes are labelled as C_1, C_2, C_3, etc. but effect event was wrongly presumed to be identical. We have wrongly thought effect is one and the same. Whenever there is slightest change in cause event effect, event also changes. Death due to bullet injury is of different kind than the death due to poisoning. If all the deaths would have been of the same kind, then why post-mortem is done to determine the right cause of death.

The crops failed due to flood are of different kind than the crops failed due to insects, or lack of proper care. Similarly sunlight is different from moon light. Candle light is of a unique type, and is different from the rest of other types of light. As the sources of light are different, nature of light is also different. Against the plurality theory of causation, the unique theory of causation ('same' cause produces 'same' effect) appears to be more logical and consistent.

C_1 --------------→ E_1

C_2 --------------→ E_2

C_3 --------------→ E_3

The unique theory of causation is also compatible with scientific interpretation of causation which is in terms of conditions. A set of certain conditions produces a certain effect, and the slightest variation in those conditions makes difference to the effect event.

The concept of cause as the set of certain conditions responsible for producing an effect, however, no longer fascinates a scientist. This conception of causation in terms of conditions is replaced by the latest concept of 'functional dependence'. The word 'function' is widely used in mathematics. In an effort to be more accurate and certain, the scientists express causal relationships in terms of mathematical equations. Consequently, scientific laws are formulated in mathematical terms with mathematical framework.

You are already familiar with the notion of function as we have made use of it earlier in symbolic logic. When the value of one variable depends on the value of another variable, then the former variable is called function of the latter variable. For example, when the value of Y is determined by the value of X, then Y is called function of X. Since the occurrences of certain events depend on the occurrences of certain other events, the scientists nowadays express the causal relationships in terms of 'functional dependence'.

Exercises

1. Cause is defined as "invariable, unconditional, immediate antecedent of an effect" Explain this statement.
2. "Scientists define cause in terms of sufficient condition". Discuss.
3. Explain with examples 'Plurality theory of causation'. Is it compatible with scientists', theory of 'one cause, one effect'?
4. Write short notes on:
    1. Proximate and remote cause
    2. Invariable and unconditional antecedent
    3. Necessary conditions and sufficient conditions
    4. Distinction between cause and condition.

Chapter 18

J.S. Mill's Experimental Methods

In the previous chapter you have learnt that to discover a causal relation among facts is the primary aim of a scientist. The crucial question now is how to discover a causal relation? How do we know that A is the cause of B? How does a scientist arrive at the conclusion that the certain conditions, say, X is the cause of Y phenomenon?

The logicians believe that there are methods which help in revealing the causal connections in the nature. Francis Bacon, in the sixteenth century, was the first such logician who emphasized in the efficiency and sufficiency of these methods.

The methods of discovering causal relationships though were first suggested by him, but it was J.S. Mill who formulated and elaborated them systematically in the nineteenth century. He (Mill) for the first time clearly defined these methods and highlighted their importance in scientific investigations. The formulation and structure of the methods, as we see them today, were given by him and he called them "methods of experimental inquiry". The experimental methods given by him are as follows:

(1) Method of Agreement
(2) Method of Difference
(3) Joint Method of Agreement and Difference
(4) Method of Residues
(5) Method of Concomitant Variation

Before we discuss in detail each of these methods, it is necessary to understand certain presuppositions which Mill made regarding the causal relationship. First, Mill's methods of experimental inquiry take for granted the truth that wherever and whenever cause is present, effect is also present. Second, whenever and wherever cause is absent, effect is also absent. Third, whenever cause varies (increases or decreases), effect also varies accordingly. Fourth, whatever is the cause of something, the same cause cannot produce something else. Mill's experimental methods are intelligible only in terms of these characteristic presuppositions of causation.

Let us now discuss each of Mill's methods in detail.

Method of Agreement

The method of agreement is the most popular of all the experimental methods. It is used by common men, scientists and philosophers alike. The basis of the method of agreement is the occurrence of a certain phenomenon repeatedly. In our experiences we observe some facts occur simultaneously. Whenever one fact, say A occurs, another fact say *a* also occurs. The togetherness of two facts A and *a* leads human beings to relate them casually. The human mind becomes so accustomed and conditioned by observing togetherness of the two facts that next time whenever one sees A event, he expects *a* to follow. The strength of the method of agreement depends on the large number of instances. The greater are the instances, the more reliable is the causal relation.

The method can best be understood with the help of examples. J.S. Mill's example for the method is as follows:

In our experiences we have always found that whenever fatty oil or a fat was mixed with an alkaline substance, a soap substance was produced. This has been the case in all sorts of fatty oils mixed with all sorts of alkaline. This led to the conclusion that all cases of fatty oils mixed with all sorts of alkaline substances produce soap substance.

Take another illustration. All the members of a club are above 50 years old and none of them found any need to visit hospital since three years. In order to know the cause of this happy phenomenon, the method of agreement was applied. The common factor found among these people was that they do regular exercises and are leading a disciplined life.

Take yet another very common instance as an illustration of the method of agreement given by Irving M. Copi in slightly different way. Suppose in a party, after taking dinner, most of the guests got sick. In order to know the cause of sickness among the guests, the doctor employs the method of agreement (though he may not be aware of the fact that he is applying the method of agreement). He inquires about the food items the patients had taken. The doctor is trying to isolate a common factor, common food item which all the sick guests had consumed. The food items which the guests had taken were bread, curd, rice, mixed vegetables, salad and ice cream. After examining quite a few patients he found ice cream was the only food item taken by all sick patients. Consequently, the doctor reached to the conclusion that probably ice cream served to the guests was either a cause or part of cause of sickness among people.[1]

Mill explains the method as, "If two or more instances of the phenomenon under investigation have only one circumstance in common, the circumstance in which alone all the instances agree is the cause (or effect) of the given phenomenon".[2]

The method can also be explained symbolically as:

Number of instances	*Circumstance* (*Cause*)	*Phenomenon* (*Effect*)
1.	ABCD	abcd
2.	AMNO	amno
3.	ALHP	alhp
4.	AXYZ	axyz
"	I	I
"	I	I
"	I	I
"	I	I
"	I	I

1. Cf. Irving M. Copi, and Carl Cohen, op. cit., pp. 487-88.
2. J.S. Mill, op. cit., bk. 3, ch. 8, sec. 18.

Therefore, probably A is cause or part of cause of *a*.

The symbolical expression of the method of agreement shows that it is essentially a method of elimination. It systematically eliminates the non-causal elements in the circumstances (cause) and consequently in phenomena (effect). One by one all factors like B, C, D, M, N, O, L, H, P, X, Y, Z were eliminated as the possible cause of the phenomenon *a*. Only A was isolated as a common circumstance and *a* was isolated as common phenomenon. Hence most probably A is the cause of *a*. One selects a common invariable and relevant factor occurring in these various instances and rejecting irrelevant or accidental factors so that the real and genuine relationship can be established.

The method of agreement is also called a method of observation. In this lies its merits as well as demerits. In the field where the experiments are very dangerous to perform, the method of observation is the only available method for the investigation of causal relationship. But sometimes the phenomenon occurs so rarely that one has to wait quite a long time to observe it again. It may be possible that the phenomenon may occur once in hundred years. In that case the method of agreement is not profitable method for discovering causal connection.

Moreover, Mill's formulation of the method demands that cause and effect events should be analysed into simpler components as shown in the symbolic expression. But how do we know that our analysis of the complex events into simpler components is correct? To an irrelevant factor we may wrongly consider as relevant and vice versa. How can we then be sure that in the analysis of component events, which factors are relevant for causation and which are irrelevant? The phenomena and circumstances do not come to us carrying tags of relevance or irrelevance. One has to take the help from other sources also in order to know the relevant factors in determining causal relationship. The method of agreement, it seems, by itself may not be sufficient to determine the causal relation among facts in some cases.

Let us consider here some of those cases where the method of agreement was applied but it did not establish the right causal relationship because irrelevant common factors were wrongly thought to be the cause of facts.

Instances	*Cause*	*Effect*
1.	Cat A crossed the path of x	It proved bad luck to x
2.	Cat B crossed the path of y	It proved bad luck to y
3.	Cat C crossed the path of z	It proved bad luck to z
4.	Cat D crossed the path of m	It proved bad luck to m

Therefore, crossing the path by a cat is the cause of bad luck to a man.

It is very clear the method of agreement was applied in the above example, but at the same time nobody will deny that the path crossed by a cat is not the cause of bad luck. It is sheer a chance that some accidentally common factors occurred again and again which is actually not the real cause. But how do we know which commonly occurring factors are genuine (and establish a causal relation) and which ones are accidental and cannot be causal indicator. It is only by some other source or sources, other than method of agreement, that we realize whether the common isolated factor is in fact the real cause or not. The difficulty in isolating the common relevant circumstances in some instances was brought out beautifully by Copi.[3] XYZ drank brandy and water and got drunk. XYZ drank gin and water and got drunk. Observing that water was present in each instance of the phenomenon under investigations, they concluded that water is the cause of drunkenness and solemnly resolved to avoid consumption of that liquid in future!

The major stumbling stone in the correct application of the method of agreement is that there is no way to differentiate the situation in which two facts are occurring together just by chance

3. Cf. Irving M. Copi, and Carl Cohen, op. cit., p. 511.

or whether they are coming together because of genuine relationship. It seems superstition and scientific knowledge both began from the same point, that is, by observing certain facts occurring together. In both the situations the togetherness of the phenomena is the basis of our belief in their occurrences. But whereas the former is not rooted in causal relation the latter cannot help being rooted in it. The method of agreement can merely suggest and can never prove the causal relationship.

Moreover, by the method of agreement one cannot differentiate between cause and co-existence. For instance, day and night follow each other invariably but none of them is cause of another. They both are rather the co-effects of something else. Similar objections can be made regarding heat and light, lightning and thunder.

Sometimes, the method of agreement takes us half way in the investigation of the causal relationships. For instance, in the case where people got sick after taking dinner, the doctor may isolate two food items as possible causes of sickness but out of them which one is the real cause of trouble, the method of agreement may not be able to locate. In that situation the doctor needs another method, the method of difference to determine the cause of sickness among people.

Method of Difference (Disagreement)

The method of difference can be applied to almost all those cases where the method of agreement is applied. But whereas the method of agreement requires large number of instances, the method of difference needs just two. The two instances should be such that they resemble each other in every respect except one. For instance, if a bell is rung in a jar filled with air, the sound of the bell is heard, but if the same bell is rung in a jar from which the air has been pumped out, no sound is heard (provided other circumstances remain the same). From this, one concludes that the presence of air is an indispensable part of the cause of sound.

Take another illustration. Suppose a physician wishes to test the efficiency of a certain drug as a cure for cold. He will consider people suffering from cold and who do not take the drug and consequently continue to be ill for a fairly long time. The physician also takes into account of those patients who take the drug and get immediate relief. From these two different sets of patients the physician establishes the efficiency of the drug.[4]

In the case where people got sick after taking dinner, the doctor will take two such persons for inquiry who have taken the same food items except one. Two guests, say, P and Q have eaten B, C, D, L, M food items but whereas P has taken one more item A, Q has not taken that very item. From this the doctor concludes that probably the food item A is the cause of sickness among guests.

The canon of the method of difference stated by Mill is as "If an instance in which the phenomenon under investigation occurs, and an instance in which it does not occur, have every circumstance save one in common, that one occurring only in the former, the circumstance in which alone the two instances differ, is the effect, or the cause, or a necessary part of the cause, of the phenomenon".[5]

Symbolically the method of difference can be expressed as follows:

Instances	*Cause*	*Effect*
1.	ABCERF	Sick
2.	ABCER	Not sick

Therefore, probably F is either a cause or part of cause of sickness.

The method of difference requires two such instances which resemble each other except in one respect. In the practical state of affairs, however, such a requirement is too difficult to meet.

4. Cf. Arthur Pap, op. cit., p. 153.
5. J.S. Mill, op. cit., bk. 3, ch, 8m sec. 2.

One cannot so easily find two events resembling one another in all aspects except one. This ideal condition is impossible to fulfil at times. But in experiments such rigorous requirement can be met because there the situation is under our control, and we can create the situation artificially according to our requirements.

If the method of difference is strictly applied in conformity with its requirements, then, Mill claims, it *proves* causal relation and thus yields conclusion with utmost certainty. Some logicians believe the method of difference gives "rigorous certainty". Out of the five of Mill's methods, this is the only method by which causal relations can be established and proved conclusively. But this is a "tall claim" regarding any of the experimental inquiry. In fact, neither inductive reasoning nor any of the experimental methods can ever prove the conclusion conclusively.

The method of difference, like all other methods, suffers from certain limitations. The method cannot be successfully applied in those cases where experiments are too dangerous to conduct.

Joint Method of Agreement and Difference

This is not a new method. Since the method of agreement and the method of difference are applied to the same cases, the investigator may sometimes use both of them to establish a causal relation.

The simultaneous application of twin methods increases our faith in the conclusion drawn from the evidences. The joint method thus is certainly superior than the method of agreement alone or the method of difference alone. Symbolically then joint method can be expressed as follows:

Instance	*Circumstance*	*Phenomenon*
1.	ABCD	abcd
2.	AMNO	amno
3.	AXYZ	axyz
"	I	I
"	I	I

Therefore, probably A is cause or part of cause of *a*, and

Instance	*Circumstance*	*Phenomenon*
1.	ABCD	abcd
2.	BCD	bcd

Therefore, probably A is cause or part of cause of *a*.

Let us take once again the example of the guests who got sick after taking dinner in a party. The doctor applies dual method in order to be more certain about the poisonous food element. By the method of agreement he will make a list of patients and examine what each one had eaten:

Patients	*Food Items*	*Effect*
1.	ABCD	Sick
2.	AMCD	Sick
3.	AMCL	Sick
4.	ACBM	Sick
5.	ALDH	Sick

Therefore, probably A is either the cause or part of the cause of sickness.

The doctor makes another list of patients as follows:

Instance	*Food Items*	*Effect*
1.	BCD	Not Sick
2.	MCL	Not Sick
3.	CBM	Not Sick
4.	LDH	Not Sick

Therefore, probably A is the cause or part of the cause of sickness.

Combining the results of both the investigations the doctor finally reaches to the conclusion that food item A is most probably the cause of sickness among guests. The joint method depends on the axiom that "whenever cause occurs effect occurs and whenever cause is absent effect is also absent". In the joint method the negative instances strengthen the conclusion drawn from the positive instances. Thus in this method there is emphasis both on necessary and sufficient conditions.

Method of Residues

Mill defined the method of residues as follows:

"Subduct from any phenomenon such part as is known by previous inductions to be the effect of certain antecedents, and the residue of the phenomenon is the effect of the remaining antecedents."[6] For instance, in order to know the weight of the cargo the usual practice is to weigh empty truck and then to weigh loaded truck of cargo. The difference between the weights is the actual weight of the cargo. Here the method of residues is applied, and except this method there is no other way to weigh the cargo.

Many times at a grocer's shop you would have noticed that the shopkeeper first weighs an empty container and then he weighs container again after filling it with ghee or oil. This is yet another illustration where the method of residues is applied.

The method of residues is very widely used in sciences. Many important scientific discoveries are made with the help of this method. The famous discovery of Madam Curie's new chemical radium and the tremendous radioactivity it produces is made with the help of the method of residues.

Similarly, the calculation of the path of the planet Uranus revealed the presence of new planet Neptune, in 1846. When the scientist Leverrier calculated the path of the planet Uranus then he found there is a difference of two minutes between the path calculated by him and the actual path taken by the planet which causes the difference in the calculation of the path. Later on it was further confirmed that there is actually another planet

6. J.S. Mill, op. cit., bk. 3, ch. 8, sec. 5.

Neptune which is the outermost of the all planets in the solar system.

Symbolically one can express the method of residues as follows:

Instance	*Circumstance*	*Phenomenon*
1.	ABCD	abcd
2.	B	b
3.	C	c
4.	D	d

Therefore, probably A is the cause of *a*.

The complex event ABCD is the cause of complex effect abcd; and previously it has been established that B is the cause of b, C is the cause of c, and D is the cause of d. From this acquired knowledge it is inferred that A is the cause of a, the residues circumstance is the cause of residues phenomenon. The leftover event is the cause of leftover effect.

Some thinkers regard the method of residues as the method of deduction because here less observation is done and more deduction and calculations are made. But this is not correct. For, it makes use of the knowledge of the causal relations which was inductively established earlier. Like all other experimental methods, the method of residues is also not a method of proof. The method takes us only a half-way and can be "a finger-post to the unexplained", but it can never demonstratively prove a causal connection.

Method of Concomitant Variation

The four experimental methods discussed so far are methods of elimination. In order to determine the causal relation the irrelevant circumstances are systematically eliminated. But there are circumstances which cannot be eliminated altogether. For instance, heat, gravity, atmosphere, friction, pressure, etc. are the natural necessities which cannot be eliminated altogether.

Though the complete elimination of these permanent causes is not possible, yet they vary in degrees, and through the method of concomitant variation one can establish the causal relationship between them.

Mill states the method of concomitant variation as: "Whatever phenomenon varies in any manner whenever some other phenomenon varies in some particular manner is either a cause or an effect of that phenomenon or is connected with it through some fact of causation."[7]

Symbolically the method can be expressed as follows:

Instance	*Cause*	*Effect*
1.	ABC	abc
2.	A+BC[8]	a+bc
3.	A-BC	a-bc

Therefore, probably A is the cause of *a*.

The two facts when vary together (either homogeneously or heterogeneously), they suggest the causal relationship between them.

The concomitant change in the temperature and mercury helped scientists to relate them causally. Similarly, the rise of tides in the sea is causally related with the increase in the size of the moon. As the size of the moon increases, the tides in the sea rise higher. In economics, the principle of demand and supply which determine the price of a commodity makes use of the method of concomitant variation. In order to know why cases of suicides,

7. J.S. Mill, op. cit., bk. 3, ch. 8, sec. 6.
8. Homogeneous change is that in which both the facts either increase together or decrease together, and heterogeneous change is that in which two facts vary inversely, that is, if one increases the other decreases.

   A+ means A increases.

   A- means A decreases.

rape, murders, robberies and other anti-social activities are increasing in society, one gathers the facts, events and also the situations which are increasing and hence are responsible for the rise in the undesirable behaviour. These examples make it clear that in the quantitative induction method of concomitant variations is the only relevant method to determine causal relation.

However, this method like all other previous methods is not foolproof method. Sometimes two phenomena vary together but they are not causally related. They both may be the co-effects of some other cause. For example, the minute hand and the second hand in a watch vary simultaneously but the movement of hour hand is not the cause of the movement of minute hand or vice versa. Moreover, since the method of concomitant variation is the method of quantity, the method demands some scale to measure the increase or the decrease in the quantity. The scale may not be very accurate or sophisticated but certainly some scale is absolutely indispensable.

Assessment of the Methods

The study of the experimental methods may give an impression that the causal relationship among the natural phenomena can easily be established. This, however, is not always the case. The experimental methods are merely instruments, and how efficiently and successfully one makes use of these methods in discovering causal relationship, depends entirely on the skill and ability of the user.

Mill had made two claims regarding his experimental methods. First, they are the methods of discovery. That is, these methods alone are sufficient and enough to establish causal relations among facts. The scientists' skill, wisdom and imagination, it seems, have no place in establishing causal relation. Something similar Francis Bacon has also stated. He said our method for discovering causal relation in "sciences is such as leaves but little to the accurateness and strength of wits, but places all wits and understandings nearly on the level. For as in the drawing of a straight line or a perfect circle, much depends on the steadiness and practice of the hand, if it be done by aid of hand only, but it with the aid of rule or compass, little or nothing; so as it is exactly with any plan."[9]

Second, Mill claims the methods can *prove* the causal relations *demonstratively*. Inductive logic supplies, says Mill, "rules and models (such as the syllogism and its rules are for ratiocination) to which if inductive arguments conform these arguments are conclusive and not otherwise".[10] These rules and models are nothing but his experimental methods about which he claims that they have demonstrative function and has capacity to prove the causal relationship among facts just as a conclusion is proved in deductive logic.

But this is not correct. The experimental methods do not and cannot prove demonstratively the causal relationship. Since the methods make use of observations and experiments, the knowledge based on them can never be certain and demonstrative. Just as the inductive reasoning is problematic so also causal knowledge arrived through the experimental methods. Nothing in the inductive logic can claim to be demonstratively proved because inductive logic is not totally formal.

Thus both the claims which Mill made about his experimental methods are rather "big" claims, and cannot be accepted as valid. There is a "quest for certainty" in his theory of induction and because of this he made such claims. The experimental methods otherwise have an important function. They are extremely potential in suggesting a course of inquiry to a scientist, and they are important "milestones" and good "signposts" on the roads of scientific discovery, though by themselves they are neither sufficient nor complete in establishing causal relations among facts.

---

9. Francis, Bacon, *Novum*, *Organum*, bk. 1, LXI.
10. J.S. Mill, op. cit., bk. 2, ch. 3, sec. 7.

Exercises

1. Explain and illustrate the method of agreement. Highlight its merit and demerit.
2. Explain and illustrate the method of difference and point out its special features.
3. Explain and illustrate the joint method of agreement and difference. In what way it is superior to method of agreement alone?
4. Explain and illustrate the method of concomitant variations. Point out its special features.
5. Clearly bring out the limitations of Mill's methods of experimental inquiry.

Chapter 19

Hypothesis

In any scientific investigation, the scientist begins by assuming some possible explanation for the problem he is investigating. This possible explanation is called hypothesis. Using this as a starting point of his investigation, he proceeds further to collect facts through observation and experiments. If our empirical evidences support the hypothesis, then the hypothesis is accepted as correct explanation, otherwise not. A hypothesis thus is merely a tentative or provisional solution to a problem. It is not the real solution of the problem (for which the hypothesis is constituted), till verified.

A hypothesis is important for a proper and systematic scientific investigation. It points to the direction in which the scientist should make observations and conduct experiments. By framing hypothesis the research is focused on specific points and the entire energy (experiments and observations) is used to gather the evidences in favour of the hypothesis. Random investigations are of no help and only an organized investigation is fruitful. Hypothesis defines the scope of a scientific inquiry and helps in saving time and efforts of the investigators. The hypothesis serves as the starting point in the rigorous scientific research and thus a hypothesis is assumed as a guide to scientific inquiry. All scientific investigations start with the formulations of hypotheses and stop with their verification and proof. Historians, detectives, social scientists as well as natural scientists make extensive use of hypotheses.

It is not only in the branches of knowledge the hypotheses are framed, tested, verified and proved, but even in most ordinary and common practical life, we continually frame hypotheses in order to give an account for, or analyse or solve a practical problem. Suppose when I go back home and I find my son has not reached home from school which he normally does by that time, I start guessing and making tentative explanations as to what would have happened to him. I may suppose that he has missed the school bus, or his school bus is late, for it is caught in traffic. These alternative explanations, suggestions or solutions are called hypotheses.

A hypothesis is simply a suggestion or a possible explanation of a particular phenomenon. It is merely a suggestive, tentative or a provisional solution to a problem. A hypothesis is not the real solution until tested and verified. All hypotheses are subject to revision, modification or even rejection.

Since a hypothesis is extremely important in every field of investigation, let us see how it is framed. The formation of a hypothesis is not a mechanical process. No rules or criteria can be laid down for making a "relevant" or "good" hypothesis. Actual framing of a hypothesis is the work of a genius. Here the sagacity, genius and originality of a scientist play important role, for only a genius or a trained mind can see something significant in the phenomenon which others do not notice. Hypotheses are suggested, writes De Morgan, not by rules, but by sagacity of which no description can be given previously because the very owners of it do not act under any prescribed laws. S.H. Mellone adds beautifully, "Nature, herself, . . . does give broad hints as to the direction in which a fruitful hypothesis may be looked for; but only a prepared mind knows how to 'take the hint'."[1]

Nature gives "broad hints" to inquisitive mind and they are "finger-posts" in nature pointing outlines of fruitful inquiry. Induction by simple enumeration and analogy are two main sources which suggest hypotheses to a scientist. Two phenomena when repeatedly occur together, then it suggests that there is

1. S.H. Mellone, *Elements of Modern Logic*, p. 197.

some connection between them, and consequently a scientist frames a hypothesis. In chapter 16, you have learnt that induction by simple enumeration cannot prove the causal connection between the two phenomena but it does suggest a hypothesis, a line of inquiry to a scientist. Similarly analogy does not conclusively prove a causal connection though it is a fruitful source for suggesting hypotheses. When it is found that two things resemble each other in certain important respects, we frame the hypothesis that they will possibly resemble each other in other respects too. The planets, earth and mars, resemble each other in possessing similar kind of atmosphere, land, etc. On the basis of these resemblances we are led to suppose that the planet mars might resemble the earth in being inhabited by living creatures. The analogy, thus, is a very important source of making hypotheses.

Science demands a higher degree of exactness and in this sense scientific research is a rigorous investigation. For this purpose there should be a well-defined problem which needs a solution. One of the important characteristics of scientific thinking, and of all thinking having scientific spirit, is to grasp the problem and its nature before proceeding to solve it. Sometimes it comes to a scientist well defined and some other times the scientist himself sees a problem where others do not. Only attentive and intellectually curious mind sees the problem where others do not. A scientist then begins by providing possible solutions, conjectures, suppositions, hypotheses to solve the marked problem. All his energy is then focused on framing and verifying hypotheses.

Generally, a common man is inclined to treat any provisional supposition as an hypothesis. But a scientist does not consider seriously any supposed or provisional answer. A hypothesis is considered for serious discussion only if it satisfies certain conditions, though these conditions are, by no means, conclusive or exhaustive.

Conditions of Valid Hypothesis

The main characteristic of a "good", "valid" or "legitimate" hypothesis is that it should explain facts around us; it must be based on events actually occurring in nature. Valid hypothesis depends on facts in its origin and also for its verification.

Another important quality of a "good" hypothesis is that it should be verifiable with reference to observation or experience. The verifiability of a hypothesis can be done directly or indirectly. A hypothesis which lacks any verification (direct or indirect) is called "barren hypothesis", and is not for the scientific inquiries.

Besides verifiability and having approved by actual experiences, a good hypothesis must satisfy other conditions too. A hypothesis should be purposeful, and directed to solve the problem for which it is framed. Random or irrelevant hypotheses cannot be considered for serious discussions in sciences or in ordinary common life. In other words, a hypothesis must be relevant to the problem it is supposed to solve. Relevance here means the hypothesis must either be a cause or part of a cause of a phenomenon for which it is formed. If, however, a hypothesis is neither of them, then it is irrelevant hypothesis and cannot be called "good" hypothesis.

Moreover, the hypothesis must be clearly and distinctly conceivable in itself. It should be stated in the clearest of terms. The vague, obscure and ambiguous hypothesis will only compound the problem of the scientist instead of solving it.

Generally a hypothesis which needs less calculation or mapping or observation is considered good. The scientist prefers the "mathematically simplest hypothesis" available. "For example, he will assume a linear equation rather than a quadratic equation if both fit the data".[2] Copernicus suspected that complexities of the epicyclic orbits of the heavenly bodies were due to the observer's own motion. By shifting to the sun as centre of the

2. Arthur Pap, op. cit., p. 226.

coordinate system, he managed to produce a far simpler system of celestial bodies. But simplicity should not be confused with familiarity.

One of the important characteristics of a good hypothesis is that it must not contradict other established truths or laws. This condition demands that we should take into account the achievements of the past. Certain things have been established rather definitely and any novel suggestion, which contradicts one of such well-established laws, will be treated with suspicion. Knowledge of facts and laws previously ascertained gives steadiness to scientific knowledge, and any contradiction of these established laws will only raise the suspicion towards the new hypothesis.

But this condition at times can be violated and overruled. There are instances in the history of science when the established theories and cherished laws are abandoned in favour of new findings. For instance, Ptolemy's[3] theory of universe (according to which the earth is the centre of the universe, and the sun, the moon and other planets revolve around it) was once established and accepted theory. It was later challenged and replaced by Copernican[4] theory according to which sun is the centre of solar system, and the earth, and other planets move around it.

A hypothesis which conforms to the various conditions laid down above is called "legitimate", "valid" or "good" or "working" hypothesis. A scientist goes ahead in his investigations with working hypothesis. A working hypothesis is accepted as true for time being and is used as a guide for further inquiry. But a working hypothesis is accepted as the real solution (to the problem for which it is constituted) only after verification and confirmation.

Verification

A working hypothesis is to be tested and verified. Without verification a hypothesis can never be accepted as the real solution

3. Claudius Ptolemy was an Egyptian astronomer who lived about CE127.
4. Nicolaus Copernicus was Polish astronomer who lived about CE 1473-1543.

to the problem. This is the most crucial stage in the scientific investigation. There are two stages of testing the validity of a hypothesis.

1. Verification of a hypothesis
2. Proof of a hypothesis

VERIFICATION OF A HYPOTHESIS

Verification of a hypothesis means testing of the truth of the hypothesis in the light of actual facts and in the context of empirical data. The process of verification involves a comparison between the conclusion deduced from the hypothesis and facts gathered through observation. The greater the agreement between the inferences derived from the hypothesis and facts gathered through observation or experience, the stronger will be the evidences in favour of confirming the hypothesis. Verification means to find out whether the conclusion derived from the hypothesis is supported by the actual experiences or not.

Verification of a hypothesis is of two types:

(i) Direct.

(ii) Indirect.

Direct Verification: Direct verification is done by direct appeal to experiences and observations. Suppose one wants to test the hypothesis that the involvement of students in the college administration solves the discipline problem among the students. For this the behaviour of the students are studied to find out whether they respond to the responsibility given to them. If the observation shows that an increased participation in the college administration decreases the indiscipline among them, then the hypothesis is verified by direct observation.

Indirect Verification: But in many cases direct verification of hypotheses is not possible. In those cases indirect verification, and indirect evidences are looked for to verify the hypotheses. In indirect verification the consequences are deduced from the hypothesis (the one which one wants to verify) and they are then compared with the actual facts. If the deduced consequences or evidences agree with the facts actually observed, then the hypothesis is verified, otherwise it stands rejected.

There are situations in science where a scientist verifies the hypothesis indirectly, that is, by deducing evidences. Arthur Pap says, "there is no other way of testing an empirical hypothesis — especially one of highly theoretical character, such as the hypothesis of universal gravitation, or the atomic hypothesis, or the gene theory of biology than by deducing from it directly testable consequences."[5]

Indirect verification of a hypothesis is done by constructing a logical argument. If expressed in the strict logical form it becomes a hypothetical syllogism. Suppose one wants indirect verification of a hypothesis, say, H, then one will frame hypothetical syllogism as follows:

If the fact S is observed, then the hypothesis H is true.
S is observed.
Therefore, the hypothesis H is true.

Take a concrete example:

If the roads are wet, then it has rained recently.
The roads are wet.
Therefore, it has rained recently.

Take another example:

If the house is badly ransacked, then the aim of criminals was to steal.
The house was badly ransacked.
Therefore, the aim of criminals was to steal.

In all the above examples the hypotheses are verified or confirmed on the basis of certain other facts which are observed as true.

---

5. Arthur Pap, op. cit., p. 139.

The hypothetical syllogism can also be used to disconfirm or to disprove a rival hypothesis, say, H. The structure of the reasoning adopted for this purpose would be as follows:

> If hypothesis H is true, then the fact S must be observed.
> The fact S is not observed.
> Therefore, the hypothesis H is not true.

Yet another example:

> If it rained recently, then the roads are wet.
> The roads are not wet.
> Therefore, it did not rain recently.

Take another illustration:

> If the aim of criminals is to rob, then the valuables must be missing.
> But no valuables were missing.
> Therefore, the aim of criminals was not to rob.

It is evident that by disproving the rival hypothesis, no hypothesis is proved. It merely eliminates rival hypotheses to increase the probability of some other hypothesis. For example, in order to know the cause of the gruesome crime in which all the members of the family were killed, the investigating team makes a number of hypotheses, say, H_1, H_2, H_3, etc. By framing hypothetical syllogisms the rivalry hypotheses are eliminated one by one. If the investigating team wants to know whether the hypothesis H_1, that is, the robbery was the motive of the crime, then by structuring hypothetical syllogism, as we have done above, H_1 can to be ruled out. The investigating team then takes second hypothesis H_2 for verification. The hypothesis H_2 states that probably the revenge was the cause of crime. The hypothetical argument is framed as follows:

> If revenge was the cause of the crime, then the victims were known to be unpopular or unfriendly people.
> But the victims were not known to be unpopular or unfriendly people.
> Therefore, the revenge was not the possible motive of crime.

In this manner the hypothesis H_2 is also disproved and eliminated. The list of hypotheses is short-listed in this way and then the attention is paid to the remaining possible causes of the crime.

Scientists, detectives and historians use direct as well as indirect verification to justify and verify their hypotheses. The "utilitarian justification of a method of accepting and rejecting hypotheses"[6] is usually employed by them. The "utilitarian justification" of hypothesis means the "satisfaction produced" by accepting a particular hypothesis. If we get good results and it works pragmatically well in our experiences and explain the facts perfectly well, then the hypothesis is accepted as confirmed and verified. But no hypothesis is totally true or completely confirmed. There can only be a "high degree of confirmation".

PROOF OF A HYPOTHESIS

Verification (direct or indirect) is merely one step in the direction of proving a hypothesis. The hypothesis is called proved conclusively only when it stands as the only hypothesis, providing an adequate explanation for the facts or is the only solution for the problem. In verifying hypotheses, the scientist takes each alternative hypothesis one by one, and examines it in the light of available evidences. At this stage, no comparison is made among the rivalry hypotheses and as a result more than one hypothesis can be verified at a time. But while proving a hypothesis a scientist puts all the verified hypotheses together against each other to assess whether any one of them is supported by such conclusive evidences which are not available for the other hypotheses. Thus while verification is the process of evaluating each hypothesis separately on its own merits, proof is the process of comparison among the verified hypotheses. Proof of a hypothesis means a "process of elimination of competing hypotheses". After eliminating rivalry hypotheses, the best and the most acceptable hypothesis is chosen as the proved hypothesis.

---

6. Arthur Pap, op. cit., p. 234.

Hypotheses are first verified and then among verified hypotheses the best one is selected, and that chosen one is called proved hypothesis. When more than one hypothesis are verified then there is competition among them. In order to select one out of them, further investigations are done and then the best among them is chosen. This best chosen one is called *proved hypothesis*.

A proved hypothesis must adequately explain all the facts for which it has been made and it must be the only hypothesis to do so. The hypothesis, say A, is called proved when it is the only explanation or cause of the fact, say, B. The fact B does not follow from any other source except A. "We must know not merely that A is an antecedent of B, but that A is the only possible antecedent of B . . ."[7]

Moreover, a proved hypothesis must explain not only those facts for which it is framed but other related facts also. For example, the law of gravitation explains not only the falling of bodies on the earth but provides the explanation for the movements of the planets and their behaviour. In short, a proved hypothesis must be verified, and it must be adequate to explain the phenomenon under investigation, and also it should be the only hypothesis to do so.

However, in science many hypotheses remain unproved even though they have been verified. This happens because the conclusive evidences may not be available to support the facts. For instance, there are different hypotheses regarding the origin of the world. Each one of them stands verified to some extent, but none has yet been proved conclusively. The demand for absolute and conclusive proof of a hypothesis is an ideal demand which cannot be always met. However, the hypothesis that stands verified with the support of evidences is raised to the status of theory. At the same time a well approved and generally accepted theory becomes a law.

---

7. S.H. Mellone, op. cit., p. 195.

Crucial Instances

As you have seen a hypothesis stands finally approved only when it eliminates the rivalry hypotheses and provides conclusively the most logical and complete explanation of the phenomenon under investigation. If a certain observation yields an instance which finally confirms one hypothesis and provides conclusive evidence against the others, such an instance is called crucial instance. The scientist stands on a cross road, wondering as to which hypothesis provides the real explanation for the phenomenon under investigation. Since an instance or an experiment helps in choosing his way, such an instance or experiment is called crucial.

Exercises

1. Define hypothesis and point out its importance in induction.
2. Explain the conditions of a good hypothesis with suitable examples.
3. How is a hypothesis verified? Explain both direct and indirect verifications of hypothesis.
4. Distinguish between verification and proof of a hypothesis. Do you agree with the statement that without verification no hypothesis can be accepted as a real explanation for the problem though without proof a hypothesis still can be somewhat dependable?
5. Imagine you have lost your college I-card. What hypothesis you will frame and how will you verify them.

Part IV

Chapter 20

Informal Fallacies

FALLACY is an error in reasoning, it is a mistake in judgement. An argument is governed by certain rules, and violation of any one of them makes the argument invalid and fallacious. Sometimes incorrect argument deceptively appears to be correct but on the examination is found incorrect. As you know the aim of a logician is to provide methods to differentiate correct reasoning from incorrect one, he thus investigates all the sources from where the incorrectness can creep into the reasoning. A logician picks up all the holes from where the errors in the reasoning enter and then suggests how to tackle them.

The list of errors to which a human mind is prone to, is long. In logic they are divided into two categories:

1. Formal Fallacies
2. Informal Fallacies

FORMAL FALLACIES

A formal fallacy is committed when the argument has faulty structure or form. Formal reasoning such as syllogism, if it violates any of the rules of the valid categorical syllogism, then it commits the formal fallacy. Fallacy of Undistributed Middle, Illicit Major, Illicit Minor, Existential Fallacy, etc. are a few instances of formal fallacies.

INFORMAL FALLACIES

The informal fallacies are committed by every man, be he a scientist or a common man. Though the logicians disagree about the number of informal fallacies but roughly they (the fallacies) can be divided into three categories. They are:

1. Fallacies of Ambiguity
2. Fallacies of Relevance
3. Fallacies of Presumptions

Fallacies of Ambiguity

Fallacies of Ambiguity arise from the loose and mistaken ways in which words and sentences are used in arguments. Since arguments are expressed through language, there can be many ways in which errors could arise. It could be either due to wrong use of words or due to wrong construction of statements. Accordingly there are many fallacies of Ambiguity. Some of the main fallacies in this category are:

1. Fallacy of Equivocation
2. Fallacy of Amphiboly
3. Fallacy of Accent
4. Fallacy of Composition
5. Fallacy of Division

FALLACY OF EQUIVOCATION

Definition:

> The Fallacy of Equivocation occurs when same word or a phrase is used with two meanings.

The simplest way in which the Fallacy of Equivocation is committed is by giving different meanings to the same word in an argument.

See the following examples:

1. "I will follow Karan's advice because he gives sound advices". The other person says, "Yes I could hear his sound even at long distance". Therefore I can hear his advice even at long distance. Here the word 'sound' has two meanings. Firstly, it means good and reliable; he gives good and reliable advices. Secondly 'sound' means 'noise' which is created while speaking.

2. Power tends to corrupt

   Knowledge is power

   Therefore knowledge tends to corrupt

   The word 'power' has two different meanings:

   (i) It means authority to control or to influence others.

   (ii) It means strength, skill, acumenship and mental sharpness.

3. Friend A to another friend B "I am behind you" B said to A "Yes I could see you are right behind me." There are two meanings of the word 'behind'. It could mean "I am at your back. I will support you morally, emotionally and even financially". The other meaning of 'behind' is in the context of space as in queue you are right behind me.[1]

4. "This is a fine country to live in " said the poor man in 'Charlie Chaplin's film *The Great Dictator*. A policeman caught him but later on he got himself off by pleading that all he meant by fine country was that it is really very good and fine country to live in.[2] There are two meanings of the words 'fine'.

   (i) A 'fine country' means a country full of punishments.

   (ii) Second meaning of 'fine country' is good and nice country to live in.

5. One might argue that:

   The enforced payment of income tax is a deprivation of freedom.

   To be deprived of freedom is to become a slave.

Therefore anyone compelled to pay income tax is a slave.

Here the expression 'deprivation of freedom' is equivocal. In the first premiss, 'to be deprived of freedom' means a necessary

---

1. William J. Kilgore, *An Introductory Logic*, p. 68.
2. Joseph Gerard, Brennan, *A Handbook of Logic*, p. 213.

imposition of taxes in the interest of country, while in the second premiss it means a total deprivation of liberty.[3]

Look at another example:

All laws are made by government

V = at is a law of falling bodies

\ the government made V = at is law

This is incorrect reasoning, for the term 'law' is ambiguous. At one place it refers to the physical law and at another place it is used as a legislative law.[4]

Sometimes Fallacy of Equivocation is committed when one considers words derived from same root have the same meaning, or when a resemblance between ideas is established from the mere resemblance of words. Let us take often quoted example from J.S. Mill's argument.

The visible is that object which can be seen. The audible is that sound which can be heard. Therefore desirable is that which people actually desire.[5]

It is true that 'visible' means 'what can be seen' and 'audible' means 'what can be heard' but 'desirable' though it has the suffix 'able', it does not mean 'what can be desired' but it means 'what ought to be desired'.

See this example:

Since human bodies become less active and then die, from this it is inferred that political bodies to become less active and then die.[6]

Yet another example

---

3. Cf. E.W. Schipper and E. Schuh, *A first Course in Modern Logic*, pp. 49-50.
4. Cf. *The World Book Encyclopedia*, vol. 12, p. 363.
5. J.S. Mill, *Utilitarianism*, ch. 4.
6. William J. Kilgore, op. cit. p. 47.

Projector should not be trusted.
The engineer has finished valuable project.

Therefore the engineer should not be trusted.

The argument has Fallacy of Equivocation because of the resemblance of the words 'projector' and 'project'. The word 'project' means 'plan' where as 'projector' means a promoter of a scheme.

Let us take another example.

Idle men are inefficient
Idle men are incapable

Therefore, idle men are invaluable

One wrongly assumes prefix 'in' as 'not' in all cases. Similar fallacy is committed when suffix 'logy' (which means science) is attached to psychology, geology, biology, and on that basis wrongly assumes astrology to be the science of 'astros' whereas it is 'astronomy' and not 'astrology' which is science of 'astros'.

Unintentional equivocation almost inevitably creeps into arguments on religion, philosophy, ethics and politics. Words like 'right', 'wrong', 'good', 'bad', etc. are 'relative terms'. Such terms should be understood in the context in which they are used and if the context changes so do their meanings.

The meanings of 'relative terms' differ in degrees. That is why meanings of 'relative terms' cannot be same in its various occurences.

See the following examples:

Professor Singh must be a good teacher because he is a good man.

In this argument the term 'good' is 'relative term', so its use cannot be same in its every occurence.

See another example:

He is a big poet because he is from a big country.

Here 'big' is 'relative term' hence cannot have same meaning.

FALLACY OF AMPHIBOLY

Definition:

> The Fallacy of Amphiboly occurs when the construction of statement allows it to have more than one meaning.

The Fallacy of Equivocation designates the ambiguity of a word or a phrase, whereas Fallacy of Amphiboly refers to the ambiguity of statement. The Fallacy of Amphiboly is due to grammatical structure of a sentence, and not due to multiple meanings of the terms. See the following examples where fallacy of Amphiboly is committed:

1. 'Children alone are not permitted to see this movie."[7]

   One meaning of the statement is "they can go with other children" to see this movie, the other meaning is that everyone except children are permitted to see this movie.

2. "Nandita ran to meet her daughter, happy and excited". Who is happy and excited? It could be Nandita or it could be her daughter.

3. "Mrs Natrajan only promised a donation". It can have two meanings:

   (i) Only Mrs Natrajan and no one else has promised a donation.

   (ii) It could also mean that Mrs Natrajan promised only donation and not more than that such as her presence in the inauguration or use of her personal influence in getting the scheme of school building passed, etc.

4. "Save soap and waste paper" can have two meanings:

   (i) You save soap but you can waste the papers.

   (ii) It means you save both soap as well as waste papers.

Let us see yet another example from mathematics. If we are told that a number is equal to three times five plus four, the statement is amphibolous, since the answer might be either.

7. William J. Kilgore, op. cit., p. 67.

$[(3\times5)+4 = 19]$ or

$[3\times(5+4) = 27]$[8]

This shows the right punctuation is so important in mathematics.

Amphibolus statements have always proved exceedingly useful to those persons who attempt to predict future events. Predictions are worded in such a way that they cannot be falsified. Indeed anyone wishing to gain a reputation as a seer, astrologist, palmist or something similar could not do better than to become skillful at devising amphibolous statements. It is obvious that all the different meanings given to the same statement in the same context cannot be true. For example, the famous amphibolus statement, "Alexander Darius shall conquer" may mean either

"Alexander shall conquer Darius" or "Darius shall conquer Alexander". Clearly both the meanings cannot be true at the same time but which one of them is true, the Oracle never discloses.

In another famous Amphiboly King Croesus was advised that if he attacks the Persians, he would destroy a "great empire". Whether the "great empire" was his own or that of Persia, the Oracle of Delphi did not disclose. Croesus chose war with Persians and lost. He thus destroyed his own "great empire".

FALLACY OF ACCENT

Definition:-

> The Fallacy of Accent occurs when one distorts the meaning of a statement by wrongly emhasizing some part of it.

Like the Fallacy of Amphiboly, the Fallacy of Accent is not an inferential fallacy. The Fallacy of Accent is committed when the meaning of a statement is changed by wrongfully stressing words in the statements.

---

8. Cf. E.W. Schipper and E. Schuh, op. cit., p. 53.

In an attempt to derive home a point, we emphasize some word or phrase; but when a word or a phrase which is not emphasized in the original text, but is wrongly emphasized later on, then the meaning of the argument changes. Tone, accent, stress and italics can completely change the meaning of statements and render an argument fallacious.

Look at the following examples:

1. "Woman without her man would be lost."[9] This would convey different meanings to man and woman depending upon the emphasis on 'woman' or 'man'. If the emphasis is on 'woman', then the meaning of the sentence will be:

   For a woman, man is important as she will be lost without him.

   If the emphasis is on 'man' then the meaning will be that for man, woman is important as without her he will be a lost person.

2. An author conforms in his biography that through the years of his childhood he had cherished a silent devotion to a mystic, supernatural animal which his church choir sang every Sunday. The animal so celebrated was "The Consecrated Cross-Eyed Bear". But his illusions of childhood destroyed when it turned out that the choir was singing only about "The Consecrated Cross I'd bear".[10]

The fallacy is also committed by gossipmongers who repeat statements made by some poor innocent in such a malicious voice as to prejudice their hearers completely.

Emphasis when made orally or in writing to clarify meanings, then it is used in a correct way. But unfortunately sometimes it is used for the insidious purposes. Propagandists deliberately distort statements to mislead audiences. For example tabloid newspapers often use bold and large print to attract the readers'

---

9. K.T. Girdar and Mudgal, *Elementary Mordern Logic*, p. 207.
10. Joseph Gerard Brennam, op. cit., pp. 213-14.

attention. For instance, in a newspaper this type of advertisements can be seen very often.

TAKE ABSOLUTELY FREE

But somewhere it is written in an insignificant way, the contest entry form free. One should read fine prints in order to avoid traps laid down by advertizers.

FALLACY OF COMPOSITION

Difinition:

> The Fallacy of Composition occurs when the conclusion is drawn from the attributes of the parts of a whole to the attributes of whole itself.

The Fallacy of Composition occurs mainly because the arguer assumes that the whole is sum total of its parts. The whole, the comprehensive set is wrongly considered as the collection of its subsets. Let us see some examples:

1. Every book of Delhi Public Library is a good book. Therefore Delhi Public Library is a good library.
2. All the parts of the bus are light in weight and can be carried on the shoulders. Therefore the bus is light in weight and can be carried on the shoulders.
3. Every player of the Indian Cricket team is an outstanding player. Therefore, the Indian Cricket team is an outstanding team.

   Why this argument is fallacious?

   There is fallacy in the argument because for a team to be outstanding it is not enough for the team to have accomplished players. What is required for the smooth functioning of a team is quality of team spirit and its organic unity.

4. Sodium and Chlorine are "atomic components" of salt. Individually they are poisons. Therefore salt as a whole is poison.[11]

There is another form of this fallacy where one argues from a distributively used term (x) to a collective by used term (x). We commit the Fallacy of Composition whenever we argue from a premiss containing a term taken distributively to a conclusion in which that term is taken collectively.

See the following examples:

The terrorists are deadlier than the conventional criminals.

Therefore terrorists have killed more people in recent years than the conventional criminals.

This is fallacious reasoning because even though a terrorist individually is worse than the conventional criminal yet in comparison with terrorists collectively, the conventional criminals (being more in number) have killed more people than the terrorists.

Another example:

An elephant drinks more water than any other animal does.

Therefore elephants of Jim Corbett Park drink more water than all the other animals in the park.

This is wrong reasoning because though an elephant in camparison with other animals drinks more water yet collectively all other animals being more in number, consume more water than all the elephants in the Park.

One of J.S. Mill's arguments is often quoted that general happiness of people is the greatest good. "No reason can be given why the general happiness is desirable, except that each person . . . desires his own happiness . . . each person's happiness is good to that person and the general happiness therefore is good to the aggregate of all persons".[12] In other words my happines is my

11. Hurley, Patrick J., *Introduction to Logic*, p. 144.

12. J.S. Mill, *Utilitarianism, Liberty, Representative Government*, Ch. IV, pp. 32-33.

good, your happiness is your good, his happiness is his good, X's happiness is X's good. Though the argument is persuasive yet it commits the fallacy of composition. The truth of the second clause of the last sentence does not follow from the truth of the first. The good of each person may be his own happiness when taken distributively, but it is not, therefore, the case that the general happiness stands as good to all persons taken collectively.

FALLACY OF DIVISION

Definition:

> The Fallacy of Division occurs when the attributes of its parts are drawn from the attributes of whole.

The fallacy is simply the opposite of the Fallacy of Composition. It consists in predicating the qualities to the parts which can safely be predicated only to the whole. To use the same example as before one cannot reason that since a cricket team is a good team so each of its players is a good player. Numerous illustrations of both the Fallacies of Composition and Division can be found in the arguments concerning the state and its citizens. Many persons reason wrongly that what is in the interest of individual must also be in the interest of nation, thus committing the Fallacy of Composition, others commit converse Fallacy of Division by arguing that what is best for the nation must necessarily be advantageous for each citizen.

Let us take some examples: -

1. Reserve Bank of India is a "wealthy organization" therefore, Satish, who is an employee in that Bank, is also a wealthy person.
2. Germans are fond of football game.

   Hans Zint is a German.

   Therefore he is fond of football game.
3. Since Ambani's family is famous for its philanthropy, so he must be a generous man being a member of that family.

4. Books are source of instruction and pleasure. A telephone directory, therefore, must be a source of instruction and pleasure.[13]
5. Salt is non-poisonous compound. Therefore Sodium and Chlorine (its constituents) are also non-poisonous.

Fallacies of Relevance

Fallacies of relevance are committed when the premisses of an argument are found irrelevant to the conclusion for one reason or the other. The premisses appear to be relevant to the conclusion but on the close examination are found either inadequate or incomplete. The premisses may appear to be psychologically relevant but for a sound argument premisses should be logically and not psychologically relevant.

The premisses can be irrelevant to the conclusion in various ways and, therefore, there are many fallacies in this category. The main fallacies are:

1. The appeal to Emotion (*Argument Ad Populum*)
2. The Appeal to Pity (*Argument Ad Misericordiam*)
3. The Appeal to Force (*Argument Ad Baculum*)
4. The Argument from Ignorance (*Argument Ad Ignorantiam*)
5. The Appeal to Inappropriate Authority (*Argument Ad Verecundiam*)
6. The Argument Aganist a Person (*Argument Ad Hominem*)
7. Fallacy of Accident
8. Fallacy of Converse Accident
9. False Cause (*non-causa pro-causa*)
10. Irrelevant conclusion (*Ignoratio Elenchi*)

---

13. K.T. Girdar and Mudgal, op. cit., p. 215.

THE APPEAL TO EMOTION
(*Argument Ad Populum*)

Definition:

> The fallacy occurs when an argument is supported by emotions and not by reasoning.

In the Argument Ad Populum, the conclusion of an argument is supported by the sentiments and emotions. The arguments regarding important issues are accepted because of the sentiments of the masses. In such cases the premisses are so chosen as to be the instruments with which to manipulate the beliefs of the public. Sometimes an issue is emotionalized whereas some other times "emotionally toned words" are used in order to win over them. Emotional atmosphere of approval or disapproval is created by using emotionally charged phrases like "Taking the people's food", campaign for "Anti-waste", etc.

Look at the following emotionalized argument:

India should protect its sovereignty at all costs. With so much of sacrifices we got our freedom. Our forefathers had suffered inhuman treatment to achieve independence. In this respect every Indian should — make efforts to preserve the freedom and integrity of the motherland. Therefore, it is highly appreciable that in order to protect our freedom, we go in for possessing nuclear weapons.

Here the appeal is made to heart, and not to head. There can be other valid reasons also for concluding that India needs nuclear weapons other than flaming the people's emotions by arousing patriotic feelings.

The advertising agencies though do not use "emotionally toned words" yet they sometimes commit this error. The products are displayed in such a manner as to arouse the approval of the masses. Bakery products like bread and biscuits are shown consumed by smiling, chubby boys and girls. The young charming and smart girls are shown using a particular brand of shoes or jeans, etc. Uses of certain brand of cars are related with the symbol of richness, whereas use of certain drink is shown as the sign of adventurism. Sleek furniture is shown as being used by sophisticated officers. The sole idea behind all this is to influence the attitude of public, and so strong is the influence that in spite of all the efforts to resist this, one is carried by them.

In daily life often we are influenced by what others are doing, saying or buying. Others influence our decisions.

See the following examples:

1. You must agree that *Times of India* is best daily newspaper in the city because seventy per cent people read it.
2. 25% of consumers purchase Sony Television rather than any other brand. All those people cannot be wrong. Hence Sony Television is the best television brand.
3. Since everyone is aspiring to do MBA from a reputed institute, so I will also do MBA after graduation.
4. Most of the smart girls are using Dove Soap. I thought it's good idea. I will also use Dove Soap.

Above examples have the following argument form:

Since many people believe in a certain fact, say, x.

Therefore fact x is true.

From the viewpoint of logicians, such arguments are falacious because, even though we are influenced by the majority decision, the soundness of reasoning should not be examined on the basis of its popularity, but on the relevance of the premisses to the conclusion. The use of emotional or expressive language in the argument is not logically acceptable.

THE APPEAL TO PITY
(*Argument Ad Misericordiam*)

Definition:

> The fallacy occurs when one is asked to agree with the arguer on the basis of his pitiable conditions.

The argument having the fallacy of appeal to pity is a special case of the argument based on the appeal to emotions. This is a persuasive type of argument in which the relevance of the premisses to the conclusion is not considered, instead the argument is evaluated totally on the basis of pity and sympathy. Usually such type of emotional blackmailing is done when all the valid and legitimate grounds for holding the conclusion are exhausted, or when the defence attorney is unable to offer any good reasons why his client is not guilty.

Its amazing the extent to which the argument *ad misericordiam* is used by all sections of people. While collecting charity funds, or funds for any noble cause, the argument *ad misericordiam* is often used as forceful means. Also in the court in a bid to win the favour of jury, the case is presented in such a manner as to arouse sympathy and pity in their minds. The situation is so presented as to appeal to heart rather than to head.

While pleading the case of reservations in the government jobs for the underprivileged, the argument to pity is used for the approval of the jury. On "mercy appeal" the President of India can reduce the punishment of the accused as per Constitution of India.

Often it is seen that in obtaining compensation for a poor family of an accident victim every effort is made by the attorney to get the maximum amount by the appealing to pity.

Some more examples:

1. If you convict this man, who will feed the four hungry children. Thus, in the interest of poor children, pardon him.
2. A lady begs the traffic police constable that I am a single parent, and if you impound my driving license, then I will be unable to drive to work. If I cannot work, my children and I may starve to death. Therefore, you should excuse me and should not impound my driving license.

THE APPEAL TO FORCE
(*Argument Ad Baculum*)

Definition:

> The fallacy occurs when an arguer threatens his opponent with unpleasant consequences if his viewpoint is not accepted.

The threat of punishment or some sort of force is sometimes used for persuading the opponents to accept certain views. The appeal to force does not necessarily have to involve a physical threat like, "If you do not act like this, then I will hurt you". Sometimes there are "subtle" threats which force others to accept certain views or opinions. Anyone who tries to persuade the opponent to accept his dictate by threatening him, is guilty of using the argument to force. It is very old saying "When you have no case, well get angry and threaten". In other words, the best policy to defend oneself is to become offensive.

Though it is barbaric to use force for getting one's views accepted, yet in civilized society of ours, "subtle" and not so open threats are used as weapons of persuasion. Right from the domestic front to the international forum, the "subtle" threat is used as a powerful instrument. For example, the father tells his son, "Sunny, next time before giving you pocket money, I will see your report card". Many powerful nations are using "arm-twisting" policies like reducing financial aid, cutting the technical assistances, etc. if the opponent countries do not sign a particular treaty. The union workers threat the establishment that if their demands are not met they will go on strike.

In spite of the fact that the threats are used implicitly on a large scale by all sections of society, yet logically to accept a conclusion merely on the basis of threat (and not on the basis of reason), is not sound.

Examples:

1. If you don't support my candidacy for party, then I will see to it that no new schools and colleges are built in your area.

2. If you do not agree with my political opinion that Mrs Indira Gandhi was the geatest Prime Minister of free India, then you will receive F grade in this semester.
3. You will support me in this plan because if you don't, I will do everything in my power to see that you are fired.
4. Give me your bag or else look at gun in my hand.

Many political parties sometimes issue whip to their partymen to vote in favour of a particular policy in the parliament.

The general form of an argument having this fallacy is:

"If you don't accept . . . then you will face . . . consequences which are unpleasant."

"Might is right" is the basis on which one persuades others to accept one's viewpoint. Hindi movies are full of such incidents where the dictating terms are in the hands of those who hold the guns.

THE ARGUMENT FROM IGNORANCE
(*Argument Ad Ignorantiam*)

Definition:

> The fallacy occurs when the absence of proof assures the non-existence of fact and absence of disproof assumes the existence of facts.

The lack of evidences regarding a fact sometimes has been used as evidences in favour of the argument. The fallacy usually falls into two categories:

(i) Arguing from the absence of proof to the presence of disproof.

(ii) Arguing from the absence of disproof to the presence of proof.[14]

See the following examples where the Fallacy of Ignorance in commited:

---

14. Cf. E.W. Schipper and E. Schuh, op. cit., p. 32.

1. Researches could not prove conclusively that the use of mobile phone is really harmful to health. Hence it is 'reasonable' to accept that using mobile phone is not harmful to health.
2. No one has conclusively proved that there is intelligent life on the other planets. Therefore there is no intelligent life on the planets.
3. A telepathy advocate tried to convince his friend. "You must accept telepathy as a true fact, because no one has ever proved that there is nothing like telepathy".
4. Those who believe that there are flying objects (UFO) may give the following argument to convince their opponents. "Since you cannot disprove that there are flying saucers, so you should accept the reports of those who claimed to have seen such objects as reliable".
5. There is no proof that cigarette smoking causes cancer. Therefore cigarette smoking does not cause cancer.

Let us take some conventional examples.

"Ghosts do not exist" is true because so far no one has definitely proved its existence. Since no one has proved so far conclusively that "Ghosts exist", therefore, it can be concluded that "Ghosts do not exist". The argument about the non-existence of ghosts is based upon an appeal to our ignorance instead of our knowledge. But the fact that we could not definitely prove so far the existence of ghosts, that does not mean conversly the non-existence of ghosts.

A similar argument is given by an atheist. He may argue that since no one has disproved the existence of supernatural being, hence the supernatural being exists.

AN APPEAL TO INAPPROPRIATE AUTHORITY
(*Argument Ad Verecundiam*)

Definition:

> The fallacy occurs when 'cited authority' falls short of credibility.

In order to support one's opinion sometimes one takes the help of experts and there is no harm in it. Errors arise when one cites the authority of such person or agency who has no authority in that field. Some persons have achieved so great honour in their respective fields that their popularity slips over to some other fields also. The statements of doctors in the matters of health, of an economist about economics, of an attorney about law may be relevant and appropriate in an argument concerned with issues bearing on those areas. However statements of lawyer about economics, of a doctor about law, lead to the fallacy of Inappropriate Authority.

See the following example:

The growth rate of Indian Industries will go down in coming years. This is predicted by next door neighbour of our residential society Mr Kapoor. The above argument has Fallacy of Inappropriate Authority because Mr Kapoor has given his own view regarding the status of Indian industries and he is neither an economist nor an industrialist.

This fallacy is difficult to avoid at times and difficult even to expose, because some men achieve so great a status in their own field that their prestige overflows into other fields. For instance, Bertrand Russell, the greatest philosopher of the twentieth century, is an unquestionable authority in the philosophical matters. But if he says that a Pipal tree is extremely useful tree then his statement is not authoritative. For, he is not an expert in this field. Only those who deal in this area and have gained knowledge and experience are expert, and their words and statements should be treated as reliable.

Often the advertisers in the haste to promote their products, commit this error. For instance, since Sachin Tendulkar is saying a particular drink is good, so one must take his words and accept that particular brand of drink as superb. But this is wrong. Sachin is no authority in the field of cold drinks. He is authority in cricket. If he had recommended a particular brand of cricket ball or a cricket bat, then his words would have been reliable and genuinely authoritative. But in the field of cold drinks he is no better than any other man.

Sometimes the Fallacy of Inappropriate Authority is committed in spite of our best efforts. For instance, a scientist who is expert in manufacturing nuclear weapons is no authority in the international economical matters. But his words are wrongly taken as an authority in these matters. Similarly a religious leader may not be an expert in financial matters but his followers may accept his words as reliable.

THE ARGUMENT AGAINST A PERSON (*Argument Ad Hominem*)

Definition:

> The fallacy of Argument Ad Hominem is committed in the following manner. Person A makes an argument. Person B evaluates that argument. Person B shows that the argument made by A is wrong because either

(i) Person A carries a bad reputation and hence his argument cannot be sound or

(ii) Person A's circumstances are questionable hence his argument cannot be sound.

The Fallacy of Argument Ad Hominem is committed when the argument is examined not on the basis of premisses but on the basis of who is making an argument or in what circumstances one is making an argument. Personal attitudes, emotions, prejudices or some kind of subjectivity are the main source of this fallacy. The argument is judged on the basis of personal assessment rather than on the merit of the premisses. The conclusion of an argument is denied not because premisses are inadequate or non-meritorious but because it is stated by a person who either carries a bad reputation or belongs to opponent camp or his circumstances are such that it compels an arguer to hold a particular view. But the character, the nationality, the religion which an arguer holds are not relevant at all to the truth or falsity of the conclusion because the soundness of an argument is neutral to all the subjective conditions.

The conclusions in the Argument Ad Hominem are often denied or rejected (though denied or rejected on wrong footing) whereas the conclusions in many other informal fallacies are accepted (though again on wrong footing).

It may be possible that argument made by person A is unsound but the reasons given by person B is certainly fallacious. Person B attacks the argument made by A on the personal ground instead of the strength of the premisses in respect of the conclusion.

Politicians argue Ad Hominem when they criticize the opponents' policies by attacking their motives and characters instead of examining policies on their merits. Instead of evaluating the policies upheld by the opposite political parties on the rational ground, the rejection by the ruling party is purely subjective and biased.

There are two major forms of this fallacy. In the **abusive form** the conclusion of the argument is denied or rejected not because the premisses are inadequate to support the conclusion but by attacking the person who is making an argument.

See the following example:

1. I am surprised to hear that you advocate an increase in liquor tariffs. Were you not yourself in favour of the anti-drink campaign only recently?[15]

---

15. K.T. Girdar and Mudgal op. cit., p. 211.

2. Since he is leftist, he must be opposing FDI in retail sectors in India.
3. "The Government should pass minimum wages legislation so that workers do not suffer and they are "not exploited". You support this bill because you are one of the prominent leaders of Communist Party who claim themselves to be the messiah of labour class.
4. Your argument against the draft (for anti-corruption) prepared by Anna Hazare team cannot be accepted since you are pessimist and all pessimists are against the draft (for anti-corruption).

   Second form of this fallacy is *circumstantial*. Sometimes the conclusion of an argument is denied on the basis of the profession, nationality, religion or the political affiliation of an arguer.

For example:

(i) We cannot believe in Mr X argument about the increase of salaries for the Maruti Udyog workers because being an employee of Maruti Udyog he will naturally favour salary hike for workers.

(ii) The movie 'My name is Khan" is an example of this type of fallacy. The 'Junior Khan' was killed because he carried the Sirname tag of 'Khan'.

Whatever may be the form of Argument Ad Hominem, it is certain that this fallacious type of reasoning is employed by the persons who are solely cencerned with their opponents rather than with the merits of their arguments. The soundness of arguments is to be seen irrespective of personal prejudices and interest.

FALLACY OF ACCIDENT

Definition:1

> The fallacy occurs when a general rule is applied to a particular case in which 'accidental circumstances' make the rule inapplicable to it.

The Fallacy of Accident consists in applying general rule mechanically to all cases without any exception. We argue fallaciously when we apply a general rule without any regard to the special circumstance which may change its applicability in that case. Human needs, values, circumstances demand the modification of general rules in certain special cases. For example:

In the realm of morals, the Fallacy of Accident occurs if one is not careful in applying the general moral dictum. For instance, it is true lying is sin but in order to save one's life, it is not wrong to lie either. It is wrong to steal but in order to save a starving man, stealing a loaf from someone who does not need it, is not wrong. The theologicians, moralists and lawyers have to consider the distinction between general rule and a special circumstance with the greater care. Look at the following example:

All killers of men are murderers.
Soldiers are killers of men in war.
____
Therefore, the soldiers are murderers.

This is a fallacious argument, for murder is not simply killing, but taking human life wrongfully. Generally it is a crime to kill anyone; but legal execution of criminals, and the destruction of enemy soldiers in war time, present special circumstances, and "circumstances can alter the cases".

See some other examples:

1. Physical exercises are excellent for health. Therefore Mr. Anand who has heart ailments ought to take more physical exercises.
2. "Morphine is a habit forming drug; the physicians should not use this to ease out pain.[16]
3. How can Dr Mehta advise Mr Sunderajan to give some drops of brandy to a child who is suffering from cough and cold because brandy is intoxicated drug? Here is a

16. Wiliam J. Kilgore, op. cit., p. 16.

Fallacy of Accident because in exceptional cases, Brandy is treated as medicine.

"Exceptional cases are exceptions" and they do not constitute a general principle. The exceptions neither break nor define any rule.

THE FALLACY OF CONVERSE ACCIDENT

Definition:

> The fallacy occurs when we pass from a statement which is true in certain special circumstances to a statement which is supposed to be true under all circumstances.

This fallacy is simply the opposite to the Fallacy of Accident. The Fallacy of Converse Accident occurs when a general rule is formed on the basis of a few instances carelessly or deliberately. The form of this fallacy is:

Statement P is true in certain circumstances.

Therefore statement P is true in all circumstances.

For example:

To give charity to young and healthy beggar is wrong.

Therefore charity of all types is bad.

There is Fallacy of Converse Accident because though few instances of young beggars discourage us to give charity to them but one should not frame any general rule that all charities are bad. There are people who genuinely need help.

See some more examples:

1. Every person I have met in Delhi speaks Hindi. So it must be true that all people in Delhi speak Hindi. The argument is fallacious because on the basis of a few instances a generalization is formed. Persons I met in Delhi are very few in number which is like a "subset of the entire set" of Delhities.

2. The District Magistrate of city has ordered to remove religious and non-religious establishments from the accidental prone roads in order to decongest the road and also to make it broad for easy flow of traffic. Thus, the District Magistrate has a right to remove all religious or non-religious establishments in the city.
3. Dr Vardhrajan allowed Shruti to submit her home assignment one week late because last month she was suffering from jaundice. Therefore Dr Vardhrajan should allow all the students of the class to submit their home assignments one week late.
4. There is no point having a skilled worker to do this job because I found many who are regarded as skilled workers are no more skilled workers.
5. In the examination visually challenged students are given one hour extra time to finish the question paper. Therefore all the students should be given one hour extra time to complete their question papers.
6. It is necessary to imprison criminals and to lock up dangerous lunatics. Therefore, there is nothing wrong with depriving people of their freedom.[17]

FALLACY OF FALSE CAUSE
(*non-causa pro-causa*)

Definition:

> The fallacy occurs when a non-causal event is assumed to be either a cause or part of a cause of an effect.

The Fallacy of False Cause occurs when a causal relationship is assumed to exist when actually there is none.

For example:

1. My advisor told me tomorrow sun will be aligned with Mercury. So I must be extra careful otherwise I might

---

17. K.T. Girdar and Mudgal, op. cit., p. 216.

meet an accident, because of the alignment of Sun with Mercury.

2. Sameer drinks horlicks with milk everyday. That is perhaps the cause of his doing well in school.
3. The cause of fire in the factory was that there was oxygen in the factory.
4. "Rome fell because her leaders quarrelled among themselves."[18]

One form of the fallacy of False Cause is *non-causa pro-causa*. If to a non-causal event it is wrongly assumed to be the cause, then there is fallacy of *non-causa pro-causa*. All the above examples have this form fallacy.

Post hoc ergo propter hoc is another form of the Fallacy of False Cause. The fallacy means "after the thing, therefore, because of the thing". It is true, the cause is always antecedent to the effect in the time interval, but to say every or any antecedent event is the cause of the following event is wrong. Simply because one event follows another does not mean that they are related by causal relationship. For instance, when the house got burnt, sun was shining very bright, therefore, to argue that shining sun is the cause of the house burning is fallacious and suffers from the fallacy of *post hoc ergo propter hoc*.

Let us take another related example. The house got burnt because Mr X was smoking in the room. Therefore, Mr X's smoking in the room was the cause of the house burning. Now it may be possible Mr X threw the cigarette carelessly in the house and it might have spread the fire there. But before we think like that, we must carefully examine the antecedent events. *Not every antecedent event is necessarily the cause of the following event.* However, in order to ascertain the cause of certain phenomenon, it may be possible that in spite of the scientists' best efforts, genuine error of false cause is committed in some cases.

---

18. William J. Kilgore, op. cit., p. 47.

IRRELEVANT CONCLUSION
(*Ignoratio Elenchi*)

Definition:

> The fallacy occurs when the premisses do not imply the conclusion which they are supposed to, and instead they imply something else.

Ignoratio Elenchi means "ignoring the conclusion to be proved" and instead "proving the wrong conclusion." The Fallacy of Irrelevant Conclusion occurs when an argument aims to prove statement P but instead proves a different statement Q.

For example:

1. The object of war is durable peace therefore soldiers are the best peacemakers.[19]

   The argument has Fallacy of Irrelevant Conclusion because even if it is assumed that the object of war is durable peace, still it does not imply that soldiers are best peacemakers.

   The premiss misses the point. That is why this fallacy is also called "Missing the Point".

2. You must support women reservation bill in the parliament because we cannot allow women to suffer from domestic violence anymore.

   There is Fallacy of Irrelevant Conclusion in the above argument because even if we disagree with women reservation bill in the parliament, we do agree that the women should not be victim of any social injustice.

3. Abuse of Mahatma Gandhi National Rural Employment Guarantee Act (MNREGA) is rampant in many states of India, therefore, the only alternative to this is to abolish this scheme.

---

19. C. Read, *Logic — Deductive and Inductive*, p. 324.

This is fallacious reasoning because even if there are problems in the implementation of the scheme it does not mean that one should abolish it all together. What should be done instead is to make this scheme workable by framing different strategies like tightening intelligence system, etc. to carry forward this welfare scheme.

4. The survey reveals students who have professional degrees earn more in their life times than the non-professional ones. Therefore, you must join the gymnasium (gym) in order to keep yourself fit.

The Fallacy of Irrelevant Conclusion is very handy device in the courtroom. In order to protect oneself and one's client against such fallacies, alertness is required on the part of counsel.

Fallacies of Presumptions

Following are the two main fallacies of presumptions.

(i) Begging the Question (Petitio Principii)

(ii) Complex Question.

The fallacy of presumptions is committed when unnecesary or dogmatic presumptions are made before making an argument. These fallacies arise not because the premisses are irrelevant to the conclusion but because the premisses already presume what they aim to prove.

BEGGING THE QUESTION
(*Petitio Principii*)

Definition:

> The fallacy occurs when the conclusion or part of the conclusion is stated in the premiss either explicitily or in a slightly different form.

The fallacy of Petitio Principii is also called "reasoning in circle" because what we want to prove (conclusion) is already present in our evidence (premiss).

If the conclusion is already assumed in the premiss then what is the use of such reasoning? The reasoning obviously becomes trivial and superfluous. Though the fallacy is not committed deliberately but the eagerness to prove the conclusion is so strong that one unconsciously assumes (as an evidence) what one wants to prove as conclusion.

In the fallacy of Petitio Principii the premisses are not irrelevant to the conclusion but they are useless. If we assume what requires proof, then we are just beggars, begging what we ought to earn by proof.[20]

Let us see some examples where this fallacy is committed:

1. Capital punishment is inhuman as it creates fear. It creates fear because it is inhuman.
2. The scriptures are true testimonies, for superpower (God) had written them and superpower (God) exists because the scriptures say so.
3. A student complains to the teacher "This problem is wrong. It's wrong because there is a mistake in it. There is mistake in it because it is incorrect and it is incorrect because it is wrong."
4. It is obvious that the poor in this country should be given handouts from the government. After all these people earn less than the average citizen.
5. A Human Rights activist says "You must accept my belief in the freedom of speech since freedom of speech is essence of liberal principles. But why must one accept liberal principles? One must accept liberal principles because they assume freedom of speech".

---

20. Cf. A.A. Luce, *Teach Yourself Logic*, p. 168.

FALLACY OF COMPLEX QUESTION

Definition:

> The fallacy occurs when a question is asked in such a manner as to assume (presuppose) the truth of some facts hidden in it.

In the Fallacy of Complex Question a single question is asked but two or three questions are wrapped up in it. For example in the question "Have you given up the habit of taking drugs?" Two questions are mixed up. First "Did you ever have the habit of taking drugs?" The second "Have you given it up now?" That is why the fallacy of Complex Question is also called fallacy of "Many Questions". Take another example "Are you still under debt?" Even if one answers "no" it still leaves the impression that "yes, once you were".

Complex questions cannot be answered by plain "yes" or "no" because they include something which cannot be answered by "yes" or "no". But those who ask such questions insist on a simple answer of "yes" or "no".

Complex question is favourite device of lawyers who wish to confuse a witness or defendant. For example, a lawyer asks a youth, reply in "Yes" or "No" — "Are you still a leftist?" Here many questions are implicitly woven into one. For instance: (1) Were you ever a communist? If the answer to the question is yes, then (2) have you left it now? The lawyers generally would ask such questions purposely to trap a defendant into making an implicit admission of his guilt.

When the question is complex, the best way to avoid the fallacy is to refute all the presuppositions hidden in the question one by one. To a question which appears to be simple but actually implies many questions, a straight answer will lead to a position which actually the replier does not hold.

See some more examples of the Fallacy of Complex Question:

1. "You killed the man and destroyed the evidences, did you not?" Poor man if he has never met or seen the murdered

man, then he doesn't know how to answer this question. If he says "no" then obviously more questions are lined up to be answered . In order to escape from such situations it is better never to answer such questions in "yes" or "no."

2. A reporter asked Minister "Are you going to continue your policy of wasting tax payers" money for purchasing substandard telecom instruments?" The question assumes the fact that earlier the tax payers' money was wasted in buying substandard material.
3. A teacher asked the student "have you stopped "cut and paste" policy while submitting home assignments"? An affirmative answer obviously presumes that earlier the student was following the policy of, "cut and paste".
4. "Are you still neglecting your work?"— is a complex question.
5. "Have you decided to continue with this course?" is also a complex question.

The informal fallacies discussed above,are by no means exhaustive. There may be fallacious reasoning which have not fallen under any of the above discussed categories of fallacies. But it is absolutely necessary that one should make correct and straight reasoning in order to avoid confusion. The saying:

Be bright, think right

has a point.

Select Bibliography

Alexander, Peter, *An Introduction to Logic*, London: George Allen and Unwin Ltd, 1971.

Baronett, Stan and Sen, Madhucchanda, *Logic*, Pearson, Delhi 2009.

Barker, Stephen F., *The Elements of Logic*, New York: McGraw-Hill Book Company, 1965.

Basson, A.H. and D.J. 'O.Connor, *Introduction to Symbolic Logic,* London: University Tutorial Press, 1953.

Brennan, Joseph Gerard, *A Handbook of Logic*, New York: Harper and Brothers, Second Edition, 1961.

Carney, James D, *Introduction to Symbolic Logic*, New Jersey: Prentice-Hall, 1970.

Chakraborti, Chhanda, *Logic, Informal, Symbolic and Inductive* Prentice-Hall of India Private Limited, New Delhi, 2006.

Chomsky, Noam, *Knowledge of Language* (*Its Nature, Origin, and Use*).

Clark, Romane and Paul Welsh, *Introduction to Logic*, New York: D. Van Nostrand Company, 1962.

Cohen, Morris R. and Ernest Nagel, *An Introduction to Logic and Scientific Method*, New Delhi: Allied Publisher, 1972.

Copi, Irving M., *Introduction to Logic*, New York: Macmillan Publishing Co., Sixth Edition, 1982.

Copi, Irving M. and Carl Cohen, *Introduction to Logic*, New Delhi: Prentice-Hall, Ninth Edition, 1995.

Crystal, David, *Cambridge Encyclopedia of Language,* UK: Cambridge University Press, Second Edition, 1997.

Dumitriu, Anton, *History to Logic*, New Delhi: Heritage Publishers, 1991.

Harman, Gilbert, *Thought,* Princeton, New Jersey: Princeton University Press, 1973.

Hurley, Patrick J., *Introduction to Logic,* New Delhi, Cengage Learning India Private Limited 2008. Kammuisky, Jack and Alice Kammuisky, *Logic: A Philosophical Introduction*, United States of America: Addison–Wesley Publishing Company, 1974.

Kilgore, William J., *An Introductory Logic*, New York, Halt, Rinehart and Winston, Inc.

Kneale, W., and M. Kneale, *The Development of Logic*, New York: Oxford University Press: 1964.

Kreyche, Robert J., *Logic for Undergraduates*, New York: Holt, Rinehart and Winston, Third Edition, 1970.

Latta, Robert and Alexander Macbeath, *The Elements of Logic*, London: Macmillan 1956.

Luce, A.A., *Teach Yourself Logic*, London: The English Universities Press, 1968.

Mellone, S.H., *Elements of Modern Logic*, London: University Tutotial Press, Second Edition, 1970.

Mill, John Stuart, *A System of Logic* (1843), London: Longmans, Green and Co., 1925.

Pap, Arthur, *An Introduction to the Philosophy of Science*, New York: The Free Press, 1962.

Quine, W.V., *Methods of Logic*, London: Routledge and Kegan Paul, Third Edition, 1974.

Russell, Bertrand, "Logic as the Essence of Philosophy," *Essays in Logic from Aristotle to Russell*, (ed.) Ronald Jager, U.S.A.: Prentice Hall, 1963.

Schipper, Edward Schuh and Edith Watson, *A First Course in Modern Logic*, London: Routledge and Kegan Paul, 1960.

Stebbing, L. Susan, *A Modern Elementary Logic*, London: University Paperbacks, Methuen, 1961.

Stebbing, L.S., *A Modern Introduction to Logic*, New Delhi: Asia Publishing House, 1961.

Strawson, P.F., *Introduction to Logical Theory*, London: Methuen and Co., 1952.

The World Book Encyclopedia, USA, 1995.

Wittgenstein, Ludwig, *Philosophical Investigations,* trans. G.E.M. Anscombe. Oxford: Basil Blackwell; New York: Macmillan, 1958.

Wolf, A., *Textbook of Logic*, London: George Allen and Unwin, Second Edition, 1961.